Michael R. Lewin

Introduction to Psychodynamics

Other Books by Mardi J. Horowitz

Psychosocial Function in Epilepsy

Image Formation and Cognition
(first and second editions)

Stress Response Syndromes
(first and second editions)

Hysterical Personality
(editor)

Evaluation of Human Service Programs
(editor, with C. Clifford Attkisson, William Hargreaves,
and James Sorensen)

States of Mind: Configurational Analysis of Individual Psychology
(first and second editions)

Personality Styles and Brief Psychotherapy
(with Charles Marmar, Janice Krupnick,
Nancy Wilner, Nancy Kaltreider, and Robert Wallerstein)

Image Formation and Psychotherapy

Psychodynamics and Cognition
(editor)

Introduction

TO

Psychodynamics

A New Synthesis

MARDI J. HOROWITZ

Basic Books, Inc., Publishers

NEW YORK

Library of Congress Cataloging-in-Publication Data

Horowitz Mardi Jon, 1934–
   Introduction to psychodynamics.

   Bibliography: p. 229
   Includes index.
   1. Self.   2. Attitude (Psychology)   3. Emotions.
4. Consciousness.   5. Cognition.   6. Set (Psychology)
7. Social perception.   8. Social interaction.
I. Title.   [DNLM: 1. Cognition.   2. Ego.   3. Mental
Processes.   4. Psychoanalytic Theory.   WM 460 H8165i]
BJ697.H57   1988   150'.1   88–47760
ISBN   0–465–03561–2

For Carol

CONTENTS

PART II

Conscious and Unconscious Mental Processes

ACKNOWLEDGMENTS

IT MAY BE of interest to some to know the history of this book. It began as a wish, during the first year of my training to be a psychiatrist, to have a little book that one could read in bed without risk of a crushed chest, a book that would summarize psychodynamics briefly and provide an overall framework for more detailed information. I never found a suitable text. After over a decade as a teacher, investigator, psychotherapist, and psychoanalyst, I thought I knew how to outline such a work. I aimed at a syllabus for beginners that would organize in a useful way what I knew at that time. Preparing the outline shocked me; there were questions I could not answer, gaps I could not fill, that were beyond my existing personal limitations and the current stage of the field.

I did write a syllabus, however, and taught a class of elective students. That helped to clarify the gaps, but I could not come up with good material to fill the needed frame. This led to work on information processing, resulting in my book, *Stress Response Syndromes* in 1976; on states of mind, leading to a book by that title in 1979; and on schemas, leading to the book, *Personality Styles and Brief Psychotherapy* published with my colleagues in 1984.

This bit of history gives me a chance to acknowledge with much gratitude my collaborators in that work: Charles Marmar, Janice Krupnick, Nancy Wilner, Nancy Kaltreider, and Robert Wallerstein. Other important collaborators include Stephen Palmer, David Spiegel, Lester Luborsky, Howard Shevrin, Jerome Singer, Alan Skolnikoff, Daniel Weiss, Jess Ghannam, Charles Stinson, Sandra Tunis, Thomas Merluzzi, and Dianna Hartley. While I am at it, my postdoctoral students ably did their job of teaching the teacher, so I thank also Michael Hoyt, Katherine DeWitt, Lynn Campbell, Daniel Greenson, Robert Rosenbaum, Michael Windholz, and Henry Markman.

My work on states, schemas, and information processing is based on psychoanalytic theory, melded to modern psychology and neurobiology. In fact, it seems to me to fill a gap between psychoanalytic theory and cognitive psychology, so that a useful cognitive-dynamic theory can be formed. I draw upon other books to fill this gap, such as those by Erdelyi (1984), Edelson (1984), Eagle (1984), and Bowers and Meichenbaum (1984).

Attention to this gap between psychodynamics and current psychological concepts about thought, memory, and schematization of emotionally evocative themes would not have been possible without support from the John D. and Catherine T. MacArthur Foundation. I am grateful to those involved with that foundation for both a fellowship year at the Center for Advanced Study in the Behavioral Sciences at Stanford University, and for selecting me to direct their Program on Conscious and Unconscious Mental Processes. This has put me in touch with many outstanding colleagues. The staff, committee, and board members of this foundation are largely responsible for the emergence of this work. I am especially grateful for discussions with, and the confidence of, William Bevan, John Conger, Peter Nathan, Denis Prager, Idy Gitelson, Murray Gell-Mann, and Jonas Salk.

Finally, I wish to thank those who helped in marvelous ways to bring this book to fruition. Sue Silva, John Henderliter, and Lisa Eldridge typed and edited the manuscript. At Basic Books, Phoebe Hoss and JoAnn Miller provided consultation and editing. With me at the University of California at San Francisco for many years, my colleague Nancy Wilner compiled references and edited the manuscript. Henry Markman, Terry Becker, Mitchell Wilson, and Alan Cohen read and critiqued the entire text. Alan Skolnikoff, Frances Horowitz, Carol Ott, Ray Jackendoff, Stephan Stitch, Carol Krumhansl, David Olson, William McKinney, Robert Scott, Lake McClenney, Donald Nevins, Joseph Afterman, Phillip Spielman, Katherine DeWitt, Nathan Zilberg, Robert Rosenbaum, and others read portions of the manuscript and gave salient critiques.

—Mardi J. Horowitz, M.D.
San Francisco
January 1988

Introduction to Psychodynamics

INTRODUCTION

ONE'S FASCINATION with psychodynamics grows from observation of people, and deepens with concern for helping them resolve their conflicts and develop to their maximum potential. My own interest began during the 1950s, when I heard Ralph Greenson speak on the radio. At the time, I was an undergraduate at the University of California at Los Angeles, and he was a psychoanalyst who spoke to the public on such topics as "People Who Hate." He vividly described neurotic behavior and unconscious mental processes and linked psychodynamic theory directly to everyday life. Hearing him both made me a better observer of personality traits and gave me more understanding of people who were repeating self-impairing behavior. I followed up that interest by reading the writings of Sigmund Freud as exerpted in the series, Great Books of the Western World. His explanations of dreams, slips of the tongue, and jokes excited me as they clarified an underworld of meaning I sensed but could not label.

Beyond the seemingly small phenomena of dreams, slips, and jokes were patterns involving the largest themes of human life. In the passions rising from unconscious sources were the themes of man and woman over a life cycle, as they struggled to maintain both individuality and intimacy. These were the same themes I had found compelling in plays and novels, especially of ancient Greece, Shakespeare, and Dostoevsky: that is, love and hate, pride and shame, struggles between good and evil impulses, and the results of inner conflicts that bend character toward a tragic course of life.

I was already a premedical student and the decision to study psychodynamics directed me toward psychology, psychiatry, and psychoanalysis. In undergraduate psychology courses I found psychodynamics disparaged in

3

favor of experimental psychology. While the designs and mathematics of experimental psychology were compelling, the topics I was studying then seemed more neutral than emotional.

This was at a time in academic psychology when subjective experiences of consciousness were often considered a realm outside of science. An exception was found in courses on abnormal psychology, where mental symptoms were explained according to psychodynamic principles. I became very enthusiastic about the concept of how conscious insight into unconscious dynamics might bring about cure for such symptoms, and looked forward to learning how to carry out such cures when I would be eligible for psychiatric training after medical school.

That idealization lasted until I entered psychiatric training. I found then that psychiatric symptoms were harder to understand and change than I had expected. Also, the etiology of mental disorders and the mechanisms of treatment were not well understood, and the subject matter was taught in a manner I found to be disorderly in comparison with what I had anticipated.

There seemed to be different brand names for schools of thought about why mental disorders occur and how they may be relieved. Many of my colleagues chose a brand name and became that type of psychiatrist. Others wanted to find out more. A group of these residents asked Eric Berne, a group therapist on our clinical faculty, to give us a kind of training treatment in addition to his seminars. He had developed a theory called transactional analysis, which was one of the brand names available for personal identification. This was a psychodynamic theory in that it described patterns of recurrent maladaptive interpersonal behavior in terms of internal mental processes of which the subject was not consciously aware. It included the concept of various types of self-organization and the different states Paul Federn had called ego states, building on Freud's ego, id, and superego model of the mind.

A few months later, still in residency, I began a training analysis as part of my entry into the San Francisco Psychoanalytic Institute. My analyst, who saw my membership in Berne's didactic group therapy as a resistance to my psychoanalytic process with him, asked me to terminate it. When I discussed this request with Berne, who himself had trained in and dropped out of the same institute, he said that he saw my psychoanalytic treatment and training as a resistance to transactional analysis.

For a time I did both, and then I did drop out of the group therapy and found my psychoanalysis most valuable. The seminars at the institute were also of high value, but at times some teachers seemed to demand acceptance of doctrine on faith. It seemed to me then, as now, that the various schools of theory each had something true, and something false as well, to say about a large, poorly understood domain. Rather than competition between brand names, and personal identification with one of them, I sought a more ecumenical approach.

My training emphasized ego psychology; but through other teachers, I learned about Jung, the neo-Freudians, and the British object-relations school of theory about psychodynamics. My research teachers, Jurgen Ruesch and Enoch Callaway, opened the doors to cognitive science, information processing, communications, and social training theory. I read Heinz Hartmann, David Rapaport, Edith Jacobson, Otto Kernberg, and Heinz Kohut who, while arguing in various ways, seemed in the main to be pioneers attempting to put together various points of view.

Integrating diverse trends in psychodynamic theory was a gigantic task. It seemed even larger because I was interested in the revolution in cognitive science and information processing, which seemed to offer a useful language for theories about how the mind reacts to novel events in life. Also, a tremendous amount of new research on child development was revealing how social transactions and environmental stimuli might shape early personality and style. I decided to do clinical research in a smaller area, taking as a starting point the memory of a recent adult traumatic event, and seeing how it might be traced in focused exploratory psychotherapy.

In 1973, I began a research clinic at the University of California's San Francisco campus for this purpose, assembling a group of like-minded colleagues. All these faculty members joined with trainees in an intensive review of recorded cases. Again, there were competing points of view among various senior clinicians. But we endured these confusions and disagreements and analyzed the multiple perspectives and languages of our theories. In this work, knowledge of the details of the particular stress event was helpful. We could trace emergence of the memory into conscious experiences over time, and study how various aspects of the actual occurrence were associated with inner views of the person. The psychological reaction to the traumatic event was always compound: it put together elements of both the occurrence and pre-existing belief systems. We found it useful to examine the individual predisposition in terms of two major domains. One perspective focused on the past conflicts, memories, and fantasies activated by association to the traumatic event. The second focused on the person's habitual coping and defensive style as thrown into bold relief by the condition of stress. New theory and a clearer language for saying what happened in these two domains was developed.

The improved theory and language was then used to delineate more clearly the diagnoses of the stress-response syndromes, including post-traumatic stress disorders. This permitted development of a specific approach to brief dynamic psychotherapy as treatment of these disorders and, with new instruments of measurement, to study and then demonstrate the efficacy of this approach.

As a result of these efforts, I developed a systematic format for reviewing the phenomena, states of mind, self-concepts, views of others, memory themes, and habitual defenses of a person in the midst of personality change or as a consequence of working through an injury or loss. This was called *configurational analysis,* the term Erik Erikson had used for the many approaches required fully to understand the meaning of a dream. The main features of configurational analysis contained the hypothesis of multiple schemas of self and other, as major organizing principles that lead a person to be subject to particular states of mind. Shifts between states of mind were in this theory seen as the result of control processes that regulate not only the ideas and feelings entering consciousness, but the schemas used to organize all stages of information processing from perception to action.

This approach provided new ideas that might serve as bridges between diverse schools of psychodynamic thought, especially between the streams of theory called *ego psychology* and *object relations.* Concepts from cognitive science and information theory provided a useful language which would be understandable in different areas of psychology. Such concepts, however, needed to be adapted to discussions of emotional conflict and unconscious motivations. A first effort at bridge building was a theoretical effort to explain psychological responses to severe and specific stress. After my *Stress Response Syndromes* (1976; second edition, 1986), I attempted an integration—by using the configurational analysis format to describe changes in individual personality in persons having major emotional conflicts—in a series of three books: *Hysterical Personality* (1977), *States of Mind* (1979; second edition, 1987), and *Personality Styles and Brief Psychotherapy* (1984). As each book enhanced the integration, I saw, with some excitement, the chance to write up psychodynamic theory as an introductory text.

I aim for a synthesis to provide the beginner with a reasonably comprehensive basic understanding of this theory, and hope as well to show an integrative approach that will interest the more experienced reader. In order to keep the work readable, I knew I had to forgo mentioning many important figures and reduce coverage of many topics of interest. In adding my own ideas, I hope nonetheless to have done justice to the great pioneers, my mentors, and colleagues as well as to the dramatic themes of human conflict that captured my earliest interest.

The book is organized in two parts. The beginning chapters provide an orientation to conflict and the important phenomena that psychodynamic theory seeks to explain. I present these phenomena as they occur in various states of mind as organized by usually unconscious structures of knowledge.

While Part I on schemas of self and others provides a basic understanding of the enduring conflicts between wishes and fears which may be contained within one's personality, Part II examines how such conflicts influence perception, thinking, feeling, and one's choice of a course of action. Change in unconscious schemas as a consequence of new relationships is considered in Part I, and then reconsidered in relation to changes in the use of consciousness as a special decision-making and integrative tool in Part II. The final chapter shows how an understanding of psychodynamics can enable change that is self-enhancing, through integration of the diverse motives and processes that constitute a personality.

PART I

Schemas of Self
and Others

1

States of Mind

SOMETIMES one experiences an unwanted mood that seems to descend for no reason. During this mood, irrational and intrusive ideas may occur. At other times, one desires a positive state of mind but instead feels and acts in a wooden, stifled manner. Desired emotions and thoughts fail to arise. Yet everything about the brain, the body, and the surrounding world seems all right.

Generally, people are motivated to seek pleasant states of mind and to avoid unpleasant ones. Sometimes, however, they experience neither. Instead, they remain in the midst of a neutral, compromise state, avoiding both displeasing and satisfying experiences. These neutral states act as a defense against dreaded states of mind. In this chapter, I look at the spectrum of states of mind, from desired or feared to defensive or puzzling.

A state of mind is a pattern of experiences and behaviors. It has co-occurring verbal and nonverbal characteristics. When these features arise together, another person can recognize a change in state, and one may name that state oneself (Federn 1952; Berne 1961; Gaarter 1971). The following example shows the passage of Tom through several states of mind, some of which contained puzzling and unwanted experiences.

Tom is a fictitious name I will use for a man I once treated in psychotherapy. He had come to see me because of symptoms of anxiety and depression. Several months earlier, he had attended the funeral of his mother. The following episode occurred before that, and he brought up this memory during his treatment.

Tom worked as a draftsman on the West Coast. One day when he was under a lot of pressure at work he received a telephone call from his father across the continent to tell him that his mother had died suddenly. His father asked Tom to come at once. Tom told me how, hearing his father's bad news, he had laughed explosively and then said, "Damn it!" in a hard and bitter tone. Startled, his father had hung up abruptly. Tom felt numb as he arranged for coverage of his office duties and then went home to get ready to go to the funeral. He was dull and unresponsive when his five-year-old daughter tried to joke with him as he packed his clothes. Then, as she persisted, Tom suddenly snarled angrily at her. When she fled in fear, he felt a surge of remorse and burst into tears.

It was not surprising that Tom cried, but *when* he cried was—as also were his laughter and abrupt anger at the unexpected news of his mother's death, and his explosive rage at his beloved daughter. More important, these reactions were inappropriate, distressing to others, and followed by his own remorse.

While Tom loved his mother and would grieve for her in the weeks and months to come, at the moment of receiving his father's call he was feeling pressured and unsupported. The sudden news of her death was one more unfair blow, "the straw that broke the camel's back." He laughed in disbelief, as if to say, "You must be joking. Fate cannot be doing this to me now." Centered on himself, disregarding his father's feelings, Tom reacted angrily to him as the bearer of the bad news, thus offending him. Then when his daughter demanded his attention—at a time when he felt himself to be the one most in need of someone else's care—Tom experienced her as unsympathetic to him, as imposing her needs when it was he who felt like a "needy child."

Tom loved his daughter and recognized that she had a child's level of understanding. He knew she was affectionate, and that she was just trying to engage him in her own way. The view of her as selfishly demanding was incompatible with this knowledge, yet he held it as he snarled. Then he shifted to remorse for his hostility. He felt so guilty about how he had reacted to his father on the phone and to his daughter's overtures that memories remained vivid in his mind.

Tom's quick anger on hearing of his mother's death heralded entry into a state of mind he had experienced off and on. He did not like this state, which contained not just the emotion of anger but cynical, bitter, self-centered, and self-righteous qualities as well. It seemed to intrude upon his usual good mood when he was faced with external pressures, and made him lash out uncontrollably, as he had when his father called.

Tom's wife could recognize when Tom was in such a sour mood and likely to react sharply, and withdrew from him at such times. Fortunately, this cynical, bitter, angry state was not always characteristic of Tom, and he entered it only episodically. But the possibility of entering into it *was* characteristic of him, since the episodes recurred.

Psychodynamics focuses on why such maladaptive states occur and repeat themselves however unpleasant and ineffective, and on why a person may find it difficult, if not impossible, to enter or sustain a desired state of mind.

Approaching States of Mind

OBSERVATION

Observing and describing states of mind is to some degree an artificial task. Actual experience flows like a river, without any precise point of change as it moves from tranquil pools to turbulent rapids. In general, smooth transitions in states characterize a flexible person who is not stressed. More abrupt state transitions may occur when inner conflict is present, and when one is confronted with chronic strain or the sharp stress of threats, losses, or injuries.

States of mind are often described in terms of sustained emotions and for this reason are sometimes called moods. Furthermore, a given emotion can be experienced in several ways, in various states of mind. One can experience sadness in a *distraught sobbing* state, in one of *poignant but resigned melancholy,* or in one of *rigid smiling to mask despair.* One state of mind differs from another not only in terms of prevailing emotion or expressed themes, but in the apparent style or the degree of control over ideas and feelings.

A state of mind is a pattern where a composite of diverse features of experience and expression appear almost simultaneously. An observer could describe a person's particular state of mind by answering the following questions: How does the person speak during this state? Does some vocal inflection, pace, tone, or other speech quality occur more noticeably in *this* state of mind and not in that one? Does the person in this state dwell on particular themes? What facial expression, posture, gesture, action, and other qualities separate this state of mind from a contrasting one? Does the person relate to others differently in this state than in another one? Are communications in different verbal and nonverbal modes harmonious or discordant in terms of the ideas and emotions expressed? Do the expressions seem controlled, overcontrolled, or undercontrolled?

Important in describing a state of mind is the congruence or disparity between different expressive systems. In some states of mind, verbal and nonverbal messages are comparable, compatible, and complementary; while in others, there is a discrepancy between what a person says and the tone of voice, gestures, or facial expressions. Since these different systems of communication, verbal and nonverbal, may be self-regulated in different ways, the degree of such modulation is an important feature to observe. Are there lapses in control of communications and actions beyond what the person seems consciously to intend? *Well-modulated* states are those in which a person appears to be in self-command: appropriately spontaneous, openly expressive, harmonious in verbal and nonverbal communications, controlled in acting on or containing impulses. *Undermodulated* states are those in which one's expressions seem excessively impulsive, undercontrolled, or just "leaking out." *Overmodulated* states are those in which the person seems to be excessively veiled, shielded, contrived, or pretending.

A well-modulated expression of fear can be frank and direct. In an undermodulated expression of fear, the person may be striving to appear calm while conspicuously leaking signs of fear in furtive eye movements, halting speech, and sweaty palms. When overmodulated, the expression of fear can be intentional but delivered in a contrived manner of feigned nervousness. Sometimes people try to stabilize themselves in overmodulated states because they are frightened of entering into an undermodulated state of mind. The outcome may seem rigid in control, but it serves the purpose of defending against a threat. The defense has a price, the loss of spontaneity. Some periods of experience have features of several states mixed together; these may be called *shimmering* expressions of more than one state. Sometimes, during what is mainly an overmodulated state, the features of an undermodulated state emerge momentarily, as a kind of breakthrough phenomenon (Haggard and Isaacs 1966).

By recognizing and naming different recurring states, transitions between them can insightfully be observed. In this respect, the following story of Jim builds upon the angry state in the case of Tom, and allows us to examine a series of states related to that emotion.

An intelligent forty-year-old business executive, Jim, was referred for psychotherapy by a physician at the end of a three-month period of drug treatment for an anxiety disorder. The anti-anxiety medication that had been prescribed had only partially relieved his anxiety symptoms and the supportive advice that was part of that first treatment had not counteracted his phobic withdrawal from social situations. His symptoms were closely related to his fear of being fired from the firm where he worked. His severe withdrawal in the workplace made that termination a real possibility.

Jim had been successful in situations where he worked on his own within this corporation. He had been rewarded with a promotion for his creative approach to marketing the company's products. As a consequence of his promotion, Jim took on supervisory responsibilities and had to present the work of his unit to a management committee. When people he supervised did not meet his expectations, or when he was criticized by members of the management committee, Jim flew into a rage. He withdrew from his subordinates and superiors in order to avoid these explosions. Both his rages and his withdrawal from contact severely threatened his career future. He had already been warned, but could not change; he was tense and jittery in anticipation of being fired. As his anxiety states became severe, he approached a first and then a second therapist.

Jim's rage went out of control; yet he was at first very vague in describing these attacks. When he spoke of his hostility, it was clear that his angry states of mind ranged from a blind rage to a more socially acceptable state of irritation and annoyance. Yet he just spoke ambiguously of being upset at others, without further qualification. It was easy to fall in with this and say during psychotherapy, "When you get upset . . ." But such dialogue seemed confusing, since he was not just upset, but angry in different ways, and with quite different views of himself and the relationship in question in different states of mind.

As part of a careful clarification of what he felt at different times, Jim and his therapist developed a list of states in which the emotion of anger appeared in some way. These six states can be grouped roughly as those that were *well-modulated, undermodulated,* or *overmodulated.*

UNDERMODULATED STATES OF ANGER

The most maladaptive and undermodulated state for Jim was that which was, in psychotherapy, labeled *blind rage.* In this state, Jim wanted to demolish any person he was with. Overcome with destructive revenge impulses, he saw others only as frustrating to him. He was not aware that he had ever even liked the person whom he wished to destroy. He also had no awareness that his rage was a passion that would decline over time. It was as if, during this state, Jim believed he would hate the person forever.

Another undermodulated state was that labeled by Jim as one in which he *blurted out irritation.* During this state, he felt bursts of hostility. But unlike the state of blind rage, he knew this anger would not last forever. When he wanted to reduce his passion, he blurted out his irritation. Unlike his experience in the blind-rage state, he did not feel as if he were aiming to destroy the other person. He did, however, experience the blurted-out irritation state as one in which he was not in full control of himself. He felt that he became too irritated about trivial things, spoke

15

too harshly and rashly, and might generalize his reaction from one situation to another.

WELL-MODULATED STATES OF ANGER

Jim also expressed anger in two well-modulated states, which were called *annoyance* and *bantering sarcasm.* In the state of annoyance, he was aware of his anger and of how he was expressing it to others, and felt that his sharpness was appropriate and fully under his control. While expressing his annoyance, he felt that others were equal to him; he was simply mad at them. He did not generalize his annoyance to other themes, and was consciously aware of how his anger related to times that he felt well disposed toward other people.

During the bantering-sarcasm state, Jim handled feelings of hostility by teasing others in a good-tempered way. He was aware that he was being hostile, but also that he liked the other person, and that he was converting a kind of potential for anger into humor. In this state, he could tolerate being the butt of similar barbs.

OVERMODULATED STATES OF ANGER

In contrast to the undermodulated states of blind rage and blurting out irritation, and the well-modulated states of annoyance and bantering sarcasm, anger also was present for Jim in two overmodulated states. One was called his *stony* state; the other a *sullen and grudging* one. In the stony state, he felt numb. He was aware of his potential for anger but was rocklike and did not manifest his feelings to others. He discovered that his stony demeanor and aloofness were actually experienced by others as hostility; but within himself, he felt like a rock, above being irritated.

In the sullen and grudging state, Jim tended to be surly, but suppressed any direct display of irritation. This effort at suppression caused him to speak very carefully, with precise wording and little feeling in his tone of voice. He did not react spontaneously to others, but instead crept slowly through an interchange, making the other party uncomfortable.

The task of clarifying his states of mind in respect to the theme of anger or of warded-off anger provided a useful self-exploration for Jim, who had a poor acquaintance with words for naming his own emotional experiences. This task clarified both the importance of the anger as a theme and the interpersonal patterns involved in evoking rage. In the next phase of psychotherapy, Jim revealed a fantasy of what he expected from his therapist. He desired to have no further experiences of rage, to have the therapist remove this theme and emotion from contaminating his life, and thus to be completely relieved of his chronic anxiety about what problems his rage might cause.

Once this expectation was communicated to the therapist in words, it became clear to Jim, on reflection, that it was not within the range of human possibilities to be expunged of all rage and fear. Nonetheless, he was angry with the therapist and expected him to feel ashamed that he could not produce this kind of psychotherapeutic triumph. Jim's expectation that the therapist would feel shame soon led to an examination of his own potential for entry into a dreaded state of shameful mortification associated with a weak, ridiculous self-concept. Jim attempted to avoid any entry into the state of shameful mortification because it was much more painful for him to experience than anger. As already mentioned, this aim to avoid shameful mortification had a defensive purpose.

THE ROLE OF DEFENSE

Using psychodynamic theory, mental conflict can be analyzed or modeled at multiple levels. If conflict is modeled in terms of states of mind, one defines wishes as *desired* states of mind and fears as *dreaded* ones. The mind anticipates future possible states, and may defend against particular moods. These defenses may lead to *compromise* states.

A compromise state is most likely to arise because one anticipates that a desired state of mind could have bad consequences, such as bringing on a dreaded state of mind. The anticipated risk is too great, so one wards off both desired and dreaded states by maintaining the compromising level of experience and style of behavior. Even so, other moods may arise that are leakages of some unwanted emotions or expressions, yet still defensive avoidances of what one most fears. These may be called *problematic* states. They often contain symptoms that are a compromise between impulses and defenses.

For example, Jim liked a mood of joyous and *exhibitionistic excitement.* By showing his work to others, he hoped to gain their admiration and boost his self-esteem. But showing his work could lead into either the desired state of exhibitionistic excitement or the dreaded state of *shameful mortification.* If he did not present his work, he avoided shameful mortification but reduced his chances of exhibitionistic excitement. Instead of either the desired or the dreaded state, he withdrew from contact and, alone in his office, often entered a state of *ruminative rehearsal,* colored by anxious anticipation but without fantasies of humiliation or success.

This ruminative rehearsal state was a compromise; within it Jim could not achieve the pleasurable excitement he desired, because he rehearsed dully without concluding that he was really ready to present. When com-

17

pelled to confront others, this compromise did not work. Then he became *anxiously worried,* or shifted the blame for incompetence to a subordinate and entered a *blind rage,* which he later reviewed in his memory during an *anxiously worried* state. The blind rage state, a defensive compromise that avoided his own state of shameful mortification, presented its own problems as did his state of anxious worry.

These states complete a *psychodynamic configuration* in that they show a conflict between a *wish* for exhibitionistic pleasurable excitement and the *fear* that exhibition will lead instead to shame. A *defense* against that fear is to maintain the self in a state of ruminative rehearsal, but there may be *symptomatic states* in which the conflict erupts as states of uncontrolled rage or anxiety as shown in table 1.1.

The Effects of Stress on States of Mind

Serious life events such as threats, injuries, and losses, may disrupt a person's equilibrium. They may make it harder for a person to have positive states of mind. Unpleasant and distressing states of mind occur more frequently.

The first reaction to a traumatic event is often alarm. Since sudden, intense feelings often lead to a cry for help, a common first phase of psychological response to stress is called the *outcry* phase (see figure 1.1). During a sustained outcry, the individual may experience states of panicky overactivity or stunned shock, as well as emotions of sadness, rage, fear, or guilt.

Phases with more overmodulated and undermodulated states than usual

TABLE 1.1
*Jim's States of Mind Modeled
as a Psychodynamic Configuration of Conflict*

Dynamic Element	Type of State	Label for State
Wish	Desired	Exhibitionistic excitement
Fear	Dreaded	Shameful mortification
Defense	Compromise	Ruminative rehearsal
Symptom	Problem	Blind rage, Anxious worry

FIGURE 1.1

Phases of Response Often Seen after Stress-Inducing Life Events

Phases	Common States during Each Phase of Response
EVENT ──→ OUTCRY	States are high in arousal, emotion, and action.
DENIAL	States are lower in arousal and emotion as some memories or ideational implications of the stressor event are avoided.
INTRUSION	Intrusive ideas and images occur with pangs of intense feeling.
WORKING THROUGH	Oscillation occurs between states like those during phases of denial and intrusion, with gradual reduction in the degree of avoidance and sense of involuntary recollection.
COMPLETION	The person returns to states like those experienced before the stress-inducing events.

may follow. Stress is characteristically manifested by this wider range of experience. To avoid facing implications during a phase of relative *denial,* a person may have states of dazed inattention, leaden apathy, or insulated working. This numbing of emotional response may then be followed by the opposite kind of experience, with *intrusive* ideas and pangs of intense feeling. In an intrusive phase of response to stress, there seems to be less control than in the defensive states that characterize the denial phase.

INTRUSIVE EXPERIENCES DURING UNDERMODULATED STATES OF MIND

The sequence shown in figure 1.1 from *outcry* to *denial* to *intrusive* phases is a general tendency seen across large populations and in response to diverse stress events (Horowitz 1986). An outcry phase of response to stress does not always occur. The person may enter a denial phase virtually at once. Or the person may enter an extended phase of intrusive ideas and pangs of emotion. The intrusive phase often contains undermodulated states of mind.

During an undermodulated state of an intrusive phase of response to stress, ordinary perceptions may threaten the person. Common noises may trigger a startled reaction when usually the person would hear them without flinching. A strained hyperalertness may result, as the person seems to expect unwanted threats from every direction, and maintains a tense, exhausting level of preparedness to react swiftly (Janis 1969). Sometimes a perception is made into a conscious experience of threat by adding inappropriate internal elements. One example is an *illusion,* a mental imagery experience that combines external and internal elements. In an illusion, an ordinary bush may seem to be an attacking person; a branch moving at the window may be seen as a threatening face; one's own face in the mirror may seem to be the face of a loved one who has died.

One may have vivid internal visual images related to the stressful life event, of which *hallucinations* are the most intense variety. In these, one experiences an auditory, a visual, an olfactory, or a tactile mental image as if it were a real external object. A related experience is a *pseudohallucination*—"pseudo" because while one's mental image is intense and evocative of emotion, one does not appraise it as having external reality (Horowitz 1983). A fairly common example of a pseudohallucination is feeling the actual presence of someone who has recently died.

Other phenomena that occur in intrusive states are *unbidden images,* or *flashbacks,* which repeat memories of a traumatic incident. The intrusive idea or image may be difficult to dispel, disrupt concentration, and lead to a rising spiral of painful emotions.

An *intrusive state* often contains ideas and feelings warded off during a denial state. Fred, for example, had pseudohallucinations after the suicide of a man he knew. A few days before, he had been telephoned by Gregory, who seemed very depressed and asked Fred to come over to be with him. Since Gregory was not a close friend but a casual acquaintance whom Fred did not want to get to know better, he said he did not have time to get together. When he later heard that Gregory had committed suicide, Fred said to himself, "I refuse to feel guilty about that!" and put ideas about the man out of his mind.

A week later, intrusive images of Gregory's face occurred whenever Fred shut his eyes. He could sleep only with the lights on, so as to be able to see something real whenever he awoke. He so dreaded the recurrences of these threatening images that he had to change the way he washed his face, so that he wouldn't have to close his eyes to keep the soap out. These symptoms disappeared after a brief period of psychotherapy helped him confront and resolve a warded-off belief that he was partly responsible for Gregory's suicide.

The intense fear of situations that remind one of the traumatic event may lead to *phobic behavior.* In phobic behavior, the person withdraws excessively, thus reducing alarm reactions by a maladaptive avoidance of whatever is feared. The threat has been overgeneralized, and too much of life becomes fear-inducing.

In an intrusive state, one may compulsively repeat the threat, whether it was in the past or is impending in the future—a repetition that may range from tic-like gestures to acting out of the events in current life. While possibly experiencing it as intrusive, sometimes a person who expects a threat to recur purposely seeks out some analogous risk: that is, someone afraid of a car accident may take up sky diving or drive recklessly. Through this counterphobic behavior, one aims to prove that the threat is not overwhelming, that one can face it without excessive fear. Counterphobic behavior is sometimes related to a person's vigorous pursuit of some stimulating activity to escape from states containing intrusive thoughts and painful feelings about a particular threat. Such pursuits of alternative states of mind may lead to extensive use of alcohol or street drugs, to promiscuous sexuality, or to the taking of capricious risks.

REDUCTIONS IN EXPERIENCE

After the phase of initial outcry, the person who is experiencing a traumatic event may go through a phase of relative denial of its severity. During denial phases, there may be states of mind in which the person feels emotionally numb. In such states, the person may be inattentive to some stimuli, even dazed and out of touch with some aspects of the environment. Responsibility to others may be lessened or may seem stereotyped rather than spontaneous. One's own body may seem less full of sensation than usual, even to the point where one does not notice a painful injury or disability.

Post-traumatic amnesia, which occurs during denial states, consists of a failure of recollection of all or some aspects of traumatic events. It is believed to be the result of an unconscious defensive maneuver to avoid unpleasant emotions, the *repression of traumatic memories.* In a related phenomenon—*constriction of associational width*—one irrationally avoids connecting the stressful theme to directly implied meanings. The person may then operate in some ways as if the traumatic event had not happened: a widow may, for example, go on cooking and setting the table for two for months after the death of her husband. At the same time, the performance of ordinary activities may have a lifeless or mechanical quality. The person may lack spontaneity, have lapses in concentration, actively disavow the occurrence of the stressful event, or deny that he or she has heard it is likely to happen. A man may, for instance, deny that his physician has told him—and done so repeatedly—that he has cancer; or even though acknowledging the diagnosis, may disavow that his cancer could be fatal.

21

A related emotional numbness may go beyond the omission of emotional reactions, and be consciously felt. Some people have likened this feeling to being wrapped up in a cocoon or a layer of insulation against the world. During a phase of relative denial, the person may also have reduced experience of positive states of mind.

After a traumatic event, the usual sequence of phases is outcry, denial, and intrusion. These initial phases of response are followed by a long phase of working through. During this phase, various emotional themes appear and change. The person oscillates between states that feel undercontrolled, as during the intrusion phase, and states that feel overmodulated, as during the denial phase. The extremes are gradually reduced as one gains mastery over the emotional themes of psychological response to the traumatic event(s). Eventually, equilibrium is restored, and the person enters a phase of completion, at least one relevant to that particular life event. Later events may reignite the original trauma's emotional meaning, causing the cycle of phases to be repeated.

RECURRENT MALADAPTIVE STATES

After a serious life event, the highly stressed person may experience the denial and intrusive phases described earlier. During denial phases, there may be states of mind in which many usual features of experience and behavior are omitted. During intrusive phases, there may be states in which the opposite occurs, bringing more unbidden or unwanted experiences and behaviors than the person consciously intends or even feels he or she can tolerate. Both extremes of experience seem to be dictated, in part, by unconscious motives and mental processes. Similar deflections from consciously desired levels of experience may occur when the person is under stress from inner conflict, even in the absence of external stress. When the conflict persists, the person may experience recurrent unwanted or maladaptive states of mind.

Such unwanted entry into states of intrusive ideas and emotional turbulence is illustrated in the following example. Mary consciously wanted a positive state of mind to result from a situation that actually precipitated a negative one of panicky proportions. One evening, she fixed dinner in her apartment for a man whom she had known for some time and liked very much. She had decided that she wanted to make love with him. As they began to kiss, Mary became sexually excited. Suddenly her sensuous erotic state changed to panic. Her heart raced, beads of perspiration sprang on her brow, her mouth went dry, and her stomach knotted. Gasping for breath, and with a sense of great fear, she pushed him away and ran into the kitchen. He followed her, looking concerned. She burst into tears and asked him to leave. Afterward, she felt terribly dejected about her behavior because this was not a new pattern: the panic state had intruded before when erotic situations progressed toward consummation. The involuntary recurrence of this state disrupted relationships with men she liked. She could only have an extended erotic sensual experience when alone, through masturbation.

Mary's neurotic pattern, which recurred without her learning from it, was not a conscious choice of behavior and was due to psychological rather than organic causes. Her *panic* state interfered with her chances to learn: she could not find out that sexual play with a lover was pleasurable and nonthreatening, because she had to interrupt each episode.

Disordered states are roughly divided into two categories: *neurotic* and *psychotic*. Neurotic state transitions are irrational, but reflect a less flagrant break with reality than do entries into psychotic states of mind. In neurotic states one may act in unusually inhibited or impulsively excessive ways. Mary viewed her non-experience of a fully erotic state as a serious omission from her life, and her panicky state of fearful avoidance as intrusive and unwanted. That is why these aspects of her experienced states of mind could be called "neurotic" rather than "normal."

In contrast to neurotic experiences, in psychotic states hallucinations, delusions, confused thoughts, and chaotic impulsive actions are more intensively and frequently added to such intrusions and omissions. A person who enters psychotic states is not necessarily—in fact, is seldom— "always" psychotic; but may have a combination of psychotic, neurotic, stressed, and normal states of mind. The way one views social situations, thinks, and plans action may be different in each state, with the most irrational ideas, feelings, and actions found in psychotic states.

PATTERNS OF STATE-TO-STATE TRANSITION

Mary's recurrent states of mind illustrate how there may be cycles in which one state commonly leads to another state. Her panic state has already been described in terms of its abrupt movements, grimaces, sweating, anticipation of impending disaster, and frightened facial expressions. This often led to another undermodulated state: her *deflated* state, in which her speech and movements were slow and monotonous, and her facial expressions frozen; she had images of sad despair, and felt deadened and fatigued. The deflated state occurred when she consciously reflected upon her inability to be authentically sensual with men.

Mary had an overmodulated state that seemed outwardly sensual but felt inwardly unauthentic. In this *swinging* state, she dressed and acted in sexually provocative ways, while her mind felt distant from her body. The

23

pattern of state sequences was this: Mary would often begin a new relationship with a man in her swinging state. Later, under threat of sexual encounter, the panic state would occur. Following that, a persisting deflated mood state would arise as a consequence of her sense of failure, inadequacy, and hopelessness.

Mary had a well-modulated state that she enjoyed, and which, during her psychotherapy, was called her *shining* state, to label its qualities of openness and spontaneity. In this state, Mary expressed lyrical ideas and feelings, and viewed herself as authentic and admirable. She had artistic interests, and this positive state of mind would occur with a companion who shared these interests. When her competence in art or at work was threatened by such a companion, an *attacking* state would occur. In this attacking state, Mary—with a hard edge to her voice—would accuse the other of unscrupulous behavior, scowl, and feel angry. At other times in such situations, the deflated state would descend upon Mary. Since, in the attacking state, she felt in control, and in the deflated state, she did not, she preferred the attacking state.

In the nonsexual area of her work and recreational companionships, Mary tended to have a cycle that began with the shining state. She might next enter a *working* state in which her efforts were active and concerted, she experienced only mild tension, and she felt efficient and competent. Then, if any friction was introduced, the attacking or deflated state would occur. Rekindled interest in the companionship restored the shining state.

As an example of how state descriptions may be summarized for an individual, the states just reviewed for Mary are grouped in table 1.2.

Mary had inner schemas about herself and about how she expected a sequence of actions between herself and others to occur. Because these schemas contained assumptions different from actual situations, Mary failed to take advantage of good opportunities and felt her life was out of control. Each of her states of mind was organized by a different set of schemas. The next chapter will explore the topic of schemas.

The Development of States of Mind

Two of the case illustrations, those of Jim and Mary, indicated recurrent maladaptive states of mind. These states were based on inner assumptions that made external situations seem more stressful than they actually were. The problematic states of each person tended to recur. The two cases

TABLE 1.2
Six of Mary's States of Mind

Name	Description
	Undermodulated
Panic:	abrupt movements, grimaces, sweating; feeling intense fear; images of impending doom
Deflated:	monotonous, slow speech and gesture, frozen facial expression; feeling deadened, fatigued; images of despair
	Modulated
Working:	active and concerted efforts; feeling mild tension; ideas of being competent
Attacking:	hard edge to voice, scowling face; feeling angry; accusing the other
Shining:	lyrical, open behavior; feeling fresh, clean, admirable; creative ideas
	Overmodulated
Swinging:	sexually provocative dress and demeanor while feeling distant and not really erotic

contained other states of mind that also tended to recur. In a way, then, both Jim and Mary could be said to have a *repertoire of states* that they might experience again and again over time. How might such repertoires develop in the first place? The answer to this question eventually will be found in terms of biological, social, and psychological factors and how they are synthesized in the mind. While psychodynamics focuses on psychological synthesis, a brief statement about temperament should be made before I conclude this introductory chapter.

BIOLOGICAL TEMPERAMENT

Temperament includes biologically determined variations in how a person is able to regulate and consciously experience various types of emotional arousal. These will include the threshold and latency between perceiving a stressful situation and having an emotional reaction to it, as well as the time it takes to recover from a sharp arousal, such as a fit of sobbing, temper, or panic. Temperament may also include dispositions to certain ways of perceiving, representing, and thinking, as well as how the various bodily organ systems respond to nerve or chemical messages on stimulations (Plomin 1986; Thomas and Chess 1977; Rothbart and Derryberry 1981; Goldsmith and Campos 1982).

The brain uses many different neurotransmitters. These are signaling

25

systems that vary somewhat from person to person. This variation in use of neurotransmitters stems from differences in temperament and disposition. Variations in chemical influences on information processing by the brain also affect states of mind. Some positive states of mind may be impossible to achieve when certain chemical patterns are dominant, and confused information processing or negative alterations in mood or state of arousal may result (Bloom, Cooper, and Roth 1982; Reiser and Rosen 1984; Kandel 1983; Solomon 1987).

The brain influences positive and negative emotions and the ability of the person to control ideas and feelings at both conscious and unconscious levels of psychological purpose. Thus temperament constantly influences states of mind, and brain physiology influences immediate possibilities for a state of mind to occur. Both the brain and temperament, then, influence the psychology of social interaction from the very beginning of life, and the temperament of a baby affects the earliest infant-parent relationship patterns and so influences attachment (Emde and Harmon 1982).

PSYCHOLOGY AND SOCIAL MOLDING

The human baby enters the world with the built-in facility and propensity for looking at the forms that constitute a human face. The small infant will react to two eyes and a thatch of hair even if these forms are crudely painted on a board. Gradually the infant recognizes faces of particular people so that, by at least nine months of age, he or she can tell the difference between a parent and a stranger.

The growing child responds to the states of mind of caregivers and peers in two primary ways: *mimicry* and *complementarity*. In the first, the baby imitates the expression on the face of another: when whistled to, for example, the baby may purse its mouth. In the same way, by reflecting them, the baby gradually learns the states of mind observed in the caregiver (Stern 1985). In complementarity, the child forms a pattern that fits with the state of important persons in the child's life. In a sense, child and parent become an integrated pair and, as a pair, have a set of joint states of mind. To preserve the equilibrium of these shared states, roles may be exchanged, and either party may be supportive of the other. The needier party gets more care from the other. The states of the caregiver are thus complementary to and partially governed by the care receiver.

Abnormal states may affect mimicry and complementarity of moods. Clinical studies have been conducted on the children of parents who have frequent pathologically depressed states of mind. When such states have been prominent during caretaking of children younger than two years of age, those children's behavioral and mood patterns have reciprocated the depressive states of the parent, and vary from control groups of children without depressed parents (Gaensbauer et al. 1984; Zahn-Waxler et al. 1984). Some such children may exhibit a *nurturing, caregiving* state in order to sustain the distressed parent; others may enter an *avoidant* state in which contact with the parent is not sought (Zahn-Waxler et al. 1984; Davenport et al. 1979; Anthony 1975). The sad parent may evoke either a sad child (mimicry) or one who becomes animated to cheer up the parent (complementarity).

Culturally determined likes and dislikes also affect those states that the child may develop. Different societies foster certain states in their juvenile members, and attempt to dampen manifestations of other states. Societies have standards and traditions of how moods should be displayed, and what states are good or bad to exhibit under specific circumstances. Some societies are stoical, training certain members to stifle anger, grief, or even joyous excitement at critical times. Others reinforce major displays of emotion or may condone sexual or hostile acts if they are done in out-of-control states encouraged by specific holidays or ceremonies. Gender variation of specific types may also be encouraged, with some states of mind labeled as particularly masculine or feminine. Individual psychology, therefore, always develops within such social frameworks.

INTERACTION OF BIOLOGICAL, SOCIAL, AND PSYCHOLOGICAL INFLUENCES

Biological cycles take time and may continue until a metabolic sequence is completed. In certain instances, a person's state of mind cannot change from one of *tense arousal* to one of *restful repose,* even though one may recognize that an anticipated threat has not really materialized. The biological cycle of alarm and one's impulse to fight or fly may have to run its course, before tension can gradually be reduced (Cannon 1929; Selye 1976).

A woman, say, may fall into a *depressive* state because of brain changes induced by chemical intoxication or viral infection, as in influenza. Once the neural systems are restored metabolically, she may not change out of the depressive state because the emotional experience may have activated negative memories and beliefs about herself. Thoughts about personal unworthiness, helplessness, past reasons for presently feeling guilty, and morbid views of the future may now be active themes. She may need to complete a train of thought on such themes before her well-being is restored.

Or, a man may feel insulted that he did not receive an expected promotion at work. His psychological disposition might be such that he believes he would not be able to tolerate the unpleasant feelings of facing such an insult head on. Instead, he might perhaps take an early lunch and drink excessively with his meal. After several drinks, his brain function would be changed, and he would also have a psychological set for how one behaves after drinking alcohol (Nathan, Parsons, and Butters 1987). He might return to work and stage a drunken scene. Once sober again, he might feel remorse and try to apologize. In spite of his apology, his colleagues could go on reacting to him in a suspicious manner for days. The social climate would then affect him adversely; and to dim this new pain, he might repeat the pattern of lunchtime drinking. It will be helpful to remain aware of such interaction of psychological, social, and biological factors as we turn to focus on the mind and how schemas and unconscious processes influence conscious experiences of thought and emotion.

2

Self-Organization

JUST AS states of mind vary in an individual, so we all have multiple views of self, any one of which may be dominant in a situation. When a view, whether negative or positive, is dominant, it serves to organize mental life and to determine how one responds to others.

A *self-concept*, in this context, is a view of oneself that has been consciously represented and so is accessible to consciousness (Viney 1969), while a *self-schema* is a view of self whose conscious representation is not necessarily available but persists unconsciously to organize inner mental processes (Horowitz and Zilberg 1983). *Self-organization* refers to the summation of all a person's self-concepts and schemas at various levels of conscious and unconscious mental processes: the whole may be greater, as a gestalt, than the sum of the parts.

Self-Schemas

Before discussing the theory of this organization, I shall illustrate its operation in the story of the courtship of a fictional couple, John and Sue, each of whom wants to form an intimate and mutually satisfying relationship with a person of the opposite sex. For the purposes of this story, John and Sue each has just three types of self-concept: realistic, superior, and inferior. As organizers of mental life, these self-concepts say, in effect:

Superior: I am exceptionally talented and sexually attractive, irresistible to everyone.
Realistic: I am a relatively attractive and interesting individual who will appeal
to some persons.
Inferior: I am a relatively ugly and disgusting person who will repel most people.

When the superior self-concept is the dominant organizer, John and Sue are each in an especially *vivacious, excited state of mind.* When the inferior state of mind is dominant, each is *timid and afraid of contact.* When the in-between realistic self-concept is dominant, each is *open and receptive.* With this blue-print, we can trace their courtship.

At a large party, John looks across the room to see a vivacious and pretty woman, and moves to introduce himself. Sue is attracted by his charm and displays herself to advantage. They each feel excited; each enhances the most appealing characteristics of the other. They begin to go out together.

As they spend more time with each other, they are no longer always on their "best behavior." Sue learns that John is sometimes clumsy in his understanding of her, sometimes morose over his own shortcomings, and sometimes anxious and neurotically guilty that their sexuality is "bad" or "dirty"—attributes organized by his inferior self-concept. Sue is fright-ened by these aspects of John because her early enthusiasm for him was based in part on her feeling self-enhanced by being with a companion who was vigorous, competent, and known to their peers for his good qualities.

At the same time, John observes that Sue has moods in which she feels and acts like a damaged child, sometimes pouting that "too much is ex-pected of her and too little is given to her." Also, Sue is neurotically afraid to experiment with certain forms of sexual pleasure: for example, she sometimes feels too ugly to let him look at her naked body in daylight. Of course, he has similar moods, but is surprised to learn of hers, also orga-nized by her inferior self-concept.

Sue and John influence each other when they are excited, and they influence each other now, at a time when they feel unattractive. Zest, excitement, and anticipation disappear from their love affair, each now seeing the other as a person who once evoked grand feelings, and each now blaming the other for "losing the magic" in their relationship.

To regain a sense of liveliness, each turns to another person in their circle. Courtship is itself exciting; and, with the new companion, each again enters an exhilarated state of mind, acting attractive and charming because the excitement of interest in a new relationship stabilizes the superior self-concept. This return of zest convinces each of them, sepa-rately, of their "rightness" in turning away from the other to a new companion. John tells people that it turned out that Sue was "somehow bad for him"; and she does the same.

John and Sue repeat the pattern with their new companions. Each then feels dejected and lonely, and they seek each other out again. Gradually they develop more realistic views of one another and of what they can do for each other. When one has an "off" mood, the other does not see him or her as being a "bad" person. They learn to enjoy the occasional moments when they seem wonderful to each other. During times of stress, when each once tended to feel bad, ugly, and incompetent, they help stabilize each other's sense of being worthwhile, attractive, and capable.

I have presented this example to show how each individual may have several self-schemas, and varied states of mind depending upon which schema is dominant in a particular situation; and also how the actions of another person can affect the mood of the self in different ways, depending on which schema organizes one's subjective interpretation of what is happening. Moreover, one's self-schemas can change as one learns about the other, and the other's view of oneself, in a relationship.

A single person may have many self-schemas; and any self-schema in this repertoire may at any given time be the dominant organizer of one's mental life. The dominant self-schema of a state of mind acts as the organizing focus for one's perceptions, thoughts, emotions, and choices.

A self-schema is composed of a set of subordinate schemas, including ones for complex body movement (Piaget 1970; Saperstein and Gaines 1978). While each state of mind may be organized according to different self-schemas from a person's repertoire, he or she must think and act within one body. Nonetheless, that body may be mapped or sensed differently in different states of mind, even if in reality it remains anatomically the same.

The mental map and inner view of the body has long been called a person's *body image* (Schilder 1950; Fischer 1971; Horowitz 1964). As just mentioned, this body schema may not correspond to one's actual body, just as self-concepts do not always reflect real traits. The patient with anorexia nervosa and the amputee with a sensation of itching in the missing limb (the "phantom limb" phenomenon) have subjective, conscious body images based on inner schemas that do not accord with reality.

The repertoire and the hierarchical organization of self-schemas change slowly, and their relative persistence makes one's personality consistent over time. But a person does not behave in exactly the same way in all states of mind. Rather, one is "multiply stable," exhibiting different recurrent patterns. A person has several potential "I" experiences, depending upon which self-schema is active as organizer of a state of mind. As one remembers these differing "I" experiences and compares them, one can develop a more extensive "I" experience, a kind of *supraordinate self-concept*, which gives more of a sense of personal stability and continuity across different states of mind. An unconscious *supraordinate self-schema* may help the person integrate emotional reactions to diverse situations over time.

Different self-schemas may be associated with different motives, priorities, styles of controlling ideas and feelings, and values. Conflicted elements within a personality may be associated with different self-schemas, and different self-schemas may also conflict in goal, purpose, and role. Such conflicts within the personality have been described as different "parts" of self-organization in the psychoanalytic model of *id, ego,* and *superego* structures and functions.

CLASSICAL PSYCHOANALYTIC MODEL: ID, EGO, AND SUPEREGO

When Freud (1900) first examined conflict, he divided parts of self-organization into zones of thinking and remembering according to degree of reflective self-awareness. These domains were those of *conscious, preconscious,* and *unconscious* mental structures and processes. Freud postulated a boundary between each zone at which information would be regulated. Through the inhibition and facilitation of ideas at this border, conscious thoughts, feelings, and actions might be censored in various ways. For example, the conscious self might not want to know about certain wishes arising from the unconscious because they seemed immoral. Freud believed such wishes to be usually sexual or hostile in nature and repressed to avoid fear, guilt, or shame. The threat of their emergence set off anxiety, which was reduced by maintaining inhibition of the ideas related to wishes. The inhibited, repressed wishes were seen as disowned aspects of self, experienced—if at all—as self-alien. Yet the repressed wishes exerted dynamic force from the unconscious and were likely to leak out in changed form or further disguised as neurotic symptoms.

Later, Freud recognized that conflict between "parts" of the self could occur within any one of these zones of awareness and non-awareness. To give a general form to the "parts," he then divided the mind into sets of functions which he named *ego, id,* and *superego* (Freud 1923). Aspects or derivatives of each structure could be conscious, preconscious, or unconscious, although conscious representation of any derivative was seen as an ego function.

The term *ego* tended at first to mean "I," the reflected-upon self. Freud's goal was to differentiate sources of inner drives from higher functions; the "I" as opposed to "it-like" or *id* surges of biologically based appetites, such as sexual urges. These primary wishes stemmed from evolution and genetics and included aggressive rivalry, competition, self-protection, sexuality, reproduction, and the establishment and preservation of fundamental social attachments, territories, and hierarchies (Bowlby 1969, 1973, 1980; Lifton 1976).

As psychoanalytic theory evolved, the term *ego* came to refer not so much to self as to a set of functions. One of these functions was a cognitive appraisal of reality, id urges, and superego values. Other ego functions included synthesis of needs, threats, opportunities, wishes, and morals into action plans as well as restraints. The superego's functions internalized social controls of the self, maintained ideals, "insisted" that ideals, values, and morals be adhered to over time, and unconsciously sought punishment for transgressions, as through activating a sense of guilt.

The coordinated mental functions involved in ego operations included thinking, perception, logical appraisal of inner and outer reality, complex memory organizations and their recall, and other reasoning tools (Hartmann 1964; Rapaport 1967a). While id functions said, in effect, "I want it now," and superego functions said in effect, "Thou shalt not do that now or in this way," the *ego* functions had to mediate, compromise, and regulate actions to solve the conflict, while simultaneously seizing opportunities or dealing with pressures from the environment.

Thinking was regarded by Freud as having at least two forms. Since the most reality-oriented, adaptive, and rational type of thinking was a late development out of a more primary process, Freud called it *secondary-process thinking.* It was contrasted with the earlier and coexistent form called *primary-process thinking.* Primary-process thinking moved from impulses toward action by use of the memory of how similar wishes had been satisfied in the past. Associations between a stimulus and a memory were made on the basis of any similarity, without checks for the logic of the association. The primary process tended to ignore time and negatives. In contrast to primary process, *secondary-process thinking* was slower, more logical, and more orderly. Primary-process thinking moved toward more immediate gratification of wishes, even if that meant impulsive action or hallucinating the desired consummation of an appetite. Primary-process thinking might not be as adaptive, because of the tendency toward immediate action and illogical associations, yet it might lead to creative spontaneity.

Self-organization could be diagnosed as more or less mature in terms of how coherently, resiliently, and successfully ego functions synthesized the often conflicting demands of reality, id, and superego. In less mature or abnormal self-organizations, id or superego attributes might dominate, controlling the state of mind of an individual to the point where one was either too impulsive for one's own good, or too rigid, lifeless, and conforming.

CONTEMPORARY PSYCHOANALYTIC VIEWS

The most important implications of the "topographic" view of unconscious, preconscious, and conscious, are its hypothesis of unconscious schemas. These unconscious schemas influence the patterns of conscious experience and action *without* one's recognition of the powerful motives and meanings involved. In this "repressed," or dynamic, unconscious, the conscious recognition of warded-off motives and meanings is actively, unconsciously prevented. There are thus "repressed" aspects of self, omitting unwanted aspects of identity from conscious knowledge.

The id is not the same as the repressed, because the ego functions of representation and memory are involved in the ideational form of urges. Superego values are also involved in the repressed, conflictual, thematic complex. The classical structural model (id, ego, and superego) becomes unwieldy at this point. While agreed to for many years by psychoanalysts, it is insufficiently worked out to be used as a general theory for the mental processes involved in conflict for these and other reasons, as reviewed by Emanual Peterfreund (1971), John Gedo and Arnold Goldberg (1973), George Klein (1976), James Thickstun and Alan Rosenblatt (1977), and Joseph Slap and Andrew Saykin (1983). One aspect of these critiques has been a call for a better theory of self and object depiction in the mind, including a model of conflict between the main body of integrated ideas (schematized as self) and sets of repressed, active, unconscious urges and beliefs (schematized as alternative selves, dissociated selves, or warded-off components of self-organization) (Jacobson 1964; Kohut 1972, 1977; Kernberg 1976, 1980; Slap and Saykin 1983).

In the construction of such a new model, which is partly my task in this book, it is important to retain hard-won theoretical constructs that continue to work well. The id concept needs to be retained as emphasizing primary, internal motives that may activate specific schemas associated with satisfaction. The superego concept needs to be retained as emphasizing the power found in values, including unconscious values and processes of conscience. Rather than these global words *id, ego,* and *superego,* I shall speak of motivations, self-schemas, and values as they constitute types of schema.

Types of Schema

MOTIVATIONAL SCHEMAS

The word *motivation* is often used in popular psychology to indicate how to get people to do useful things, such as pay more attention to their health or work. In psychodynamics, *motivation* in its narrowest use refers to inner drives and wishes that press toward specific impulses and intentions to act. The more drivelike motives are for gratification of biologically linked needs or appetites, such as searching for water and drinking when thirsty, finding and eating food when hungry, securing a safe place to sleep when tired, and engaging in reproductive behavior when sexual objects trigger interest. Emotional systems, once highly activated, also motivate the information-processing and action-planning systems of the mind.

While animals have some instinctive templates for how to act in specific situations, they may also have to learn much from parental example or trial and error. People also have such genetic templates; but, as in many other animals as well, these hereditary givens are transformed to new modes through the process of learning. The more wishlike motives are those for expanding the capacities of self, for self-growth, and for getting certain gratifications and positions in relation to others, as in gaining social recognition and status or power.

Motivational schemas are learned sequences of ways to gain pleasure or to avoid displeasure. The first elements in a schema indicate the sensations of arousal of the need; the next elements indicate the objects of desire, as well as the actions to be taken given these conditions. These schemas are like a *script* of how to proceed from wish to satisfaction in terms of a series of step-by-step sequences. Each person may have a set of different scripts for how to eat and drink in different circumstances. In the repertoire of human beings, there are even more complex sets of motivational schemas that contain the sequences of what to do when "hungry for sex," "starving for companionship," "burning for recognition," or "thirsting for revenge" (Berne 1961; Schank and Abelson 1977; and Tomkins 1979).

In a larger sense, motivation also involves an aim at safety and coping with threat. Motivational schemas may also refer to cues of danger, and how to overcome the standard obstacles and interferences to accomplishing an aim. Motivational schemas act as programs of how to go from a less desirable state of mind to another more desirable one. Wishes are one form

35

of motive; the aim to get out of dreaded situations or states is another. Thus, motivational schemas include models of how to escape from threat situations such as different types of attack, how to hide from shame, or how to grieve and so reduce states of pining sorrow. Cultures vary in the forms used, and human beings learn schemas from their cultural circumstances.

What are the prime motives of human beings? Freud (1905) focused much of his early attention on sexual drives *(libido)* as a prime motive for thought and action. Early psychoanalytic theory focused mainly on sexual drives as motives developing first toward sensory gratification in oral satisfactions, then toward self-control of urinary and anal expulsions and containments, and finally toward genitally based urges (Freud 1903). Finding sexual motives too limiting as a primary category of what people want, Freud later (1920) added aggressive drives as a basic striving, and speculated even about alternative life and death instincts. Later theorists also found the sexual drive theory, while powerful in human life, too limiting as a categorization of basic motives. Most emphasized self-development and integration itself, as a basic striving that changes in nature over the entire life cycle, from birth to death (Murray 1937; Jung 1959; Erikson 1950, 1958, 1959; Kohut 1972, 1977; G.S. Klein 1976; Kagan and Moss 1983; Stevens 1982; Colarusso and Nemiroff 1981; Levinson 1978; Weiss and Sampson 1986).

These theories of motivation suggest certain general principles: the mind works to increase pleasure *and* to avoid displeasure; the ways of doing this become schematized; the schemas as a whole are an important aspect of self as a unique personality; the types of pleasure sought and displeasure avoided evolve with development over the whole life cycle. Early in development, one learns pleasure of the senses in terms of good and bad feelings. Appetites are a bit more complex, and are pleasurable if they occur *and* are satisfiable, but displeasurable if constantly frustrated. Sexuality is a powerful appetite, exerting unconscious pressure even when consciously denied, and affecting a great deal in personality and social connectedness. From raw sexual appetites, more refined modes evolve, blending with other capabilities of self.

Pleasure is found in many forms of self-development, especially in learning to do anything well. Incompetence is a source of displeasure, whether at work, lovemaking, in a sport, caregiving, or in a creative pursuit. A fundamental human motive is also the desire to be of interest to others: people strive for attention even if they want sometimes to be alone or withdraw to avoid the displeasure of being ignored, scorned, or misunderstood. People also strive, in a fundamental way, to do good for others, and dislike being frustrated or ignored in this aim (Symington 1986). Some desires to seek pleasure and avoid displeasure are paired, as shown in table 2.1.

Motives become schemas as the self develops. Eventually one has an intrinsic wish to integrate motives and schemas, so as to reduce conflict, but also to get an aesthetic pleasure in the harmony of self as a unity. The obverse is painful: a sense of fragmentation, identity diffusion, and doubt about self-worth. There may also be satisfaction in moving beyond coherent self-integration, as in transpersonal and spiritual experiences of being part of a greater whole.

SCHEMAS RELATING THE SELF WITH THE WORLD

All motivations involve some articulation of the self with the surrounding world. Many motivations involve the search for relationships from which one may obtain sensory pleasure, appetite gratification, security, empathy, friendship, love, and a sense of shared purpose and commitment. Hence, important aspects of self-organization are the *role schemas* of self in relation to others.

A *role* is a set of customary functions derived from repeated social transactions of the past. In a way, a role is like a learned, habitual series of actions (Skinner 1953). A character enacts a role by performing these

TABLE 2.1
Some Motivating Wishes for Pleasure and to Avoid Displeasure

Domain	Pleasure	Displeasure
The five senses	good sensations (e.g., smells, touch, warmth, sounds, tastes)	bad sensations (e.g., pain, cold, noise, odors)
Appetites	rise of appetite and gratification with decline of appetite	rise of appetite and frustration with tension of unconsummated appetite
Capabilities of self	doing better and better; gaining competence and power	incapable or doing worse and worse
Self as of interest to others	getting attention, finding relationships (e.g., love, being of help, being seen as worthwhile, gaining status)	losing attention and relationships (e.g., being ignored, scorned, unliked, unloved, seen as worthless)
Integration of diverse motives in the self	synthesis, harmony, reconciliation	sense of fragmentation, conflict, doubt
Beyond the self	union and mystical experiences	chaotic sense of loss of boundaries; fear of death

functions or actions once again—as in the "baby role" in a family. The role of "baby" is to be small, cute, and, because of relative helplessness, to be in need of care. The complementary role is that of parent, whose role as caregiver includes the functions of competence, responsibility, and empathic concern. The baby sends signals of need to the parent and receives care from the parent; the baby responds by expressing signs of satisfaction.

In a given family, each member may at times take on the baby role, even though the youngest member may enact this role most frequently. The father may at times act cute or sick, be relatively helpless, and signal the need for care. He may not only playact the behavior, as in dissembling sickness, but have all the conscious, subjective inner experiences of the role as well, while in that state of mind. The mother or an older child may assume parental function for him as "baby." The term *role* is, thus, useful for it allows us to refer to the schemas for a set of social functions as well as inner experiences without insisting that the same person is always acting that role.

In addition to roles and scripts that relate the self to others, inner models relate the self to the rest of the world. Such models of the world surrounding self represent learned distinctions about locations in space, as being in home, home city, or state. Schematic distinctions are made between edible and poisonous plants and animals, kin and stranger, safe and unsafe atmospheric patterns, and permitted or taboo paths through terrain. Intangible forms such as social order are also schematized. Hierarchies of dominance aid automatic decision making because the schemas say, in effect, when to defer to the demands of others and when to expect to have one's own way. These are often referred to, in the history of class structure, as a person's "station in life" and are equivalent to the "God-given" order in the deterministic theories of the Calvinists, to the class system in nineteenth-century England, or to the caste system of the Hindus. Today we see these hierarchies as schematic forms passed on by a culture about the behavior expected from individuals. Thus, the individual, the society, and the ecology all determine the schemas included and emphasized in an individual's personality. These schemas contribute to and stabilize self-organization.

VALUE SCHEMAS

Value schemas help a person decide which of conflicting motives to choose. One assesses, often unconsciously, potential actions and their probable outcomes according to whether they are moral or immoral, good or bad, sanctioned or taboo, safe or dangerous. Values determine which goals are best if all are "good." One aspect of value is an *ideal self*, a schema sometimes called the *ego ideal*.

An idealized self-schema may be diametrically opposite to schema of the self as bad or evil. The individual compares a current self-concept derived from self-observation with ideal self-concepts and with bad, dreaded self-concepts. Pleasure such as self-satisfaction is felt when the self is closer to the good views; displeasure such as plummeting self-esteem, when the comparison shows the self as far from ideals and closer to what is devalued.

Multiple Self-Schemas

As I have said, we each have a repertoire of self-roles and may, in different states of mind, experience any one of several self-concepts. Again, it is most useful, to begin with, to illustrate this point in a fictional story drawn from everyday life.

One morning Ken boards the bus and sits down next to the friend with whom he usually rides. Turning to George, he says brightly, "Nice day today!" But, to Ken's surprise, George replies sarcastically, "Nice for *you*, maybe!" Maintaining his facial composure, Ken looks out the window, away from George. With a change of tone, George says earnestly and plaintively, "Ken, I'm sorry, I'm not myself today."

Ken looks back. "Is it something I can help with?"

"No," George says, "just the blahs. Just trouble and more trouble ahead with my boss. You sure have it better!" he exclaims bitterly, referring to Ken's position as a leader of a small unit in their company.

Ken nods skeptically. He decides not to ask further about the matter, and George does not pursue it. Both ride on, silent and withdrawn from each other.

Ken knows George fairly well. He knows that George is usually in an amiable state of mind, but occasionally has snappy, irritable moods. In these moods George tends to be envious, talking to Ken as if Ken has some special advantage in life that has been unfairly denied to George. Ken knows what George is like when "himself" (amiable) and "not himself" (envious and irritable)—two states that can be contrasted as follows:

Amiable state: In this state, George views himself as a friend and peer of Ken; he
   is likely to be realistic in describing his work, with all its problems, and to be
   warm and friendly with Ken.
Irritable state: In this state, George regards himself as an unfairly injured party, one

with fewer advantages than Ken; he is likely to exaggerate both the problems caused him by his boss or co-workers, and Ken's success at his own job, and to be unkind to Ken.

In this story of friendship, as in the love story of John and Sue, the state of mind of one party is likely to influence the response of the other. When George is in his amiable state, Ken is likely to feel happily responsive. In the face of George's irritability, Ken knows he can respond in several ways, depending in part on his own pre-existing mood. He can respond sympathetically to George's sarcastic and nasty griping—a response that will soothe George, who will gradually return to his amiable state. At other times, Ken can gripe about his own work, and the two men may then enjoy sharing their dislike of "bosses." Ken can also choose, as he has, to ignore George's bad temper and just look out the window.

George's state of mind is not just an expression of one of his emotions, but a patterning of many features. Some features also elicit certain responses from his friend. The response from Ken leads to further reactions from George. George may be relieved if Ken soothes him, his state may worsen to rage if Ken ridicules him, and he does remain irritable when Ken ignores him.

So far I have discussed what Ken knows about George because he is his friend and has observed George's repeated patterns. Ken also knows, or at least infers, more about some aspects of George's self-schemas than the latter may know about himself.

Of George's many possible states of mind as seen by Ken, the two in question here are "amiable" and "irritable." During each state, George tends to assume a particular role (good companion in the amiable state; unfairly disadvantaged man in the irritable) and to assign one to Ken (good companion in the amiable state; unfairly advantaged man in the irritable). Also likely in each state is a certain social interaction, a style of how information about events at work is expressed, and a schema showing which value is uppermost during each state. Thus, in the amiable state, George shows an interest in Ken's activities, accurately reports events, and believes that the highest value is to tell the truth; while in the irritable state, he complains, interprets events so that all blame is assigned to others, and considers that the best course is to avoid blame.

Of course, these fictional examples involve only a few of the states of mind possible in the human personality. Particular states of mind are closely associated with role-relationship models, as I shall discuss in the next chapter.

3

Role-Relationship Models

People are likely to clash when they view quite differently a shared situation, and their various roles in it. Such was the case of Alice and Loni, and the "diaper station."

Alice's daughter, Loni, had recently married and even more recently given birth to her first child. It was a difficult labor, leading to a caesarean section. Loni invited Alice to come and help when she came home, but Alice came at once, arriving while Loni was still in the hospital. She busied herself cleaning house and then prepared a convenient place where the baby could be diapered and bathed. While preparing what she named the "diaper station," Alice had a pleasurable fantasy based on memories of her previous experiences when her daughter was a baby. In these expectant fantasies, Loni was grateful for Alice's creative efforts, and Alice viewed Loni as the beaming little daughter who, as a child, had given her mother sudden hugs whenever delighted by a special present. Alice imagined the same pleasure when Loni came home and saw all that Alice had done to help her, especially the "diaper station."

The actual moment came to pass. Loni saw the "diaper station" and spoke irritably to Alice, saying that she had planned to set it up herself in a different way. Alice had a sharp change in mood and became cold and pouting for days. She had tried to help, but miscalculated the situation, and then was stung and hurt by what she perceived as Loni's criticism. She sullenly felt herself to be a hard-working, unappreciated mother and Loni an ungrateful, selfish daughter. During this mood, Alice struggled to prevent herself from acting on the impulse to leave at once for her own home.

Alice's fantasy of Loni as an admiring little girl rather than an adult mother led to a sharp discrepancy between Alice's expectations and Loni's actual behavior. True, Loni was irritable, but that might be expected in a fatigued woman shortly after childbirth and hospitalization.

A view of Loni as an adult would not have led to such a flagrant change in Alice's mood. Had she not been expecting an admiring and awe-filled child, enthusiastic about the "diaper station," she would have been more readily able to understand and tolerate Loni's irritable mood, as well as the latter's wish to choose how to take care of her own first child. In that case, Alice would have been able to sustain her own sense of well-being and provide empathic understanding to Loni.

Loni and Alice clashed because they each entered the situation with a different set of expectations and a different working model of their respective roles in the relationship. Discrepant expectations are, of course, not the only factor in determining the outcome of a situation; also contributing are the actual circumstances—in this case, the new baby, the feeling state of Loni, how Alice had been doing before in her own home, and so on.

A working model of a relationship is a schema in the mind that allows one to interpret what others are intending. Ken understood George, in the example in the last chapter, because he had a working model of their relationship. The wrong model, as in the instance of Alice and Loni, may lead one to misunderstand a given situation and to react inappropriately within it. By observing especially such inappropriate actions and misunderstandings, a psychotherapist can make inferences about a patient's enduring schemas of self and others, schemas that are applied repetitively but erroneously. It may also be possible to speculate about why a particular relationship model has been used, for instance, because one has intense wishes that could be gratified by it or intense fears that it exemplifies.

Enduring schemas of this sort may be called *role-relationship models.* A role-relationship model is a mental schematization of the relative characteristics of self and other, and a sort of script of what each may do to the other in a sequence of interactions. This sequence of expected transaction may begin with a wish of the self to express feelings or to act in relation to another person; the next element in such a script may be the expected responses of the other; and the third, the expected reactions of the self. In the "diaper station" story, Alice had a role-relationship model as the competent mother. Her wish was to give good care to a younger daughter, and to have the latter respond with gratitude, leading to Alice's own pleasure. Alice also had another role-relationship model that organized her feelings when Loni spoke irritably about her own plans for the diaper station: then Alice viewed herself as the hard-working and unappreciated mother, who had given help to an ungrateful and selfish daughter who was responding with hostility. Alice viewed herself, in reaction to that hostility, as being justifiably expressive of hurt feelings. She could have organized her responses to Loni according to a different role-relationship model. For example, she could have seen herself as the competent mother who had offered good care to her adult daughter; and Loni as the adult daughter who is tired and irritable and expressing irritation; and finally, with herself reacting with tactful agreement, drawing back from insisting on her way of organizing the situation. In that way, Alice would have responded softly to Loni's irritation, rather than with the cold, sullen state that endured for days and worsened the situation between them.

Some role-relationship models have places and actions involving more than two people. For example, in a common three-party role-relationship model, the self is expected to compete with another person for the interest of a third. The third person is expected to become interested in the self, and less interested in the second person. The second person is then expected to be jealous of the new bond of intimacy between the self and the third person.

Like other schemas, role-relationship models have certain properties. Once a role-relationship model is set in motion as an organizer of a state of mind, one tends to act according to the sequences contained within its script and to expect response from the other accordingly. Role-relationship models help in constructing available social perceptions into a whole picture. Because the schema adds "missing information" to one's perception of the outside world, it helps one size up a social situation quickly. Of course, the added information may be in error and not accord well with the actual properties of a situation. This vulnerability to error, owing to rapid organization from a schema, is compensated for, in part, by the use of multiple schemas. For example, at the onset of a new social encounter, one may "size up" the other person and the current situation by applying different role-relationship models to both. This process proceeds unconsciously, and only the schema with the "best fit" to the situation may become a working model of the relationship. I will discuss this further later on in this chapter and again in chapter 9 under "Parallel Processing." For the moment, suffice it to say that role-relationship models are in general a useful tool in human functioning in the world in a variety of circumstances. These schemas become a problem only when used too rigidly or when they do not match the situation and the expectations of others.

States of Mind and Role-Relationship Models

A specific state of mind may seem the same in its constellation of features whenever it recurs because the same schemas, especially the same role-relationship models, may be the most active organizers of ideas and feelings. Take, for example, the case of Jim (see chapter 1), the man described as having states of blind rage, as well as a defensive state of *ruminative rehearsal* that took him away from interpersonal contacts. In his state of blind rage, he was like a righteous avenger aiming to harm his subordinates, whom he believed made him look foolish. In this state, he saw their inept actions as malicious: they were marauders intent on harming him by destroying his prestige.

The ruminative-rehearsal state involved a different self-schema—not as a righteous avenger, but as a capable loner doing his work. Also vaguely in mind during this state of working in isolation was a view of perfectionistic others who would eventually appraise his work. At times in the ruminative-rehearsal state, Jim would imagine another desired state. In the desired exhibitionist-excitement state, he would star as he showed off his outstanding work to an admiring group.

As described in that earlier chapter, Jim dreaded a state close to the desired one: that is, a state in which, while he was showing his work to a group, he would receive scorn rather than admiration. This feared state was also imagined during the states of ruminative rehearsal, and his self-concept of that fantasy was as a foolish jerk enduring *shameful mortification.* This simplification allows us to consider motivation in terms of role-relationship models that one desires, fears, or uses as defensive compromises. In chapter 1, I examined four of Jim's states in terms of what he desired, what he dreaded, what was a compromise achieving neither wish nor arriving at a feared state, and what was a problem: his blind rage at others because he feared they would make him look like a foolish jerk. Each of these states has a role-relationship model (see figure 3.1).

A person's repertoire of self-schemas and role-relationship models plays a part in determining his or her character traits, symptoms, career choice, and selection of friends and spouse. For example, among Jim's traits were self-isolation and hostility. His blind rages and his anxiety about the effect of these rages were severely impairing and so could be regarded as psychiatric symptoms. His career choice and his selection of friends and of a wife were determined in part by his need to assure himself he would only be admired without the risk of ever being scorned.

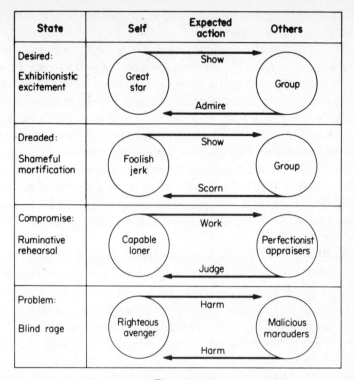

State	Self	Expected action	Others
Desired: Exhibitionistic excitement	Great star	Show → ← Admire	Group
Dreaded: Shameful mortification	Foolish jerk	Show → ← Scorn	Group
Compromise: Ruminative rehearsal	Capable loner	Work → ← Judge	Perfectionist appraisers
Problem: Blind rage	Righteous avenger	Harm → ← Harm	Malicious marauders

Figure 3.1

The Association of States with Role-Relationship Models

Properties of Role-Relationship Models

THE ETERNAL TRIANGLE

As already mentioned, role-relationship models may include three-party situations. These are so commonly the source of conflict and drama in plays, movies, and novels that they have been called "eternal triangles." Triangles of relationships are common in families. Even if there is only one child, there are often two parents; while a single parent may have a close friend or lover. The child may be jealous of the bond between the two adults. One adult may be jealous of the bond between the child and the other adult. If there is more than one child, one sibling may envy the other sibling the parent's attention. From repeated interactions in these everyday three-way situations, the child forms the schemas called role-relationship models. The growing child and, later, the adult increasingly tend to interpret three-party situations—whether romantic, among friends, or at the

45

workplace—according to the role-relationship models schematized from repetitive childhood transactions.

When three people are involved, the self may have schematic attitudes toward the bond between the other two persons, as well as toward the role of each of them. Figure 3.2 is a schema for various stories in which one woman desires to form an intimate relationship with an idealized man, for whom she is competing with another woman. If the man forms a bond with the other woman, the one who is rejected may feel envy that the two have gotten together and shame from the idea that the other two, or other people, might see her as being undesirable and rejected. In the relationship with the idealized man, the rejected woman may find that her efforts toward love have elicited a response that she has perceived as scornful from the idealized man. She will respond to him both with shame and with rage.

Because she has wished to have the bond between the man and the desired woman, the rejected woman may aim for some identification with the desired woman. Should the latter respond with contempt, however, the rejected woman may react first with hostility and then with guilt that she has been too angry. This is just one possible schema in such a triangle; variation of any of the roles—or of any aim, response, or reaction—would lead to many other schemas.

If a triangular schema of a specific sort is developed in a rivalry between a child and one parent for the attentions of another, then the schema may be a pattern used to interpret the meaning in triangular situations later in life. If the schema is used repeatedly as a working model for a series of situations, the assumptions the schema contains become automatic beliefs about what is happening. The person may not be conscious that his or her perceptions and responses are dictated by inner forms rather than by outer realities.

LIFELONG SCRIPTS

Some scripts involve schematic knowledge of short sequences of action. For example, a restaurant script contains knowledge of how to order food, pay the bill, add a tip, and generally behave in that setting; and one may have different restaurant scripts for different types of food-serving establishments or for dining out in particular cultures. Lifelong scripts tend to dictate one's repeated behavior over time in relationships with others.

Like other schematic forms, lifelong scripts may operate outside of awareness and yet dynamically affect a person's choices. The operation of such schematic forms has been called "games" (Berne 1972), "complexes"

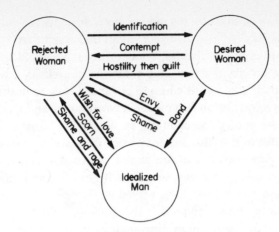

Figure 3.2
Triangular Role-Relationship Model

(Charcot 1877; Jung 1959), "unconscious fantasies" (Freud 1915; Arlow 1969), "schemactive cores" of individual personality (Knapp 1974), "core conflictual relationship themes" (Luborsky 1977), and "plans" (Weiss and Sampson 1986).

Children suffer if they are not loved. Even if caregivers are unable to love because of illness or stressful outside circumstances, the children may blame themselves. The child develops a schematic attitude that says in effect, "I have not been loved because I am, at the core, unlovable" (Wurmser 1981). This degraded self-schema may predict the future ("I shall never be loved" [Beck et al. 1976]), and do so because the role of self is inscribed in such a schema ("I am unlovable because I am weak, dirty, and defective"). Even with such beliefs, one may retain a sense of hope. Lifelong scripts may be based on a strong intention of creative accomplishment or heroic self-sacrifice in order to convince others that the self is finally worthy of love.

Many life plans are simply progressive: to achieve desired goals, such as a successful career. Other life plans are based on scripts of ways to compensate for past deficiencies; or to make up for, magically undo, or realistically prevent the recurrence of previous traumas. Psychodynamics is most concerned with these, as such unconscious agendas are the ones most likely to be maladaptive in relation to real opportunities.

Conflicted aims and feared responses to them can sometimes be resolved by rationalizations: that is, by excuses that permit expression of a desire that one has otherwise to ward off as being improper. For example, a boy may want to be cuddled by his mother because he feels lonely; yet, at the same time, he may have formed peer values that assert that "cuddling" and "mommy" are only for "babies," not for boys. To avoid the ridicule he expects from others, the boy may fantasize himself as a wounded soldier—a role that would entitle him to be nursed back to health by a caring woman. This role-relationship model between nurse and wounded soldier would be close enough to cuddling to satisfy his wish for that kind of closeness. Later in life, the boy may unconsciously seek to be injured as a means of being nursed, a means as self-destructive as it is maladaptive. Hero fantasies along this line, usually with erotic sexual components as nurse and hero fall in love, have served as the frame for many works of fiction, indicating how universal is this lifelong script.

Lifelong scripts may contain unconscious beliefs that can lead to dissatisfaction. For example, a girl may believe: "My dad is proud of how well I'm learning to play the violin. But he plays the oboe even better than I play the violin. I want to grow up and play the violin even better than he plays the oboe. However, were I to play better than he does, he might feel envious of me as I now feel envious of him. That might hurt him just as I sometimes feel mortified by my mistakes, compared to how he plays. So I will not try very hard, I will stop short." Or: "So, I will do my very best but then I will find some way to punish myself in order to make it up to him." Such a person, upon succeeding as an adult, may unconsciously throw away new opportunities afforded by that success or become depressed rather than satisfied.

Life-plan scripts are complex, in that they involve a sequence of role-relationship models, including a shift in self-schemas. For example, André, as an adolescent, had multiple views, or role-relationship models, of how he might relate to a woman: one depicting romantic spirituality in which he was good and heroic, in a state of mutual admiration and devotion to a fine but asexual young woman; one of himself as a lusting male stud taking advantage of a woman who was unable to prevent her sexual excitation from leading her into erotic acts she otherwise would think bad; and one of a powerful and consuming woman sexually attracted to him, a woman who would then cast a spell upon him—enmeshing, smothering, trapping, and ensnaring him.

André had a life plan that combined these three role-relationship models into a fixed, sequential script. Its repetitions became apparent during his psychotherapy as an adult. In the beginning of one of these repetitive and maladaptive interpersonal patterns, he would approach an alluring woman, thinking of her according to the romantic-relationship model. In fantasies based on this script, he would first rescue her from a molester and she would therefore love him. In the daydream, they would then share sexual acts. After sexual consummation, he imagined that she would change from the desirable and devoted woman into a domineering and demanding one. Now she would control and use him, and he would hate that. His self-concept and role changed from hero to helpless victim as this script unfolded into any specific daydream.

This script led André to a double standard in which he stereotyped all women as either "good" or "bad." With "good" women he was unable to feel erotic because that would make him want to commit sexual acts they would regard as dirty, and he would then have to feel guilty or ashamed. With "bad" women he felt unable to feel intimate warmth because they would regard him as something they could own, as a possession for their own purposes. Later in life, André was able to react physically to sexually attractive women, but he then deserted them before they could, as he saw it, entrap him. He quickly conceptualized each new woman as being one or another of his limited stereotypes, instead of appraising her according to her real characteristics. The result was André's maladaptive repetition of a rigid pattern and failure to learn intimate loving.

NEW ENCOUNTERS AND WORKING MODELS OF THE RELATIONSHIP

When a new opportunity for an interpersonal relationship occurs, one should, ideally, be ready to make new observations, including recognition of the other person's behavior with inferences about his or her intentions and motives. A sagacious person utilizes both such new observations and existing schemas of how people tend to behave to develop a *working model* of the current relationship, a temporary concept of the interaction with a new person from both observation and inner schemas (Bowlby 1973). Such working models organize decisions about how to respond at each new moment, or instance, in an encounter.

Working models of a relationship are modified as an encounter continues. While one unconsciously makes these decisions to modify the working model, at difficult junctures one consciously attends to solving problems or to choosing among multiple alternatives. The repetitions over time of working models can alter enduring schemas such as role-relationship models.

A person may be handicapped by two kinds of deflection from the sagacious position of being able to use both enduring role-relationship models and new observations to form working models. On the one hand, one may make excessive use of enduring schemas, so that inappropriate

49

scripts intrude into the unfolding reality situation. Rather than a new opportunity, the encounter is then distorted from its realistic possibilities into a recurrent maladaptive behavioral pattern (Peterfreund 1971; Luborsky 1984; Strupp and Binder 1984; Horowitz 1987). On the other hand, by making too little use of interpersonal knowledge retained as schemas, one may be unable to penetrate beneath the other's surface behavior and read that person's covert intentions.

The relationship between actual transactions in an encounter with another person and the internal representations of that transaction is shown diagramatically in figure 3.3. The pattern between self and other in terms of real actions is what occurs in the large box of that figure. What goes on in the mind of the subject about the self and the object is shown in the circle to the left, symbolizing the subject.

Within the mind of the subject, perceiving, thinking, emoting, schematizing, and planning actions are all organized by various types of schemas. One type of schema is the working model of the social transaction; another type is the set of enduring schemas about such social interactions. The working model is affected by perception of the actual properties of the social situation, and affects actions of the self within that situation.

The working model is also affected by enduring schemas. For any type of situation the subject may have available a variety of role-relationship models that might influence and organize understanding of what is going on. At any given moment in the real situation, the subject might have a working model relatively dominated by the role-relationship model, or enduring schema, that had the best fit to the properties observed, and also to the situational properties wanted or dreaded by the subject. This dominant role-relationship model in organizing a working model is shown by the heavy arrow in figure 3.3.

Other role-relationship models may be enduring schemas that simultaneously, in parallel, organize potential views of the social transaction, but that do not achieve control over action by influencing consciousness. Their effects might emerge later, as when the transaction appears in dreams or daydreams as a kind of review of what might have been. These parallel processing role-relationship models are shown in contact with the working model through dotted lines. The main concept is that multiple schemas are available for, and possibly partially active in, forming a working model of a situation. Some elements in a repertoire of enduring schemas may be dormant in terms of such activity, as symbolized by a lack of lines between enduring role-relationship models and the working model.

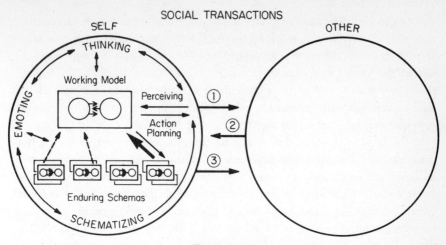

Figure 3.3
Social Transactions Modeled Within the Mind

Processes Involving Role-Relationship Models

PARALLEL PROCESSING

In *parallel processing,* a single interpersonal situation can be interpreted by an individual according to several role-relationship models at once. These schemas may operate simultaneously and unconsciously and may compete to become the dominant and conscious organizing view of a situation as was shown in figure 3.3. An example of parallel processing on a given theme is provided by the case of Adam, a graduate student in physics who delayed getting his doctorate because of procrastination in completing his thesis.

In working on his thesis, Adam had to consult with his graduate supervisor, a professor of physics at his university. Adam often delayed presenting the current status of his work to the professor, and instead, while alone in his room, would enter a state of *unproductive and ruminative worry* on the theme of his pending presentation. He sometimes reproduced this state of ruminative worry during the discussions with his professor, and often did reproduce it in discussions with his psychotherapist on the theme of procrastination. As with his psychotherapy, a session with his graduate supervisor would often begin with Adam exposing a current problem. He did not always worry about how this exposure would be met; he sometimes expected and received help. At such times, Adam was in a *working* state. There were two other states of mind, *excited reverie* and *passive complaining,* that also began with the idea of communicating a current problem to another man. Ruminative worry, working, excited reverie, and passive complaining were states with different role-relationship models, even if the first act of self in the model was exposure of a problem. Adam might be in any of these four states, using any of these four working models of the relationship, when with the professor, when discussing the situation with the psychotherapist, and when alone.

In the working state, Adam was a halting, sincere student, exposing his problem, and expecting the professor to maintain the role as earnest and patient teacher. As long as Adam was organizing his experience according to this role-relationship model, the expected script in which the teacher would provide help, and Adam would continue to work, tended to operate to organize what he did and how he felt. This role-relationship model is diagrammed in the top row of figure 3.4 where it may be compared with the other schemas relevant to this type of situation. Unfortunately triggers either from within Adam or from the teacher might lead to Adam's organizing the situation according to another role-relationship model. For example, if the teacher became impatient or abrupt, Adam might shift to the role-relationship model of his state of ruminative worry, shown in the second row of figure 3.4. In this role-relationship model, he schematized himself as an incompetent child in relation to a superior authority. With the same beginning of a script—that is, exposing his problem of procrastination—he then expected the superior authority to label his shortcomings in such a scornful way that Adam would then feel like giving up.

Most of the time Adam was either in the working state or that of ruminative worry, with the latter occurring too frequently to allow him to meet the necessary deadlines on his dissertation. The more he delayed, the more he worried! There were, however, two other states which occasionally emerged. One was a state of excited reverie, in which he imagined that he was a great scientist exposing the problem to his professor, whom he saw somewhat contemptuously as only an ordinary scientist. As an ordinary scientist, the professor was unable to help him, but suddenly Adam would provide a great solution, catapulting him to fame. While usually this was a pleasant daydream which actually encouraged him to get on with some work, at other times it became an absorbing preoccupation that prevented work. It rarely emerged during the confrontations with the teacher or the psychotherapist, during which Adam would get somewhat overexcited about a relatively minor forward movement.

The fourth role-relationship model prominent in Adam's theme of procrastination underlay a state in which he was *passive and complaining,* often annoying others with a kind of whining demandingness. In this state, he

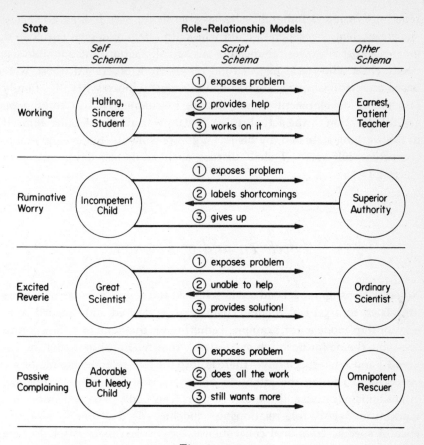

State	Role-Relationship Models		
	Self Schema	*Script Schema*	*Other Schema*
Working	Halting, Sincere Student	① exposes problem / ② provides help / ③ works on it	Earnest, Patient Teacher
Ruminative Worry	Incompetent Child	① exposes problem / ② labels shortcomings / ③ gives up	Superior Authority
Excited Reverie	Great Scientist	① exposes problem / ② unable to help / ③ provides solution!	Ordinary Scientist
Passive Complaining	Adorable But Needy Child	① exposes problem / ② does all the work / ③ still wants more	Omnipotent Rescuer

Figure 3.4
Role-Relationship Models Related to the Theme of Procrastination

conceptualized himself not as a whiner but rather as an adorable but needy child, who in exposing his problem was expecting an omnipotent rescuer to do all the work for him. When that happened, he still wanted more because all problems were not fully solved for him. Only in retrospect, after an interview with his professor, might Adam recognize this behavior, and then he would feel disgusted with himself.

To recapitulate, each of Adam's role-relationship models, as in figure 3.4, begins with the first step of the script being an exposure of the problem of procrastination in doing his doctoral thesis work. The way Adam organized his communications, including his emotional vocal tone and visual expressions, depended on the underlying role-relationship model instantiated at the time. This, in turn, depended in part on Adam's repertoire and in part on how the professor behaved in the actual situation. Adam's repertoire included four self-schemas (see figure 3.4): halting adult and sincere student, incompetent child who didn't belong in graduate school, great scientist who was far ahead of his actual position, and adorable but needy child who could expect total rescue from others. All these were based on relationships Adam had had during childhood within his family (a topic of development I shall discuss in chapter 7). By working on careful attention to the actual reality, Adam was able to stabilize himself in the working state and, by his real accomplishments, to develop a more competent self-view. (I shall discuss such adult self-development in chapter 11.)

Effects on and of Emotion

Role-relationship models, like self-schemas and scripts in general, may be associated to a general theme. There may be desired and dreaded role-relationship models: for example, centering on the issue of exhibition of self—the theme for both Jim and Adam's role-relationship models in figures 3.1 and 3.4, respectively—there is both the role-relationship model for success and gaining the attention of others, and for failure where the attention is negative and the person then feels badly. The activation to a working model of a role-relationship model may lead to conscious experience of specific emotional consequences: joy, when there is felt to be a positive response to self-exhibition, for example; and shame, when there is felt to be a negative attention from others or from self as self-observer. These emotions of joy or shame act as motivators; shame causes the individual to want to hide; joy may cause the person to wish to join further with others in triumphant exhibitions, as in the rituals of football players on making a touchdown, or athletes in other team sports on achieving victory (Lewis and Berman 1965; Lewis 1971; Wurmser 1981).

Similar pairings occur with guilt and hostility. There may be role-relationship models in which the self is an aggressor and the other is the target of the aggression. There may be more exciting and even joyous role-relationship models of hostility, in which the self is seen as a righteous hero and the other as a monster deserving of destruction. In a guilt-evoking role-relationship model, the other is seen as relatively innocent and the self as being too hostile in relation to the situation. As guilt increases, there is a reduction in the tendency to use the more righteously hostile role-relationship model as a working model. Emotional potentials are contained in the schemas called role-relationship models. Activated schemas, or working models, may activate emotional systems. The latter affect the body itself, and bodily sensation then provides another input into conscious awareness. The person may dread certain states of conscious experience and so seek to reduce that emotional input by putting the damper on a situation, or a working model of the situation.

In addition to having these feedback effects on activity of various role-relationship models, aroused emotions are signals to others. An expression of shame may reduce the scorn of others unless they are especially sadistic and want to tread on weaker persons. An expression of guilty remorse may appease others who are angry at the subject. The change in others affects the external situation, and that affects the subject's working model of the situation. The emission of such emotional signals to both the self and others is usually not consciously controlled, but is rather due to unconscious mental processes. Such unconsciously formed emotional expressions include blushing in a state of shame, and facial and bodily expressions of remorse. Aroused emotional systems affect motor behavior and organ physiology leading to conscious experience of these cues of emotional arousal. There may then be secondary emotional responses, such as shame or anger at blushing.

Anticipation of actions and fantasy or inner rehearsal also activate emotions, which may then alter what one plans. For example, when Adam fantasized an exciting solution to his scientific problems, he became more eager to present his work to his professor; but, as was more likely, when he anticipated being criticized for falling far short of necessary accomplishments, he wanted to remain withdrawn.

REGRESSION AND PROGRESSION

Regression, the opposite of *progression,* means retreat or return. Movement in either direction can occur in respect to role-relationship models. Take this case of a busy physician who developed a serious injury requiring long hospitalization and convalescence: Having been habitually active, hard working, and involved in helping others, Sam was forced into passive receptivity after a fracture of his spine and pelvis in an automobile accident. Long ago he had a role-relationship model as a passive child receiving care when sick, but this model had been dormant for a long time. He now regressed to use of this earlier view of himself as a *child,* rather than as a sick *adult.* He tried to compensate for feeling too childlike by aggressively rejecting his caregivers.

A progression would have been for Sam to learn adaptive acceptance of his new condition, instantiating a new role-relationship model as an injured adult justified in being passively cared for. A regression was his return to the child and caretaker role-relationship model. Both progressive and regressive patterns occurred during his recovery: first regression; then modification of the role-relationship model of receiving care so that his self-concept gained adult, if partially disabled and dependent, characteristics.

Sam eventually progressed even further in development of his self-organization as a consequence of working through the psychological response to stress induced by his traumatic experiences during and after the accident. For a long time, he had organized his behavior around a self-concept as an expert, responsible, "in charge" physician. He had used this "doctor" self-concept in order to master and rise above otherwise threatening feelings of worthlessness he had had in childhood. The "worthless child" self-schema remained dormant in his repertoire, associated with a value belief that "individuals who do not produce are worthless and not deserving of care by others." The conversion from a regressive working model of himself as dependent on others to a new, progressive one for the same real situation of disability required learning alternatives to such habitual but irrational attitudes. The concept of being all right while "doing nothing" became a new value schema. After Sam's recovery, this new attitude modified his views of his own patients, and he became more sympathetic and compassionate. The change allowed him to have more adult-to-adult encounters with them, rather than his usual previous parental stance in which he regarded sick adult patients as helpless children, and sometimes as worthless and lazy.

ROLE REVERSAL

Before his accident, Sam had insisted on viewing himself only as the strong and competent one in a role-relationship model between a caregiver and a needy person. He learned to occupy either role in the course of developing a working model appropriate to his disabled situation, and thus became more flexible as a person.

Usually, a person in forming a working model from an enduring role-relationship model can place the self in any role of the schema. Some roles, occupied by the self, may lead to more negative emotions than others. In general, if a weak person is threatened by a strong person, the weak person would prefer to reverse roles. Learning the role of the stronger person in repeated transactions occurs through a process called *identification*. Because of identification with parents, one learns to be a parent. This learning from the roles of others is unconscious as well as conscious. Thus, some adults are surprised when they observe themselves following parenting patterns that they disliked in their parents as a child, and vowed to avoid when they occupied that role. One identifies as well by observing teachers, friends, peers, movie stars, and admired characters in books. The words *incorporation* and *introjection* have also been used for *internalization* of a role into one's self-organization. The routes to development of schemas of self will be discussed in chapter 6, and to development of role-relationship models in chapter 7.

Once both roles in a two-person working model have been learned through identification, role reversal can serve a defensive purpose. Thus, Adam, in order to avoid being criticized by his professor, could occupy the latter's role of superior scientist and criticize him; and Sam, reversing a role he felt to be unpleasant, chose to be a doctor and take care of others, rather than be a weak child.

Play can aid in forming new positions of the self in working models of situations. The repetitions found in play allow experiments of role reversal and learning by identification. For example, four-year-old Eve suffered the stress of having her parents away for two weeks on a long trip. After the initial reunion when her parents returned, Eve wanted to play at being the one who leaves and returns. She accomplished this by hiding in the house. There were many repetitions of the happy reunion each time she was found. Eve repeated this game over and over again; and, though her parents tired of it before she did, they continued with it as long as she needed its reassurance.

TRANSFERENCE AND COUNTERTRANSFERENCE

The application of erroneous inner motives and role-relationship models onto people and situations has been called *transference.* Freud (1912) named such phenomena in psychoanalysis *transference reactions* because the person was seen as transferring an aim formed in respect, or reaction, to an early developmentally important figure such as a parent or sibling. This continuation of early wishes and fears, as a script for reactions, was assumed to proceed without the subject's being conscious of transferring the inappropriate motives, ideas, and feelings to the new person.

In interpersonal transactions, transference behavior patterns can elicit a complementary response. The other person may respond according to a working model of the relationship similar in some ways to the working model of the person exhibiting the transference pattern. The second party is said to have a *countertransference reaction.*

Certain common transference patterns in psychotherapy include the following: *Negative transference reactions* are unrealistic expectations that the therapist will be hostile, critical, abandoning, negligent, stupid, or exploitative. In a *positive transference,* one falls in love with the therapist while having the unrealistic expectation that the therapist will be loving, all-providing, omnipotent, admiring, erotic, or exalted by this form of contact with the patient. A *maternal transference* is the unrealistic expectation that the engagement with the therapist will repeat role-relationship models developed with the mother. Similarly, a *paternal or sibling transference* involves expectation of reenactment of fantasies, scripts, and role-relationship models related to the father, or to brothers or sisters. *Pre-oedipal transferences* involve themes of nurturance and control without issues of sexual longing or rivalry. *Oedipal transferences* are sexually thematic ones involving the erotic urges, envies, and jealousies of the "eternal triangle" discussed earlier (Greenson 1967). *Mirror transferences* are those in which the patient has persistent unrealistic views that the therapist's only role is to reflect an admiring response to self-exhibition. In an *idealizing transference,* a patient unrealistically expects self-enhancement from being merely associated with a great therapist; and in a *twinship transference* one views as self-restorative a continuing contiguity with the other (Kohut 1972, 1977, 1984).

Conclusion

Schemas of persons organize information about how transactions and expressions of feeling take place. Role-relationship models are an important type of person schema because they contain the attributes of self and other, as well as the script-like sequence of probable interaction. Sometimes an insistent use of inappropriate role-relationship models seems to occur, resulting in recurrent maladaptive patterns of interpersonal behavior. At other times, something new happens in the environment, creating a poor fit between external demands and available role-relationship models. The outcome may be the states of stress described in chapter 1.

The discrepancy in information between the characteristics of the real situation and available enduring schemas means that, in order to reduce stress and attain more adaptive states, the person under this kind of stress must observe the situation closely and construct in his or her mind a new working model. Eventually the information in this new working model will, by repetition, alter the enduring schemas so that they fit the new realities. That process is the topic of the next chapter.

4

The Impact of Stress
on Self-Schemas
and Role-Relationship
Models

INJURY, violence, and confrontation with sudden death are shocking experiences. To adapt to a drastic and unexpected event, one has to absorb its implications and revise existing schemas. Between the event and this revision, the person experiences the signs and symptoms of stress described in chapter 1. In this chapter, I will discuss several symptoms and emotional themes that can affect a person after a serious event until schemas of self and other catch up to new realities. I will use bereavement as an example, discussing it in some detail, because mourning is a process of schematic change that everyone experiences at one time or another. The difference between normal and pathological grief, in this context, may be used to illustrate how one can judge a psychological reaction to be "normal" or "abnormal."

The discrepancy between the stressful event and one's usual life and expectations may also lead to feelings of estrangement from one's own identity—a symptom called *depersonalization*—or that the situation is not real—a symptom called *derealization* (Brauer, Harrow, and Tucker 1970; Horowitz 1986). The case of Irv illustrates some aspects of these mental responses to stress.

Irv was out of town on a business trip when, to his surprise, he ran into his college roommate at a coffee shop. Gordon and he had not seen each other for fifteen years. They had a meal together, and were both excited and interested in catching up with each other's lives. During the meal, two burly men approached their table and began to threaten Gordon because he had not paid a gambling debt. One of the men grabbed him by his jacket lapels and yanked him up from his chair. Irv, as if by protective reflex, rose to his feet, but was shoved back into his chair by the man's companion.

Then, as Irv later recalled, he just sat there for a while with a silly and conciliatory smile on his face. He had a momentary feeling of unreality and thought, "This isn't happening to me." While feeling that this situation was unreal, he was nonetheless vigilantly scanning it for its threatening possibilities.

While Irv sat immobile, Gordon suddenly punched his assailant, and a scuffle followed. Although Irv recalled fighting with the other man, he could not recall the interval from sitting to fighting. The police arrived, and all four men were arrested because the restaurant furnishings had been damaged. Irv felt alert and very competent while telling the police his story. Each of the four men was released on a misdemeanor charge and wrote out a check for the damages. The two assailants went off together, after glaring ferociously at Irv and Gordon. Irv returned alone to his motel.

Lying on his bed, he felt that he himself was strangely unreal, as if he were viewing himself from afar as a detached other being: this was *depersonalization*. In addition, he felt as if the memory of the fight and the police was itself unreal, as if it were a dream or fantasy: this was *derealization*. He tried to puzzle over his memory of the scuffle. He could recall the story as it had occurred, remembering how he had been a victim, a fighter, and then treated as a possible criminal. All these roles seemed foreign to him.

In the ensuing weeks, Irv had vivid flashbacks and pictorial images of the event. He also turned the memory over in his mind, thinking about what it meant, and telling himself what really happened. Gradually it became as real as his other memories and lost the strange quality of seeming unreal and not a part of his life.

Memories of a stressful event remain in the mind, to recur as vivid mental images, as in the case of Irv's experience with violence. During the repetitions in memory, inner meanings accrue to the stressful life event as both rational and irrational interpretations of its causes and implications.

In such mental reviews, certain themes are "universal" in that many (but not all) persons touch upon them in the course of integrating the stressful event with self-schemas. These themes include fear of repetition, shame at one's helplessness, rage with ensuing guilt, survivor guilt, fear of identification with victims, and the threat of loss.

Recurrent Themes Following
Stressful Life Events

FEAR OF REPETITION

The person who has had one bad accident is likely to be gripped with the fear that he or she may have another. To cope with this fear, one may have to modify existing self-schemas, since most of us carry an unconscious sense of personal invulnerability until something traumatic happens to us. The self-view may then shift to being more realistic or even to feeling excessively vulnerable. Expectations may shift beyond reasonable caution to unrealistic fear.

SHAME AT ONE'S HELPLESSNESS

Because a stressful event usually involves or threatens loss, fear, or pain, it makes a person feel helpless. One may then feel ashamed of being helpless, if that has become an aspect of one of the person's role-relationship models. In some cases, a component in the precipitating life event supports the sense of personal incompetence, as when the person has looked away from traffic and so caused an automobile accident. Even one who has had no control over events may still ruminate about the failure to avoid them, seeking to explain why one let oneself in for what turned out to be a bad circumstance: a woman in a car crash, for example, may worry about why she took the particular route that led to the car crash or why she got in the car in the first place.

RAGE AT THE "CAUSE" AND ENSUING GUILT

A common reaction to frustration is to rage at any cause that one can identify as being responsible for it. One may blame any nearby person for an injury that occurred entirely without that person's involvement: after an accident, say, one may rage at an ambulance attendant, who has come on the scene only afterward.

After expressing such rage, one may then feel guilty to have reacted so.

Destructive fantasies are common after psychic trauma, and some people fear they will lose control over them and act them out. A man who has been assaulted by a member of a specific cultural subgroup, for example, may be frightened that he will act out revengeful fantasies on innocent members of the same subgroup.

SURVIVOR GUILT

When others have been injured or killed in a disaster, the person who has not been harmed may respond with immediate relief at having been spared. The survivor may also equate this relief with pleasure that others were the victims. The wish to survive conflicts with the moral injunction, developed in families, that one should share the fate of others. The result of this is guilt. The survivor may even engage in magical thinking and conclude that the wish to be spared occurred before the event, and thus that he or she is to blame for others' death or injury. Just the memory of a relieved thought—"I'm glad to be alive!"—can lead to a sense of being selfish or too fortunate after a disaster.

FEAR OF IDENTIFICATION OR MERGER WITH VICTIMS

One may fear that the self will be placed in the same role as the victim of a harmful experience even when the victim is unknown. For example, one who witnesses a suicide may become frightened that one is oneself suicidal, or will become so, perhaps by activation of some otherwise latent source of personal despair. If a loved one has fallen ill and died, it is not uncommon for the survivor to fear death from the same illness at some time during the mourning period. The belief in identical fate is based on "we" schemas, where the self is joined to others in a shared affiliation. This happens not only in families and bands of peers but as a social tendency in human beings, especially when threatened. At a pathological level one may experience an irrational sense of being fused with a victim, a merger sensation to be discussed further in chapter 5.

THE THREAT OF LOSS

Stressful events usually entail actual or threatened loss, such as of honor or wealth, or of a body part or a loved one. The self may suddenly feel diminished and terrified by the possibility of never recovering from the event.

Each of the themes just mentioned can occur as a transitory preoccupation following a stressful life event. Usually the theme is considered and then resolved positively, as the fear of repetition gives way to a sense of safety; one again feels effective and competent, rather than shamed, help-less, guilty, or vulnerable. Inner conflict and schemas of the self as weak, defective, or bad may impede such forward movement, however, in resolv-ing themes brought to mind in efforts to understand a potentially trau-matic experience.

The Ability to Cope with Major Stress

While everyone dreads illness, loss, and impairment, some of us are more vulnerable to succumbing to one kind of stressful life event and especially resilient to another. These vulnerabilities and strengths depend in part on existing schemas. A woman who has a self-schema as competent caregiver may readily rise to the occasion when someone else falls ill. While sympa-thetic to the distress of her patient, she may nonetheless enjoy a sense of enhanced self-esteem as she provides appropriate care. If this same woman has a role-relationship model in which she becomes shamefully humiliated in competition, she may be more strained in a stressful struggle for achievement.

As mentioned earlier, irrationally weak self-concepts may hinder adap-tation to stress. But a stronger self-concept does not necessarily lead to greater resiliency. Matthew, for example, was usually quite hypochondria-cal, fearing that a minor twitch of pain or a pimple meant he had a serious disease. An unusual heartbeat, a gas pain, or a weight loss of one or two pounds sent him to his physician for reassurance. His hypochondriasis was based in part on a previously developed self-schema of vulnerability to physical damage and an enduring attitude that he would have a loss of adult bodily competence because he was a bad boy, "abusing" himself by masturbating as a young adolescent.

Matthew's brother Bill did not have such a vulnerable self-schema of bodily damage. The two men worked together as truck drivers, taking turns driving so that they could cover long distances. Crossing an icy mountain pass, their tank truck skidded on the shoulder of the road and overturned. Due to a rupture in the pipes, a cloud of toxic chlorine gas was released. As a result, they both had lengthy hospitalizations due to serious lung damage, followed by a long convalescence.

As they recovered, each man had episodes of frightening difficulty in breathing. During this illness, Matthew showed a greater ability than Bill to cooperate with the treatment and more stamina in enduring the periodic discomforts and frights. This surprised everyone in the family, since they would have expected the opposite owing to Matthew's history of hypochondriasis before the accident.

Many factors seemed to account for the stark reversal in behavior, among which was the fact that Matthew had already rehearsed the role of being ill. His script in this role did not include death as an outcome; he saw the illness, rather, as a period of retribution that would cleanse him of previous contamination from evil sexual acts. When this long-feared period now occurred in reality, it almost seemed like a relief, a penance long overdue, a cleansing of his guilt.

Bill, in contrast, had regarded himself as invulnerable. He felt that any illness, if it finally came, would strike only his brother. His previous attitudes did not include the expectation of personal illness, and he did not know how to cope with his disability. The abrupt change from his usual healthy bodily feelings to fear of sudden death during the periods of difficult breathing was terrifying. He had a recurrent anxiety-provoking fantasy of being unable to breathe, of being pronounced dead and buried while still alive.

After they recovered sufficiently, the respiratory capacity of both brothers still had some residual impairment. They tired easily and could not exercise vigorously. During the slow rehabilitation over several years, Bill began to feel more resilient than Matthew, eventually regaining his zest for life, while Matthew continued to have episodic anxiety and hypochondriasis.

Thus, personal injury, as in the case of Matthew and Bill, creates a discrepancy between what used to be and now is the actual body, and between the actual body and the existing schema for it. This discrepancy is resolved through change either in the current situation so that it accords with schemas, or in schemas so that they come closer to the current reality.

The Stress of Bereavement

Mourning the death of a loved one involves a revision of schemas that is prototypical of other types of stress-induced change. Mourning, in general, is both a giving-up and a learning process. During mourning, one abandons certain schemas and learns new ones.

The terms *grief* and *mourning* have been used in many ways. Usually *grief* refers to subjective experiences, and *mourning* to processes through which a state of grief is attenuated. *Pathological grief* is the intensification of a state of grief to the degree that a person is overwhelmed, exhibits maladaptive behavior, or remains interminably grief-stricken.

Karl Abraham (1924) and Sigmund Freud (1917) differentiated normal from pathological grief. They characterized normal grief as feelings of painful dejection, with loss of interest in life functions and inhibition of activities; and pathological grief as lasting an excessive period and as exhibiting panic, hostility toward the self, regression to narcissistic forms of self-preoccupation, and other signs of deflated self-esteem. These additional features were explained by a theory that postulated a pre-existing relationship with the deceased characterized by ambivalent (loving and hating) role-relationship models. After the death, the ambivalence was thought to be internalized, leading to self-hatred. Self-hatred, felt as depression, was also self-punishment on the grounds, supported by magical thinking, that the hatred of the other led to the death, and thus the self was at fault.

Subsequent field studies and continued clinical investigations of bereavement indicate that hostility toward the self, characterized as pathogenic by Abraham and Freud, is not an uncommon grief reaction in persons who do not otherwise warrant diagnoses as mentally disordered (Raphael 1982; Parkes 1972; Horowitz 1986). Periods of self-blame, hatred, and disgust may occur in normal grief. States of mind characterized by inertia, hypochondriasis, numbness, irritability, feelings of worthlessness, and apathy have also been noted in normal grief reactions (Jacobson 1946, 1971; Schmale and Engel 1975; Horowitz 1986). These experiences are probably conscious manifestations of the unconscious review of the assault upon self-organization occasioned by the loss and other threats, as well as transient appraisals that the situation may be hopeless in terms of personal recovery.

As one works through the loss, restoring self-organization and schemas to an acceptable accord with reality, one's sense of mastery of life returns. This sense is, of course, only relative—no one is ever the master of life; and some aspects of grief and mourning persist. Excessive persistence of the feelings of inertia, hypochondriasis, self-hatred, worthlessness, and intolerable pining for the deceased, or excessive intensity of these experiences, indicates that a pathological reaction is present, one that may require professional consultation and help.

The phases of grief are a variant on the states of mind common after any stress or life event, having periods of outcry and intrusion as well as periods of denial, emotional numbing, and warding off of implications. Whether these are normal or pathological experiences depends to a large extent on how much the loss damages existing self-schemas and role-relationship models, on which usually dormant self-schemas and role-relationship models may be activated by the reactions to the loss, and on which situational deficits or social supports follow upon the loss.

The distinction between a normal response to stress and its pathological intensification, variation, or derailment will now be illustrated by breaking down a mourning process into typical phases of response during the grief of many (but not all) persons.

OUTCRY

As illustrated in figure 4.1 the first phase of psychological response to traumatic news, such as the death of a loved one, is often one in which there is intense expression of emotion: hence the label *outcry.* Interpersonal patterns often include turning to others for help and feeling a sense of close connection with them, although sometimes the opposite occurs, and the bereaved person isolates himself or herself in a self-succoring effort. In a pathological intensification of emotional response to such tragic news, some people may enter a *panic state* where behavior is erratic, and self-coherence is lost in a flood of uncontrolled fear and grief. Withdrawal, which can be a normal turning inward, may be exaggerated into a *dissociative state,* in which the person loses a sense of connection with memories of times just past or with relationships that are needed and available. The bereaved may enter a *reactive psychotic state,* expressing highly irrational and bizarre beliefs about why the death happened, or what it means to him or her. Weird attributions about one's role in the death can occur during such psychotic states. These states may resolve themselves quickly, and this form of pathological grief reaction does not mean that the person has a psychotic disorder like schizophrenia.

The states of mind that might occur during the outcry phase of response to news of a death are the result of strong emotions activated by a mismatch between an *enduring schema* and the *current working model* of the immediate situation. The enduring schema is a role-relationship model of the self being together with the person. The working model shows the relationship threatened by the death of the other. This discrepancy activates emotional systems, contributing to the various phenomena felt consciously by the person, or observed by others, during the outcry phase.

The working model is not necessarily an accurate depiction of the external reality; it may depict the loved one not as dead but rather as under great threat of harm. Part of the intense emotional arousal is in reaction to this threat, evoking wishes and plans to protect the deceased, along with a fear that rescue is impossible. During the outcry phase, for that reason, there may be many intense states of mind, with emotions like high alarm, rage, or remorse, as well as sudden grief. There may be frantic behaviors as the person undertakes hopeless actions to protect the deceased from dying, since the working model may depict the deceased as not yet dead but rather as still being "torn away" from life. Some funeral rituals serve the need of the living to "do something" for the deceased, although such rituals have other important functions as well.

DENIAL PHASE

A normal grief response may go from an outcry of sorrow to a phase of increased control over ideas and feelings. During this phase of mourning, one may avoid reminders of the deceased and focus attention on other themes. An *emotional blunting,* even *numbness,* may occur. This effort to retain a sense of self-competency will, when successful, lead to the next phase, where one will contemplate, perhaps intrusively, the warded-off ideas and feelings. But it is not always possible to maintain such unconscious control efforts within adaptive limits, and states may occur that include abnormal symptoms or maladaptive qualities. These states can include overuse of drugs or alcohol to anesthetize the person to pain. Some persons may seek to jam all channels of consciousness with stimuli, avoiding thinking and feeling about the death. To escape feeling dead and unreal, one may engage in frenzied sexual, athletic, work, thrill-seeking, or risk-taking activities.

During denial phases, one may preserve the enduring role-relationship model of the deceased as alive, with the potential to interact with the self. Working models incorporating the idea of the deceased as dead may develop, but are not always used. This may lead to discussion of the deceased with others as if the deceased were still alive, as in describing a vacation that one might take with the deceased in the future or speaking of "we" to include the deceased in present and future activities. The person separates working models of the deceased as dead and working models of the deceased as alive. When the latter are in effect, the person may engage in expectant behavior at times when the deceased was likely to appear, as at the end of the working day.

INTRUSION PHASE

An intrusive phase often follows a period of relative denial and emotional blunting. During normal grief, one may go through a time of intrusive experiences, including recollections of negative relationship experiences with the deceased, *bad dreams,* and daytime *preoccupations* that may interfere with concentration on other tasks. In *pathological grief,* there may be intensification of such experiences, to the point where one feels secondarily frightened by the loss of control over conscious ideas and feelings. Night terrors, or recurring nightmares, may disrupt sleep, and the person may become distraught from fatigue and the *intrusion of undermodulated states* with moods of rage, despair, shame, guilt, and fear. Pathological grief is also marked by failure to work gradually through these themes, with an extension of the intrusion phase for many months or even years, rather than a gradual reduction in intrusiveness of memories and fantasies.

During the intrusive phase, there are especially strong pangs of feeling and undercontrolled states of mind if the bereaved spent a lot of time with the deceased before his or her death. In such cases, the situation is "empty," the working model does not have the structure of the enduring role-relationship model, and the result is an emotion in reaction to the difference. This emotion is usually a piercing pang of intense sadness, but sometimes takes the form of rage or self-disgust, depending on who or what is blamed as the source of the emptiness. In response, working models of searching for the deceased may develop as the person pines for and seeks what is missing. This is, in effect, a last-ditch effort at wish fulfillment in the face of the reality of death.

As the intrusive phase continues, there may be an oscillation between warding off of some themes, as was conspicuous in denial phases, intrusion of some themes, and attenuation of both extremes during what may then be called a *working-through* phase. In pathological grief, some themes occur that the person feels unable to integrate. The death may lead to a sense of personal fragility that seems incompatible with a self-concept showing one as capable, whole, and coherent. Persistent shamed, guilty, depressed, anxious, or bitter moods may lead to maladaptive behaviors and unacceptable discomfort. Psychophysiological disorders can occur or, if preexisting, can be exacerbated. Inability to work through the death then impedes one's ability to work, care for others, create, or experience positive states of mind.

As an aspect of the working-through process, the person who has been yearning for a relationship with the deceased may begin to have a change in schemas, leading to a deep emotional realization that the death is actual. One may want a new relationship with a new person who embodies some of the same features as the deceased in the pre-death relationship. The widow or widower may want to date a new person, the caregiver may seek a new person to take care of, the dependent person may desire a new parental figure. In such instances, the new relationship may build upon a role-relationship model that has endured from the relationship with the deceased. Working models, based on that enduring role-relationship model, may lead to some *misperceptions* and *unrealistic expectations* about the new person. Only gradually will the working models embody real aspects of the new relationship, modifying accordingly the enduring role-relationship model for that type of encounter. During the learning process, the person may make mistakes, perhaps calling the new person by the deceased's name, or feel awkward for having no automatic scripts of behavioral sequences with the new person, as with the deceased.

These sequences of change in schematizations of self and other during the phases of mourning are summarized in figure 4.1.

CHANGE IN SCHEMAS DURING MOURNING

John Bowlby has described in three volumes (1969, 1973, 1980) research and theory on the importance of attachment in human life. Attachment bonding is a matter of schema formation and association of motivational schemas with specific role-relationship models. Loss of the person in real life means one must revise schemas. This revision takes time, and mourning processes are seldom completed in less than a year. The shifts that take place in schemas are accomplished in unconscious mental processing, and are reflected as derivatives in patterns of conscious experience and behavior like those just summarized.

Any loss is a disruption of self-organization. During the period of adaptation, one searches through the repertoire of self-schemas to see which may be the most appropriate organizers for interpreting the new situation. Self-schemas that have been dormant as potential organizers for a long time may be used. The activation of these latent schemas may lead to a regression to states of mind that seem immature.

Among the more common deflections from normal states of mind are those in which the person has unusually intense and extended fearful worry, or unusually intense and extended irritability, or outbursts of rage during mourning. In tense states of fearful worry, often associated with pangs of utter despair or moments of giving up on life, the person may act according to schemas in which the self is weaker, more defective, and less capable than is actually the case. This person may have suffered intense separation anxiety in childhood or adolescence whenever separated from a nurturing caregiver. Now they feel not only loss, but as if suffering an abandonment beyond their ability to tolerate.

Such role-relationship models as that between an abandoned waif and an absent caregiver are never completely erased. Rather, they become dormant, available for reactivation. The childhood fear of abandonment, and the childhood states of separation anxiety, have been subdued by development of role-relationship models in which the self is adequately

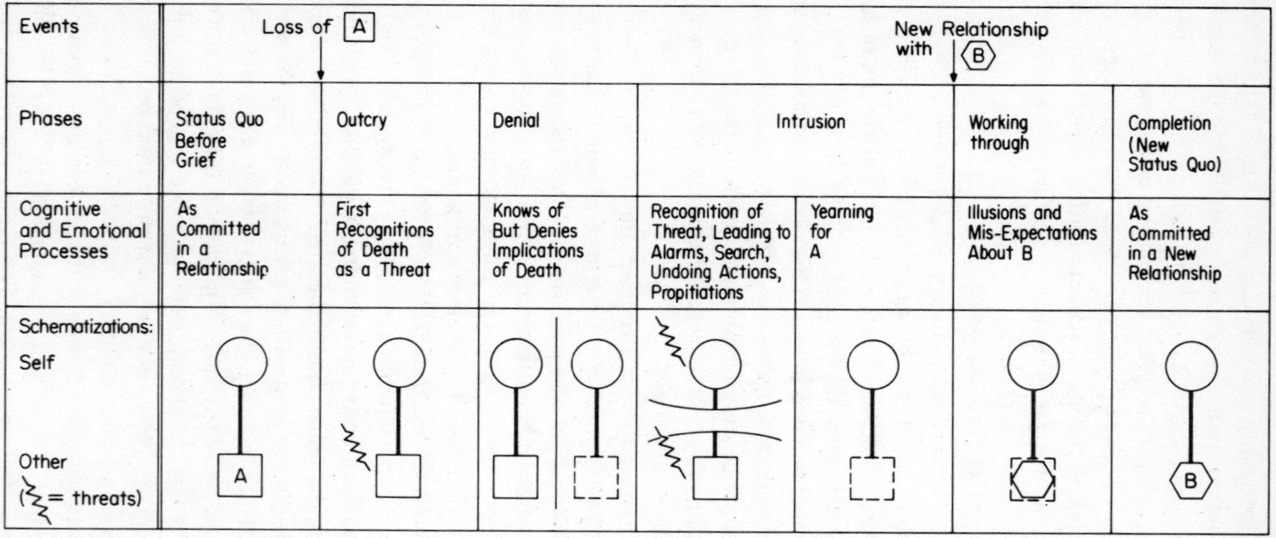

Events	Loss of A →			New Relationship with B →		
Phases	Status Quo Before Grief	Outcry	Denial	Intrusion	Working through	Completion (New Status Quo)
Cognitive and Emotional Processes	As Committed in a Relationship	First Recognitions of Death as a Threat	Knows of But Denies Implications of Death	Recognition of Threat, Leading to Alarms, Search, Undoing Actions, Propitiations / Yearning for A	Illusions and Mis-Expectations About B	As Committed in a New Relationship
Schematizations: Self / Other (⟿ = threats)						

Figure 4.1

Change in Schemas During the Mourning Process

cared for, often in situations of reciprocal caregiving, with the self as equally capable of assuming that role of being a caregiver for self or other. Now death has destabilized this mature role-relationship model, and reactivated the early role-relationship model, causing intense fear that the self cannot survive a separation from a loved one (Horowitz et al. 1984).

AMBIVALENCE

A loss to the self is interpreted by the mind as an insult or an injury to the self, even when that loss is the death of another person, a loved one. One of the normal responses to insult to the self is anger. The expression of this emotion signals hostility to an unwanted situation, and says, "Back off." Normally, the anger that occurs as a part of mourning begins to emerge after the early stages of sorrow, and even after stages of fear for the self such as those just mentioned. One may experience pangs of anger toward the deceased as well as toward other people involved with the self who cannot undo the loss, and who have not shared the loss with the self.

In normal grief reactions, the bereaved experiences the pangs of anger, modulates its expression, and does not remain in intense or prolonged rageful states of mind. In pathological grief reactions, the rage is more intense, lasts longer, or both. In such instances it is likely that pre-existing role-relationship models contained a lot of ambivalence. Even when ambivalent role-relationship models have been dormant and everyday life organized by loving and kindly role-relationship models, the loss may reactivate the latent forms, leading to a state organized by these earlier forms.

The term *ambivalence* denotes the simultaneous existence of opposing tendencies, such as the desire to approach and to avoid another person at the same time, or as the experience simultaneously of both attraction and repulsion, love and hate, caregiving and destructive aims. Ambivalence is a common human condition and is not a sign of significant psychopathology. Those who love want love in return, and are frustrated if they do not get all they desire. In development one learns to master the anger that may occur in response to that frustration. As I shall discuss in later chapters, persons at different developmental levels have varied ways of organizing their ambivalences, and some ways are pathological. In some instances, the pathological symptoms and interpersonal patterns are caused not just by the dual feelings of affectionate yearning and hostile wishes but by the defenses one uses to pretend that a polarity of the dual feelings is nonexistent.

The death of a loved one leads to sorrow and the massive frustration of affectionate yearnings. That frustration often leads to anger and to memories associated with anger. One recalls, in some states of mind, all the pleasant satisfactions and, in other states, all the slights, insults, and shortcomings of the relationship. The unpleasant memories are also worked over during the mourning process. The more ambivalent a person is, as well as the more shame and guilt one feels about the hostile components of this ambivalence, the more difficult it may be to review these memories and accept the death.

A person who has been ambivalent toward the deceased may feel not only sorrow at the death but also some gladness that the relationship has ended. The more susceptible the person is to shame and guilt about the hostility in the relationship, the less one can tolerate this reaction of gladness, and the less one can tolerate a burst of anger at the deceased (such as saying mentally to the deceased "Why didn't you take better care of yourself, you so-and-so!" or "Why did you leave me now!"—feelings not uncommon in normal grief reactions). The person who cannot tolerate the experience of rage may experience either intrusive episodes of feeling flooded and out of control over diffusely expressed hostility, or such marked inhibitions of thought and feeling as to stifle the mourning process and thus prolong it without resolution.

A man, say, has had a good relationship with a woman friend, now deceased, but an ambivalent one with his sister, who has earlier filled many of the functions of the deceased. Owing to a good relationship with the deceased, the man has a role-relationship model schematizing both the self and the other as kind and good, and the script of interaction as one of mutual exchanges of love. The shock of his woman friend's death then may activate the earlier role-relationship model with his sister. As a result, the man may return, or regress, during bereavement to neurotic states of hostility and guilt, states organized by role-relationship models from an earlier time, but remaining dormant until activated by the stress of mourning.

A pathological role-relationship model that could be regressively activated in such a situation is one in which the self is a betrayed and needy child, the other an evil deserter. The self reacts to the betrayal of togetherness with rage. Once the self is hostile in the script, the strong and weak, good and bad roles can be reversed, so the hostile self is now in the role of evil destroyer, feeling guilty for having harmed the other through rage; the other is now viewed more as innocent victim than evil deserter. Such pairs of role-relationship models may develop during earlier dependent relationships in which one regarded the other as desirable but also as causing the self to suffer.

In childhood, the person may have felt separations from a caregiver, such as the mother, as painful interludes and also may have viewed the mother as causing these periods on purpose. The child might first be hostile toward the mother, and then feel that anger as undesirable and as the cause of the mother leaving the self. The child would swallow that anger and try to placate the mother to secure her caregiving attention and her proximity to the self.

In this ambivalent script, loving yearning for the mother is coupled with hateful destructiveness, guilt, and reconciliation. As an adult, this person may learn that a loving attachment with a spouse or a companion neither merits nor requires hostility. The death of that companion may, however, be interpreted not only by the kind and good role-relationship model; it may fit the usually latent role-relationship models of the ambivalent script all too well. The earlier neurotic patterns of wish, frustration, rage, guilt, and reconciliation may be reactivated during mourning.

At some point during the mourning process, the survivor has to think, "Why did the deceased leave me?" The rational answer to this question is usually that the death was not sought by the deceased, and that it had its realistic causes. One may, however, temporarily consider such irrational answers as: "The deceased left me because I am unworthy, or hateful. I did not appreciate their love enough, I was too demanding, giving too little." This answer may be irrational in several respects, including its endowment of the deceased with the omnipotent ability to forestall death. This attitude, when in conjunction with a hostile and ambivalent role-relationship model, may be difficult to set aside as inappropriate; and one may recall and dwell upon various memories of being frustrating to and frustrated by the deceased, with a compounding of sorrow by guilt and anger.

IDENTIFICATION WITH THE DECEASED

The survivor may have to take on functions of the deceased. The surviving spouse may have to be both mother and father to the children, handle all the finances, make all the decisions. Beyond these necessities, the survivor may want to hold on to the personality attributes of the deceased by imagining his or her presence, by projecting these qualities onto other companions, or by personal mimicry of the qualities. Wanting the attributes, and practicing versions of them, may lead to new self-schemas; and as a consequence, one may become the source of strength for others as well as oneself.

These processes born of stress can lead to the growth and strengthening of character (Pollack 1978, 1982). For example, as a result of mourning, one who previously could stabilize self-concepts of goodness only within a protective relationship may independently learn to view oneself as good, even without such support.

BIOLOGICAL AND SOCIAL FACTORS

Regressions to role-relationship models characterized by weak or ambivalent self-schemas are, however, not only psychological in origin. There may be a complex interplay between mind, brain, and body, as well as with external factors such as social situations. During bereavement there is high physical stress from sleep disturbances, extended emotional arousal, and a variety of deprivations of restorative situations. The immune system changes during periods of grief, as may various endocrine functions (Osterweis, Solomon, and Green 1984). When brain physiology is disrupted, a regression is more likely to occur. In addition, some bereaved persons are ignored rather than supported by their social networks, as relatives and friends seek to avoid contagion with death and suffering. A widow may not be invited to parties that she would otherwise have attended had her husband still been alive to make a couple. Loss of social supports can contribute to regression. Finally, a variety of factors may combine in a vicious cycle, as when the bereaved person is less vivacious and more irritable than customary, and friends stay away, making one feel more isolated and stressed.

Regression and Progression in Self-Schemas

Regressive and progressive changes in schemas may, as in mourning, follow many other types of stressful life event, such as separation from friends, divorce, departure of children to college, retirement, illness, injury, and physical aging. Success can also be a stress, owing to new demands of responsibility and productivity; and other positive life events may also lead to regressions and progressions in self-schemas.

While we are not surprised when loss of something good leads to stress, we are very much indeed when loss of something unpleasant does. Such odd experiences may occur on removal or recovery from a long-standing affliction: a person blind for decades has an operation and regains sight; an epileptic is relieved of seizures; a person with long-standing angina pectoris has surgery that relieves pain; a person with trigeminal neuralgia (tic doloreux) has an injection that arrests the condition; a person taking care of a brain-damaged, unresponsive invalid is "freed" by the latter's death;

a prisoner is released to return to his family. In each instance, conditions as they have been schematized are changed. One may experience a mourning reaction for the "old, bad, but familiar," with regressions or progressions in self-schemas as well (Penman 1954; Horowitz 1970; Sacks 1983).

In summary, it is a general principle that a stressful event presents a person with stimuli that drastically conflict with inner schemas. Continued confrontation with the new situation requires a change in schemas. New schemas are built up only slowly. In the process, one may try out dormant schemas to see how well they fit the new situation, and provide internal input to a temporary working model. Emotional states of mind in response to stress are due *in part* to the discord between the new situation and enduring schemas.

Stress can combine with personality predispositions to produce symptoms and signs of psychopathology. Less dormant personality predispositions may lead to recurrent maladaptive patterns even in the absence of acute stress.

5

Recurrent Maladaptive Interpersonal Relationship Patterns

E ACH PERSON DEVELOPS, over time, a repertoire of schemas. When one is engaged with another person, the working model of that situation will be constructed using available schemas. Persistent use of an inappropriate role-relationship model in constructing a working model will mean that the working model will deviate from the situation, or at least the other person's view of it. In spite of this fact, one may continue to use the same working model again and again. The result may be psychological pathology.

This habitual pattern—a recurrent, maladaptive interpersonal behavioral pattern—was illustrated in case examples in chapters 1 through 4. A review of the common maladaptive patterns will be presented in chapter 7. I will introduce in this chapter more ideas about how mental models can distort real situations. I will begin with aberrant working models as constructed in some psychotic states of mind, and then deal with those in less drastic states, such as those occurring in persons with borderline, narcissistic, and neurotic levels of personality development.

Some Aberrant Working Models in
Psychotic States of Mind

Irrational beliefs that are distinctly discrepant from reality, and persist after repeated confrontations with reality, are *delusions*. In some delusions, one views others as being much more concerned with the self than is actually the case, and becomes preoccupied with the irrational notions— *ideas of reference*—that others are talking about or acting against the self.

In this section, I shall describe some of the delusions and confusions of views of self and others that may occur in states of psychosis such as schizophrenia, paranoia, or psychotic levels of depressive disorders. Although the cause of the disturbances may be biological—induced by organic changes in the brain, from toxins, hallucinogens, tumors, inflammations, or vascular impairment—the form of their mental contents will be influenced by psychodynamics.

DELUSIONS ABOUT THE SELF

Some delusions make the self seem far more important than the real situation would permit. Many delusions involve either the grandeur of the self or its centrality as a target of persecution from others—as in the case of Donald, a young man with a persistent view that Satan was especially interested in corrupting him, and controlling the movement of his left arm. Since Donald also believed that he himself no longer possessed the left arm, this delusion involved a loss of self to the devil. The delusion was not always apparent but was manifest when he was in a psychotic state, and his thinking was disordered. In other ways, this irrational belief and its consequences were not evident. With each recurrence, however, the delusion was approximately the same: his left arm, never his right, was an evil apparatus acting beyond his personal control. Only by enormous acts of will could he prevent it from balling into a fist to strike others or claw at himself, and then all he could do was to hold it rigidly away from his body in a strange gesture. He could render it immobile, protecting others and himself, but could not use his hand constructively for work.

Donald's fear of the evil arm was extreme when this delusional view organized his experience. To exorcise the devil within it, he inflicted pain on his left arm by cutting it superficially with razors or burning it with lighted cigarettes. The persistence of the delusion was evident from the

77

scars Donald had accumulated on the surface of his arm over several years. He had been told repeatedly that his view was inaccurate, and that he ought to stop mutilating himself. He believed the psychiatrists who told him this, but when the delusional belief took hold, it grew in power. At first he would feel tension, then conflict over whether to attack his arm. Finally, he would attack his left arm, and feel not only pain, but a rush of relief, and would shift out of his state of extreme agitation for a time.

The dynamics behind Donald's delusion involved his feeling that he was to blame for bad acts, or even bad impulses, and that the evil flowed from himself to his unowned left side. The left arm was chosen because it was not "his" as much as was his right arm and hand, which he used for writing and precise work. At an earlier period, he had allowed some "bad acts" such as masturbation, which he felt was wrong, to be performed by his left hand, preserving his right and main arm as "innocent."

In this instance, blame was sent from the self outward. Even other people were spared; the devil was at fault, rather than a fellow human. This displacement of "blaming the devil" has a long history. Demonic possessions were commonly investigated during the Middle Ages, and women and men said to be witches and warlocks were burned at the stake to cleanse society of imagined sources of evil. The psychotic delusion of the man with the satanic arm is not far from what is possible for normal persons caught up in a powerful social belief system.

The man with a satanic arm had a *persecutory delusion*. As I said to begin with, *delusions of grandeur* may also involve imposition onto a working model of irrational views of self and other, views based on recurrent use of schemas that may be active in psychotic states of mind and dormant in other states of mind. Such was the case of Thomas, a young man who had recurrent psychotic states of mind during which he had the delusion that he was Jesus. He insisted that others pay deferential attention to him, and preached weird sermons to them. Yet at times the sermons were quite coherent and beautiful, full of eloquent moral precepts. While Thomas sometimes had a beatific state of mind, he could not stabilize it, and entered into states of intense panic and dread of self-fragmentation. Within these states, his thoughts were dominated by a confusion of jumbled images of world devastation. People who fear self-dissolution often both symbolize and displace this fear to the larger social or environmental sphere, and predict external chaos.

As Thomas recovered from his current schizophrenic disorder, his delusion of grandeur underwent a transformation. He soon described himself as helplessly lost in a world that did not contain a place for him. He talked of his co-workers at the post office and how they seemed to listen to him as if he were talking weirdly. By seeing others as equally alienated lost sheep, he had, he now realized, forged a view of himself as a restorer and savior of the world. Thomas imagined Jesus had gone through this kind of transformation, and wanted it for himself.

As he recovered, Thomas described how he had been intensely miserable during adolescence. He gained solace at church by staring fixedly at the crucifix. He had an experience in which he was the one hung on the crucifix, surveying the crowd assembled below. In this view of himself—above the crowd yet connected to it by their attention—his self-esteem felt vastly enhanced. It was a saving alternative to the view of himself as having a mind deranged, a personality that was coming apart, and gave him a social status detached from human connection but looked at and adored. As Jesus, he was complete: he was giving to others and providing goodness for all out of his own suffering.

While we do not know all the biological, psychological, and social factors that cause states in which delusions are likely to occur, we do know that when thought processes are disrupted a delusion can function to restore a sense of coherence. Suppose a mentally impaired person is faced with experiencing two alternatives: a chaotic jumble of ideas, a fragmenting sense of identity, and great fear of losing control; or thinking in terms of a delusional story with a sense of getting attention, being in a definite role, and feeling a clear emotion such as anger at another person. With no other choice available, owing to the mental impairment, the person may well unconsciously choose the delusion. The mind seems to have an intrinsic property of preferring order and regulation to disorder and dysregulation. The schemas used to restore order may lead to irrational working models and beliefs if schemas that lead to rational ones are for some reason unavailable. In addition, there may be an organically induced impairment in brain function which, at the level of processing of psychological information, may reduce the person's capacity for comparing working models with external situations. This has been called *impaired reality testing* in psychotic states of mind.

All persons seem to have at least some vulnerability to states of anxious worry that their sense of selfhood or identity is disintegrating. Sometimes this concern is represented in the mind as a symbolic image of the body falling or coming apart. Some people may alleviate such worries by rest, sharing good experiences with others, doing things that reflect well on the self as in work, creativity, and sport; while others may drink alcohol, smoke, eat, take drugs, or seek sexual or adventurous thrills, even fights

79

in order to bolster a coherent self-concept. Delusions can also serve as a desperate way to restore a lapsing sense of identity. Delusions often incorporate real stimuli, current or past, and thus may contain an element of truth along with the irrational. The person seen as a persecutor may actually have ignored or disliked the self. A delusion is seldom just an impairment of reality testing without other motives.

Once a person has had extended episodes of experiencing psychotic states of mind, one's memory of it may be like a psychological trauma. As with other stressful life events, one may earnestly hope never to repeat the behavior and states of mind of the illness and, to prevent it, may defensively stabilize working models, leading to a compromise state of mind. This happened with Georgia, who had psychotic states of mind during a schizophrenic disorder. A wife and mother, she had—in an irrational, psychotic state of mind—developed the delusion that her children had become agents of evil, and she felt urges to harm them. In fact, she continued to care for their safety, and did not harm them, although they became agitated by her incomprehensible speech, sudden changes in facial expression, and unusually violent verbal accusations. She recovered and was not delusional. Yet she recalled the ideas, emotions, and urges constructed from aberrant working models during her psychotic states of mind, and rigidly governed her behavior toward her children. She was so frightened of being irritated, much less angry at them, that she avoided such expressions totally. She consciously focused on herself as a careful mother giving good care to nice children. As a consequence she lost spontaneity and behaved in a woodenly "kind" way which struck observers as remote rather than warm and sympathetic.

DELUSIONS ABOUT OTHERS

During psychotic states of mind, working models may contain views of others and their motives that are very different from those that the situation warrants—as in a delusion of persecution, for example. The view of the other may refer to attributes that a person wants to delete from self-conceptualization. In the defense mechanism *projection,* there is just such a dislocation of attributes. A feeling, such as hostility, that is dreaded in the self may be projected onto the other person, as if it were the latter's motive. Any unacceptable thought, feeling, impulse, or even memory of past behavior of the self may be planted in the working model of the other. Through repetition, this placement can become an aspect of enduring role-relationship models. In that case, one may repeat maladaptive behaviors in which one always sees others as consumed with perverse sexual desires or impulsive, destructive aims.

CONFUSION OF ATTRIBUTES BETWEEN SELF AND OTHER

Among the more uncanny vagaries of human communication are those in which a person mixes up attributes of who is who, and assumes that one has another's characteristics or another has one's own. Such experiences are difficult to believe unless actually witnessed—as occurred in the case of Thomas when, after recovering from a psychotic episode in which he thought he was Jesus, he was discussing his interpersonal relationships during a period of psychotherapy. His treatment was aimed at improving his relationships with others and providing support during his period of turmoil. His therapist was accustomed to the fact that Thomas spoke in such vague generalities that his meanings were frequently unclear. But the therapist began to notice that some of the generalities were caused by lack of pronoun specificity, so that it was unclear whether Thomas was talking of "I" or "you"—a confusion that showed up clearly in respect to the theme of cigarette smoking. The therapist did not smoke, but Thomas was smoking in the therapist's office and talking vaguely about how people who smoke risk their health. By his demeanor he seemed to be criticizing the therapist, not himself. To the therapist's surprise, Thomas then urged him to stop smoking. Thomas then revealed that he was feeling frightened owing to his increasing sense of emotional closeness to the therapist. He felt a sense of blending body into body with the therapist, and the therapist understood that he was losing his identity in an extreme depersonalization, or *merger sensation.* In the midst of this experience, Thomas felt confused about who was who, as was reflected in his alternation of pronouns.

Normal states of mind may also contain merger sensations. Such episodes may occur during the climax of sexual intercourse.

WANTING BUT DREADING TOGETHERNESS

When alone, a person vulnerable to psychotic states of mind may be unable to tolerate loneliness without feeling a loss of cohesion in self-concept. To avoid a sense of disintegration in intolerably unpleasant states of mind, the person may indulge in an irrational but reparative fantasy life in which others are added to the working model of the lonely situation. Others may be imagined as focused on the self, either favorably or hostilely. This fantasy life, often repeated, can lead to fixed delusions such as I have already illustrated. Another route toward reducing the dread of being alone, and of fragmenting identity, is the compulsive search for contacts with others. This may take bizarre forms; for example, the men and women who spend all day in cafeterias to be close to strangers or who chant slogans to passers-by on street corners. They may have a bizarre working model of what is actually happening.

Even though a person with a lack of coherence in self-organization may sometimes be intolerant of being alone, he or she may also be intolerant of closeness to another person at other times—as if the identity of the other person might engulf one, obliterating one's own distinctness, and contributing in that way to the sense of identity chaos (Modell 1976; Jacobson 1964). As a result, one may wholly deny the presence of the other person, or how he or she is feeling, as well as engage in bizarre self-restraints that may even look like a paralysis of movement. When frustrated by another person, one may experience a dangerous switch to viewing that person as demoniacally evil, or to other extremes of suspiciousness.

Aberrant Working Models in Borderline or Narcissistic Personality Styles

Persons with borderline and narcissistic personality disturbances may also have states of mind in which thought, expressed feelings, and actions are organized by working models sharply out of accord with the actual, current social situation. These terms, *borderline* and *narcissistic,* are loosely applied to persons with more impaired reality testing than persons with neurotic disorders, but who do not frequently or for long periods have psychotic states of mind because they can make adjustments in working models so that in many states of mind their models do accord more with actual situations.

When alone, such persons may at times enter a state of uncontrollable apathy, so that they cannot rouse themselves to recreation or work. They may engage in perverse autoerotic sexual activities because of the sense of depersonalization or loss of self-coherence that may occur with social deprivation. This increase in perverse activities or apathy will not happen in every instance of isolation; being alone often reduces anxiety evoked by a close social contact that one feels as intolerable.

Persons with a borderline level of disturbance may enter a state of uncontrollable excitement during some relationships. When frustrated by other people not conforming to what one wants, one may develop an exaggerated working model of the self, or of the relationship, as being very bad, even "all bad" (Kernberg 1975, 1976, 1980, 1985; Gunderson and

Singer 1975). Construction of such an "all-bad" working model involves blatant denial of the other person's actual intentions, recent good acts, and the particular social situation (Greenberg and Mitchell 1983). Fearing entry into such sudden crises of "badness in the world," such persons may also unrealistically and blatantly ignore actions that fall short of ideal: for example, denying that a friend has borrowed money and is refusing now to pay it back. Hence, such persons with borderline personality structures are said to *split* apart good and bad views in an at times totalistic fashion (Kernberg 1975; Horowitz 1983; Marmar and Horowitz 1986). Unlike normal and neurotic personalities, the person at this level of character is less able to temper the bad with memories of the good, and seems to have less of a chance to develop supraordinate schemas that mingle pleasant and frustrating role-relationship models.

The tendency to organize memories and schemas into all-good and all-bad sets means that persons with borderline self-organization may be vulnerable to explosive shifts in state of mind. Sudden rages and sudden blissfully sweet states of gratitude may occur during the same interlude. Such persons thus tend to have a recurrent maladaptive pattern of intense but unstable friendships and love affairs, and an uncertain grasp on personal identity.

The narcissistic style personalities are those usually able to stabilize themselves short of these explosive situations, except under severe stress. They may accomplish such self-coherence by treating another person as a supplement to themselves. Heinz Kohut (1972) has used the word *selfobject* to describe this treatment of another person in a working model as if he or she were not a separate center of initiative but rather an extension of the self. In other words, one does not view the other fully as having wishes, fears, purposes, and feelings that are independent in origin. Such selfobjects may be viewed as if they were ideal, as if they were intensely interested in admiring and catering to the self, or as if they were *alter egos,* teamed up in an alliance or twinship with the self as two against the world. As a result of such relationship schemas, one may have an idealized engagement with another, regarding that person as a reflecting mirror or as a twin to the self (Kohut 1977). Sometimes, in an *as if* identification with an admired other, one lives a masquerade: one may act like a specific film star or other role model, but the imitation lacks a firm inner sense of identity (Deutsche 1965).

Other types of compensatory schema may, when active as working models, lead to states of mind in which a person acts in a *grandiose* manner, presenting the self to others as being unique, great, extraordinarily talented or attractive. When constant attention and admiration are unavailable, the person may shift to a state of cool indifference, rage, or leaden apathy. One's *sense of entitlement* leads to exploitation of others. Since one also views others as not fully independent, one tends to have relationships that end after an initial period of romantic or idealized work involvement. One's constant need for fantasies of unlimited success, power, brilliance, beauty, or ideal love may interfere with the work of developing the skills necessary for moving one toward more realistic aspects of these goals; hence, work and creativity may also be impaired though idealized. The result may, after a time, be a depressed state of mind.

Aberrant Working Models in Neurotic States of Mind

Persons whose characters have neurotic schematic attributes also have states of mind organized by working models not fully in accord with the realities and opportunities of the actual situation, and may be motivated to use such inappropriate role-relationship models in order to undo past traumas, to make up for past deficits, or to regain some relationship they had or almost had in the developmental past. Where the healthy person is able to experience—at least sometimes—being alone as a sweet and meaningful time, the neurotic person is more likely to have unwarranted fears and compulsive self-indulgences. With other people, one may have recurrent maladaptive behavior patterns characterized by seemingly unnecessary defensive inhibitions. Working through stressful situations may be impaired by cycles of rage, guilt, and unnecessary reparations. These actions are less extreme, and there is less intrusive explosiveness than in the narcissistically vulnerable, borderline, or psychotic personality.

There is thus a spectrum from the unusual elicitations of sympathy and irritable responses of the healthy person under stress, to greater difficulties with conflicts over affection and rage in the neurotic person, to the more intense and unrealistic demands, tantrums, or destructive explosions possible in the highly disturbed personality. Although the thoughts and feelings of the neurotic personality may be based on aberrant working models, one's impulse control is better, and one can check reality so that blatant and bizarre errors seldom occur.

The neurotic misuse of a role-relationship model to organize a working model to a social situation may be illustrated by the case of Murray, a young financial district professional who got a stomachache every time he had to present his work plans. His firm developed and sold new stocks and bonds. While Murray had an excellent record for his performance of these tasks, he was not advancing in his career because, whenever the time came for him to present to his supervisor, he procrastinated. One reason was that he had a fantasy in which he imagined that his supervisor would scoff at his work and ridicule him as an incompetent.

The anticipated ridicule never occurred at this job. In psychotherapy Murray told of earlier sources of his fantasy. When he was fourteen, he went to work after school with his father and discovered that in the office his father fiddled and dithered. Murray was surprised since, at home at the dinner table, he had heard his father boast of his small business. Murray had an urge to tell other family members of his father's actual low competence at work. While doing so would express his anger with his father for failing to meet his own high standards, it would also hurt his father, whom Murray did love. For this reason, and also lest he spark a destructive confrontation with his father, Murray avoided both telling and competing.

Now, Murray's present work situation did not in reality seem comparable to the earlier relationship between him and his father. The supervisor, a kind and intelligent man, was quite competent. He was unlikely to castigate Murray and was likely to warmly praise good work. Despite the real attributes of the situation, Murray persisted in his conscious expectations of being terribly humiliated by the supervisor. During psychotherapy, these views were modified; and there emerged a feeling Murray had warded off—a sense of guilty rivalry with the supervisor, as with his father. Murray wanted to find and surpass a senior rival, but could not complete this plan without anxiety over defeat or guilt over success. Caught at the conflictual midpoint, and stymied by the lack of a clear conscious concept of the problem, Murray could not act. Once he was clearly conscious of his patterns of behavior, he cooperated with his supervisor, reduced procrastination, endured being judged, and sought competition in safe and socially acceptable ways, without impairing his career.

Thus, Murray's maladaptive pattern of procrastination was based on unconscious use of a role-relationship model to construct a working model inappropriate to his current situation. His wish to excel was in conflict with a fear of surpassing and also a fear of failing. Procrastination was a compromise, preventing his fears in the short run but leading toward eventual failure.

Motivation for Aberrant Use of Role-Relationship Models

Wishes and fears may be so intense as to activate a role-relationship model, which is then imposed inappropriately onto a working model of interpersonal situations. A man terribly frightened of derision tends to imagine rejection when hearing a pair of friends laugh, thinking they are laughing at him. The fear can become a self-fulfilling prophecy when he accuses the friends in a way they find to be ridiculous, and they later do laugh at him mockingly.

One of the most tragic instances of misuse of role-relationship models and their implicit scripts occurs when a parent feels in need of sexual pleasure and feels sensually close to his or her child. The erotic desire activates sexualized working models for relating to the child. The child may then be seduced by the parent to sexual transactions despite the taboo against incest. Thus is created a situation harmful to all parties.

Table 2.1 (page 37) summarizes motives in terms of wishes for pleasure and aims to avoid displeasure. Each motive can be related to various possible goals and schemas for how to relate the self to the goals in question. Conscious and unconscious thought processes select which goals and schemas achieve priority as working models of situations and intentions. The more intense the motive, the more likely the schema with a good fit to its particular needs will be activated, and perhaps the schema will then be used inappropriately in constructing a working model. Emotional systems, once activated, also may affect the competitions between schemas. Emotions prime memories, and priming of certain memories will also make some schemas more likely than others to be imposed onto situations (Bower 1986). I will consider this feature in the construction of aberrant working models in greater depth in chapter 9.

Rigid Script Sequences

The rigidity of role-relationship model sequences may impair realistic construction of working models of situations. An obligatory following of schematic script sequences can be illustrated by the case of Marsha, who had dynamics somewhat similar to Murray's, with additional elements.

A woman in her mid-twenties, Marsha had a recurrent maladaptive pattern with father figures, and with her actual father who was alive and important in her life. She very much wanted to further her skills and achieve success as a journalist and novelist. She worked at a newspaper for a living, and at night wrote short stories or sections of a book she hoped to finish. At her job she vacillated between being a submissive copywriter and a more independent person with her own slant on stories. She could rationalize her banal work on some newspaper stories as not just being meekly responsive to every small direction from her supervisor, but as a means of keeping her energy intact for her own work at night. Yet at night she sometimes also did very "meek" work, not trying to be creative but only repeating what she already knew how to do from the work of others.

In a similar manner, she could find no comfortable position in her relationships with the older men who were her usual lovers. She was sometimes almost abrasively demanding of her own way, and would not honor the time of appointments with them because she had to make her own schedule at the spur of the moment. At other times, she was almost cloyingly submissive, letting the men take over too many decisions. Most disruptive of all, she would oscillate between seeking more closeness and then demanding more independence of action, between showing off her work to pretending she had given up her writing.

As an adolescent, Marsha had imagined future success as a creative writer. Yet now, as an adult, when she tried to imagine this as a pleasant daydream, her conscious fantasy would turn sour. She would imagine her success as pleasing her father, but her fantasy then showed how it would hurt him. Although he had wanted to be a writer, he worked in an automobile factory writing technical manuals for new fabrication procedures. It was now too late for his earlier ambitions, and his self-esteem seemed very brittle. Marsha wanted him to be pleased with her success, but knew how bitter he was as he talked of relatives who had "made it." She fantasized he would feel belittled by her success.

During adolescence, Marsha's mother did not support her and seemed only to worry about her daughter's sexual activities. Marsha did not want to be anything like her mother, whom she saw as a defeated housewife, submitting to a husband who made up for his own falling short of life goals by tyrannizing his docile wife.

Marsha wanted desperately to leave the tightly controlling atmosphere of her home, with the incessant criticism of her dating habits, of her staying up late in her room or reading at the dinner table. Writing would be her ticket to independence not only from her parents but from all bosses. This wish to become autonomous was linked, however, to a continuing wish to establish a close, loving relationship with her father, perhaps by having him admire her success in a craft he valued greatly.

The result of such situations during Marsha's development was a configuration of role-relationship models that contained a conflict between a wish and a fear. A schematic script went from one role-relationship model to another within this configuration. The rigidity of that script meant there was no easy resting place between a desirable working model and one with dreaded features.

Suppose, for example, Marsha were to have reason to view herself realistically as a person who had just had a success in her writing. She would then get into a situation that would be organized by herself showing off this success to a man from whom she wished admiring closeness as a response, a wish she originally had for her father. The first step of the script would be to show the father surrogate (or her real father) some of her success as an independent writer, with her own ideas expressed for all to see and admire. While she wanted love and admiration, she also expected, as a potential response in another working model, that the father figure might express mortification over his own failure which she, by her success, only highlighted.

To her chagrin and surprise, this kind of behavior had occurred in past times in situations with her father when she had performed well in school. Then she had learned another step to appease him, and this step was now part of this schema. Anxious over the threat of causing him pain and vague anger with her, she would lower herself to be more like her mother, subordinate to his wishes and stature in the family. Thus, in situations that began with a working model of showing off and receiving a proud response from the other, she might then change to a working model of inflicting pain, and so to a working model in which she had to appease the vanity of the other person.

In Marsha's case the role-relationship model that contains the wish to show success had, by mortifying rather than gratifying her father, provoked anxiety in her and self-criticism for having caused her father pain. Through her rigid use of this role-relationship model, she misinterpreted situations outside of her family. If a peer was envious of her work, she tended to respond maladaptively and reduce her own efforts to submit to that person's needs. This was the next step in the script sequence: the assumption of submissive stance to reduce anxiety and guilt over success.

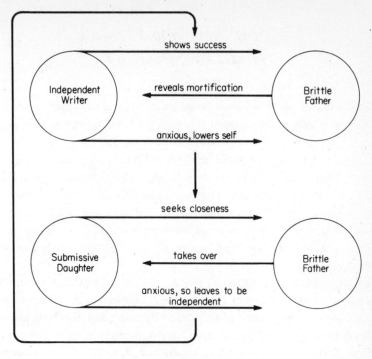

Figure 5.1
A Sequence of Two Role-Relationship Models

The role-relationship model in which her self-schema was that of a submissive daughter also contained a wish—to be closely loved and connected with her father. He would reward her with praise for being a good daughter in this script. Yet within this role-relationship model, there was a feared response—of being taken over by her father; it would make her anxious about losing autonomy. She would criticize herself for being too much the good little girl, too little the strong woman, and would shift again to the independent writer self-concept.

Where most people wish for both independence and dependence, Marsha rigidly linked these two role-relationship models. She could not have a single wish and expect a positive response, but instead would go back and forth through the whole scenario, as if inexorably, always leading to the maladaptive and rapid oscillations in her relations with older men. This overall cycle of working model sequences is shown in figure 5.1; especially significant is the sequence denoted by the arrow leading from the bottom to the top of the figure.

Deficient Input into Working
Models of Situations

Some people, for reasons I shall consider in the next chapter, reach adult life with relatively meager sets of schemas for developing working models with which to interpret interpersonal situations. Since schemas are necessary in order to organize rapid understanding and response to a social situation, some schema is better than none, and a poor fit is preferable to entering a state of confusion. The person in this situation may not have learned schemas of self and others easily and well in the first place; and if there are obstacles in the way of learning more adaptive schemas, one may not be able to escape from repetitive, maladaptive interpersonal behavioral patterns.

Working models are affected by two sources of information: the external situation as well as internal schemas and memories. It is important to maintain the working model of a situation by using and matching information from both sources. Some people have impaired ability to perform this function, and certain biological states such as drug-altered consciousness may affect it. The result may be a failure in fusion of internal and external sources of information, with a preponderance of inner view (as hallucinations or delusions) or an enthrallment with external perceptions whose personal significance, however, cannot be deciphered.

While we know little about the cognitive processes that fuse internal and external sources of information into a working model, we do know that sensory loss or deprivation leads people to increase input of internal schemas in forming conscious perceptions. One may elaborate spots seen from reflections of blood vessels in the eye, or bits of debris within the fluid portion of the eyeball, into small animals. Or one may elaborate noises generated within the inner ear itself into voices of people (Horowitz 1983), as occurred in the case of Herbert, a factory foreman whose hearing had been partially destroyed by an explosion of chemicals near his work station. Since he was not otherwise injured, he returned to the factory after a brief leave. Because of his hearing impairment, he had to step down as foreman, although he continued responsible work in putting together ingredients for chemical reactions. He had a sense of rushing noises that waxed and waned, but increased when people talked in his vicinity. These noises were probably the result of damage to his middle ear and auditory nerve. He felt a frustrated rage at the accident and his loss, but suppressed any expression of it. Feeling that the noises were people talking about him, he had an interval of intense suspicion. This was resolved in a brief therapy aimed at helping him work through his stress-response syndrome and accept the change in his hearing.

A working model can be constantly altered through a process of checking the inner views with the actual transaction taking place. As already mentioned, this process, which may proceed unconsciously, is an aspect of *reality testing:* that is, the normal ability to see whether inner views accord with external situations (Freud 1911; Weisman 1958). Deprivation of interpersonal feedback reduces one's ability to test the reality of a working model. The gap in external input is usually filled with internal input, and the role-relationship models that relate to unmet current wishes and unmastered fears are the ones most likely to be used.

Some situations are constructed for this purpose; and, while not initially instituted to do so, the psychoanalyst sitting behind the patient on a couch turned out to create this kind of deprivation situation. In it, an intense transference into the analytic situation may occur. These transferences are usually warded-off patterns based on working models organized mostly by motivated role-relationship models. Patients capable of reality testing can compare the felt experiences organized by these transferred role-relationship models to a more realistic view of the situation with the analyst. This gradually builds a new working model, often called a *therapeutic alliance* because it contains somewhat more realistic views of roles of patient and therapist. The working model of the alliance can then be contrasted with the working model of the transference (Basch 1980; Malan 1979; Luborsky 1984; Strupp and Binder 1984). This comparison can also revise memories and beliefs about people currently important in the patient's life as well as important in earlier phases of a life story (Stone 1961).

In psychotherapy, the face-to-face situation provides more feedback on the immediate reality of the therapist, and of the patient's relationship with him or her, so that reality will not be colored by as many or as intense transference enactments; this procedure allows other types of therapeutic work to take place. Many psychotherapies also involve attention to transference and how it contrasts with the working model of a therapeutic alliance, but do not encourage the regressive transference experiences that are promoted by interpretation of resistances to them in psychoanalysis.

Because the deprivation of feedback evokes transference reactions, it is seldom used in the treatment of those persons with psychotic disorders who cannot at least sometimes correct inappropriate views through reality testing. Nor are such procedures as deprivation of feedback from the therapist much used in the brief psychotherapies, family therapies, or in the behaviorally and cognitively oriented ones.

The ability to test reality and to have realistic perceptions may still exist in a person who has an irrational view of a situation based on a working model. If the working model is sharply out of accord with perceived reality, the person may have a sense of estrangement from reality, as in *derealization* or *depersonalization* experiences. In a sense, not only do motives to force certain role-relationship models onto a situation, or loss of capacity correctly to model current external situations, create pathological working models, but the irrationality of the views that are then expressed leads to stress. A vicious cycle may lead to increasing strain, more irrationality, symptomatic states of mind, and then diagnosis of a mental disorder.

Summary

So far in this text I have considered states of mind as caused, in part, by the kind of working model the person develops, often unconsciously, out of elements from inside and outside the mind. The external situation and environment provide the elements from outside the mind, insofar as the person can perceive them. That perception itself is a constructive process, involving schemas, and will be considered in more detail in chapter 8. The elements inside the mind include schemas, memories, impulses, needs, values, and intentions. Of these, self-schemas and role-relationship models have been emphasized, as they have to do with interpersonal relationships and patterns of self-esteem.

In the course of discussing schemas of persons, I have covered a range of states of mind from normal to psychotic. It is, I think, important to discuss this range, but hard to do so without offending people, because placing anyone anywhere in this range necessarily calls for a value judgment. Psychological science may forever deal with shades of gray, not either/or methods of labeling a behavior pattern "normal" or "abnormal." Usually any behavior makes some sense when it is understood, and therefore no episode can be seen as purely abnormal or pathological. Keep in mind the metaphor of "shades of gray," as I make some sweeping statements to summarize the issues covered thus far.

The judgment of normality or mental health of a person under scrutiny for an interval of time can be made by that person in self-observation, or by others who observe him or her. Having different vantage points, though, they might not agree. Nonetheless, from any vantage point, the judgment itself often has to do with how closely the behavior of the subject conforms to reality, in relation to what might be most adaptive to the welfare of the subject. When working models of situations lead to behavioral patterns that appear to foster personal aims and acknowledge the real properties of situations, one is judged mentally healthy.

When, however, there is some discrepancy between working models and actual situations, the person may be judged to be on a range from strained or stressed by situations, to neurotic, pathologically narcissistic or border-line, or psychotic, in terms of psychological capacity (Blanck and Blanck 1979; Stolorow and Lachmann 1980; Blatt and Lerner 1983). In this summary, I will review some generalizations that have been made about this range without getting into the specific signs and symptoms that are part of psychiatric diagnosis.

At a psychotic level of functioning, one may act on an experience, a conscious idea, or feelings, in patterns organized by working models totally unrelated to external situations. To the extent that psychotic states of mind are a repeated characteristic of an individual, it might be that one has schemas that predispose one to working models that do not accord with reality. That person might then be said to have, in this regard (although there are other factors), a psychotic character or personality structure (Gedo and Goldberg 1975; Volkan 1976).

This character or personality structure consists, in part, of schemas. These schemas might be such that the person is sometimes unable to tolerate being alone without developing working models that are repara-tive but that lead to irrational consequences. When frustrated in an inter-personal situation, a person with such a disposition might be more likely than others to develop extreme ideas, such as that either the self or the other is demoniacally evil. There may be irrational actions, or extreme withdrawals and paralyses of action, to avoid the destructive potential in such beliefs. Even when the situation is not inherently frustrating, the inability to form a working model that allows intimacy and closeness can make it frustrating. Imposing closeness on such persons may lead them to engage in extreme efforts at withdrawal or self-protection. Criticism may lead to fragmentation of a sense of identity.

In contrast, the working models developed by persons sometimes la-beled by others as having pathologically narcissistic or borderline character structures may be moderately unrelated to real situations. Alone, the per-son may be unusually vulnerable to a chaotic dread of fragmentation of self-concept. With other people, the role-relationship models that are activated may lead to working models with blatant distortions of the intentions of others. When frustrated in interpersonal situations and when criticism is in the air, the person may organize views of the situation by working models that depict the self and others as globally bad (Kernberg 1975, 1987; Rosenfeld and Sprince 1963). These working models may lead the person to repeat now and again a pattern of impulsive, destructive action. It is hard for such persons to contain rage in a working model that depicts both the good and bad attributes of self and others. In other instances, self-criticism is avoided by making working models in which others are all to blame.

In conditions judged to be neurotic, working models that are also unrelated to the situations occur and lead to repetitive, maladaptive behavior patterns. When alone, the person may engage in unwarranted fears or compulsive self-indulgences. When with others, the behavior organized by neurotic types of working models may be characterized by defensive avoidances of gratifications that might otherwise be achieved. In frustrating interpersonal transactions, which are promoted by the use of neurotic types of role-relationship models to form working models, the person may repeat cycles of rage, guilt, reparation, restored intimacy, and frustration. In that way, relationships may be formed and then destroyed, reconciled and then ruptured, again and again.

In contrast to the conditions judged to be further from mental health, the neurotic conditions tend to have more impulse control because they can contain rage at frustration with others in ambivalent working models: they know of good traits of others, even while angry at them. Criticism can be leveled at the self, sometimes too harshly or with excessive perfectionism, but with recognition that self is not all bad.

Such persons have more capacity than those in psychotic states to test the reality of internal views of a situation. Nonetheless, irrational working models of the situation may lead to felt emotions that prevent the experience or expression of more positive feelings and create problems both internally and in transactions with others.

In contrast to these psychopathological conditions, relatively normal persons, when they are under stress, may also have working models at least mildly unrelated to external situations. During a period of strain, it may be harder to be alone than usual, and the person may seek more support than usual, only to misapply some inner schemas to the supportive situation when it is obtained. The normal person under stress will have a reduced tolerance for frustration and will be more likely to respond irritably.

When not under strain, the normal person is able to be alone in positive states of mind and with a firm sense of identity. He or she is able to share intimacy, and can compete or even fight with others freely when situations really warrant such actions.

We have no certain science to explain the range of states and personality structures from normal to abnormal. We do know some of the effects of stress and some of the mechanisms underlying some recurrent maladaptive patterns. In this summary, I have addressed the judgment of mental health problems in a preliminary way, to approximate how mental health professionals currently operate. Now we can turn to issues of how the schemas of self and others, called into question here, may develop throughout life.

6

The Development of Self-Schemas

THE CHILD ENTERS the world with built-in tendencies to perceive and relate to others, and also built-in tendencies on how to react independently of them. Ultimate self-organization depends on the fate of both urges to socialize and to be autonomous. In optimal development of self-schemas, the child develops a harmonious sense of self as separate from others as well as intimately connected with them. Biological impairment, psychologically traumatic events, deficiencies in the social environment, and deviant relationship patterns on the part of caregivers may lead to deflections from this optimum harmony. The self-organization may be incomplete, contain irrational elements, or make necessary excessive reliance on other persons.

In this chapter, some aspects of forming self-schemas will be described, along with some impediments to optimum development and defensive manuevers that might distort reality to protect a sense of identity. In the next chapter, I will cover similar themes about developing models of interpersonal relationships.

Social Shaping of the Self

Each new baby has many potential future identities. The self is organized according to many factors, including roles permitted or endorsed by society for men and women. These roles shape the child not only later, as it emerges from the family, but early on because they have shaped the child's parents, as in this case reported by Hermann Beland (1987):

An adult psychoanalytic patient had been, as a baby, cared for only by her mother, an unmarried woman living alone in a crowded neighborhood. The patient's mother had two simultaneously conflicting concerns: one was spoken of as "living only for her child"; the other was her immense attention to what the neighbors thought of her and her "illegitimate child." The latter concern included not "spoiling" the child by feeding her when she cried, and also stifling crying noises, in order to get the neighbors' approval for not being a nuisance.

To her mother, the patient developed a submissive attitude that she experienced as suffering a diminishment of her own identity. As an adult, she strove for her own satisfaction with her own identity, yet she herself pulled back from full initiative. When she was assertive, she experienced inner voices resembling her mother, telling her that she was bad and rebellious, and urging her to punish or even kill herself. Sometimes when she was expressing herself, she even felt choked by the invisible hand of her mother, as in memories of her mother trying to stifle her crying as a baby.

She now had many problems. If she felt faithful to her boyfriend, she became less aroused sexually with him in order to make herself feel more independent by preserving distance. If she felt secure in her job, she became less productive at it to show she was not overly absorbed in it. In a transference reaction to her psychoanalyst, this patient became intensely preoccupied with a role-relationship model similar to that with her mother: that is, she felt she would be crushed by the analyst's neglect or her forced submission because the analyst would be concerned more with doing the analysis "correctly" (for the analyst's neighbors, other analysts) than with being there to help her as a unique person. If the analyst seemed expertly competent, then she felt the analyst was not helping her; if the analyst was quiet, that was too quiet; if the analyst spoke, that was saying too much and taking over her identity.

This case indicates in part how the mother's contradictory attitudes were remembered by a patient as an adult who felt these socially conditioned attitudes had shaped her own self-concept.

THE UNFOLDING OF GENETIC INFORMATION

The gametes of egg and sperm provide the genetic code for the new baby, which includes some aspects of socially important behavior patterns. The infant with a normal set of brain functions automatically has schemas for how to cry, suckle the breast, look for faces, and snuggle up against caregivers. These patterns stimulate parents to give various types of care. As the brain unfolds in its functions, the baby is able to smile and coo, enhancing the social interaction. How this is done rests in part on the temperament of the particular baby (Bowlby 1969; Goldsmith and Campos 1982; Watson 1978; Stern 1985; Emde, Gaensbauer, and Harmon 1976).

Temperament includes biologically determined dispositions to individual variations in how a person is able to evoke, regulate, and tolerate various types of emotional arousal. This will include the threshold and latency between stimulation and emotional reactions, the rate at which such reactions as fear or anger may occur, and the time it takes to recover from a sharp arousal of emotion such as a fit of sobbing, temper, or panic. The genetics that influence temperament probably include dispositions to perception, thinking, and emotion but not these processes themselves (Thomas and Chess 1977; Rothbart and Derryberry 1981; Goldsmith and Campos 1982).

Bodily systems—that is, the unfolding of the modules of the brain and the later unfolding of genetic activity within the nuclei of the cells of neurons—affect temperament in interaction with the sensitivity of neuroendocrine organs and perhaps muscular structure itself. Temperament will then affect the earliest infant-parent relationship patterns and so influence attachment. From the patterns of relationship, the infant will develop the first schemas of self and other, and these schemas will affect the organization of experience and action, including the important, adaptive or maladaptive components of emotional expression and control of mood states.

Temperament also will affect emotion as well as the general regulatory capacity over ideas, feelings, and action patterns. The emotions experienced during development, including development of new recognitions of reality during adult life, also affect the development, change, and stability of schemas. Thus, temperament, a body property, becomes mind: a property of how ideas and feelings are regulated and what types of schemas are more likely to form.

A relatively high neural capacity may be necessary for one ever to achieve a psychological sense of continuing personal identity. For example, the sense of self as psychologically distinct probably occurs only in the more evolved primates. When a chimpanzee, painted with a spot of color on its forehead, is shown itself in a mirror, it will pick at or wipe away the spot—a response less evolved monkeys will not usually exhibit (Gallup 1979). Children between fifteen and twenty months will exhibit self-recognizing behavior similar to that of the chimpanzees (Amsterdam 1972; Kagan 1981).

Developing Self-Constancy

In Daniel Stern's (1985) review of research on early development of self-schemas, the first stage appears to be between birth and two months of age in normal babies. During this stage, there seems to be some sense of emergence of self as related to the mother, involving especially looking at the face of the mother, and in the mouth-breast contact, or other surface contacts in the case of bottle feeding.

The next stage of new self-realization seems to take place between two and six months of age, when one gains the sense of being a coherent, willful physical entity. This sense of the core bodily self probably relates to some primitive view of the mother as also a separate agency of action. Then between seven and nine months, the infant seems to develop a more subjective sense of self, to be able to hold in mind a schema of other actions than are immediately present, to know the possibility of other states of mind. There is more of the new ability to tune in to the mental states of others, probably through the emotional colorations of vocal tone, facial expressions, and bodily movements.

The sense of a verbal self that can relate to others through meaningful utterances such as words seems to be much enhanced between fifteen and eighteen months. The child appears to be developing a storehouse of information about role-relationship models, and to manipulate this knowledge internally in order to decide how to act in different situations. There is a rudimentary view of the self with a firmer differentiation of self as an agent of action different from all others.

In Stern's view, the self and the object are differentiated from the start of infancy, and a sense of individuality and a sense of attachment or connectedness develop in parallel. In contrast, Margaret Mahler postulated a gradual separation of a sense of self from an early matrix of fusion with the mother.

Margaret Mahler (1968; Mahler, Pine, and Bergman 1975) postulated an early stage of *symbiotic union* with the mother which would be altered by the unfolding of the locomotor abilities. Between the first seven to ten months, the baby learns to crawl and walk, and so to move away from the caregiver. This marks entry into a phase of increasing *differentiation* of the self in mental representation, probably with a first sense of *self-constancy,* or continuity of "I" over time (Sandler and Rosenblatt 1962; White 1985; Lichtenberg 1975). These explorations may lead to discovery and pleasurable excitement or to threat and retreat because of fear. When the baby becomes fearful, he or she returns for what Mahler called "emotional refueling."

The child practices leaving and returning to the mother. Between fifteen and twenty-four months occurs a pattern that Mahler called *rapprochement.* The normal toddler has perfected upright locomotion by fourteen to sixteen months. Through movement, he or she has developed an increasing sense of self and self-competence. The child also suddenly begins to seek more contact with the mother. It is inferred that the toddler, with any increasing sense of self, has an increasing awareness of separation and feelings about its implications. The toddler does not always feel connected when separate and may return to the mother for reassurance that she will remain attentive. The less secure the sense of connection, the more fragile the sense of self; and the less likely the mother is to be attentive in a soothing way, the more vulnerable may be the toddler to becoming very anxious or alarmed in unfamiliar situations (Mahler 1968; Bowlby 1969; Stolorow and Lachmann 1980; Lichtenberg 1983). The return to the mother, which is what is meant by the word *rapprochement,* may be seen as an interruption of exploring the world in these less normal children.

Certain milestone behavior signals a normal development of brain function and associated development of psychological schemas of persons. An interesting milestone occurs at seven to ten months of age when the infant may begin to exhibit *stranger anxiety.* If a stranger enters, especially when the baby is not in the arms of the caregiver, the baby may show a startled response indicated by staring, a fearful facial expression, or even crying. The child may also turn to look at the face of a familiar figure, as if looking for emotional cues on how to respond. Stranger anxiety indicates the presence in the baby of (1) an attachment bond to the caregivers, (2) inner person schemas against which the baby matches perceptions, (3) a differentiation of self from caregivers, and (4) a differentiation between caregivers and strangers.

The ability to recognize the difference between familiar caregivers and strangers is a biological, psychological, and social achievement of the child. The development of this ability also places the child at risk emotionally, in that it can feel frightened by the departure of familiar figures and the entry of alien ones. Ultimately, provided it is not disabling or overwhelming, this fear reaction may be adaptive. On the other hand, it also is an assault on the sense of safety of the self as separate from others.

Recent research in child development has studied different typologies of apparent attachment of the child to the primary caregiver, using such fear responses to strange stimuli as one of the indices that might allow one to place the child in a category. The categories found useful in predicting a variety of future behaviors were those of the securely attached, insecure or anxiously attached, insecurely attached ambivalent, and socially resistant child (Ainsworth 1973; Ainsworth et al. 1978; Main 1975; Sroufe and Fleeson 1986; Bretherton and Waters 1985). The securely attached child could tolerate more "strangeness" and short separations from the mother. The anxiously attached child seemed to have less confidence, and showed more maternal clinging to achieve a sense of security. The ambivalently attached child seemed to have in part given up on the mother as a security-providing figure, and to be more likely than others to exhibit detachment.

The way in which these early typological categorizations of children might predict later behavior, including the comfort and serenity in caring for a baby when that child itself becomes a parent, suggests that early schemas of self are an important substrate upon which later role-relationship models are built. Temperament may dictate how easily the child is frightened and how quickly it may recover equilibrium after a fright. Experience with caregivers will also influence early schemas having to do with security when separate and with attachment to others. Both together, nature and nurture, are important co-determinants of early personality.

Throughout childhood there is further unfolding of biological capacities which then relate to social and psychological experiences in forming personality structure. As the brain is ready, and as psychology unfolds, the child is ready to play with other children, develop friendships, affiliate with peer groups, and experience all the feedback this provides for self-schematization.

While aspects of childhood and adolescence that have to do with the development of the self-schemas in the context of role-relationship models will be reviewed next in chapter 7, a point is to be made here about adolescent change and self-schematization. At adolescence a burst of change occurs as the body develops new sexual characteristics and the brain develops new capacities to generalize among sets of information, allowing for new levels of abstract thinking, including heightened capacity for self-reflection (Mussen, Conger, and Kagan 1980).

The capacity to generalize allows the normal adolescent to form schemas of schemas, and so to form *supraordinate self-schemas,* ones that can contain, in a unit, the diverse elements of subordinate self-schemas. Love and hate, dependence and independence, good intentions and bad consequences, can now be understood (at times) as aspects of one identity. Personality may become a chord whose tones are beginning to harmonize.

With solidification of identity, pathological behaviors may be more apparent because they are repeated again and again. Occasionally the delinquent preadolescent may become a persistently delinquent adolescent; and repetitive maladaptive behaviors may lead to a diagnosis of a personality disorder. Persons who cannot develop supraordinate self-schemas may be vulnerable to explosive shifts in states, as they switch radically from one type of self-schema as organizer of experience to another.

Learning Body Boundaries

Let us turn to how the body as a physical reality relates to a mental view of the body, the body-schema, and to the self as an agent of will to action which occupies that body. As the baby acquires control over the body, he or she learns to operate upon objects and the bodily self. That which can be most directly operated—that is, the body—comes to be taken as the core of self; a central body-schema develops which generalizes from innumerable bodily sensations and feedback from movements (Freud 1914, 1923; Schilder 1950; Van der Velde 1985). Through grasping hand movements, rolling over deliberately, finding and mouthing objects, and similar behavior, the baby learns the self in action.

Much of the play of very young children has to do with what body part belongs to the self or to the other. Both mother and child play often with each other's hands. The baby may want to control all of the hands; not only his or her own, but the mother's hands as well. In learning which hands belongs to the self and which to the mother, the baby gains crucial knowledge of the *separation between self and other as sources of initiative and as different bodies* (Mahler 1968).

Mother and baby stimulate, please, and displease each other in a series of transactions: that is, they cause each other's behavior to occur in complex sequences. A woman with an engorged breast desires that the baby suck, just as the hungry baby has the complementary urge. These bodily interactions are influenced by the temperament of both mother and child. Because of temperamental differences, some babies prefer certain modes of touch and perception; and some mothers, other modes of sensation. Each may have different thresholds for what is too much or too little stimulation or body contact. Ernst Kris and his colleagues (1955; as reviewed also by Stern 1985; Shapiro 1981; Emde, Gaensbauer, and Harmon 1976) have described such perfect and imperfect matches between the disposition or temperament of a new baby and the habit patterns of a new mother. A mother who wants to cuddle a lot may be perfect for one baby and overstimulating for a baby who wants only to gaze at her. Overstimulation may disrupt self-organization; understimulation may undermine opportunities for intellectual growth.

Because of the recombination of genetic material in forming the fetus, there are many possible babies for any one mother. Not all will be "perfect" for her in terms of fit of temperament. The flexibility and resilience of both mother and baby will determine to what extent they can form a harmonious union by mutually shaping each other's behavior. In such operational learning, both mother and child are influenced by feedback (Skinner 1953). Both gradually learn action patterns that gratify wishes and avoid fears, that lead to pleasure and reduce displeasure, to the point where the behavior becomes automatic as the information in those patterned sequences is schematized.

The child develops a body-schema from repeated bodily sensations. Bodily awareness becomes increasingly specific, as coming from a particular body part. Certain areas such as the mouth, nose, and genitals are loaded with nerve endings. During the first two years of life, the child experiences stimuli from the area of the genitals through anal/urethral sphincter activities and from frequent cleaning of these areas by caregivers. The child is able to touch its genitals and to observe the genital differences between the sexes (Roiphe and Galenson 1981). Gender identity has early substrates in schemas from this era. Bodily injury, illness, or peculiar behavior by caregivers can interfere with this early phase of genital awareness. Use of the baby as an instrument of erotic pleasure for the parent, as in rubbing the baby on the parent's genitals, would be an example of such peculiar behavior that might affect the baby's schematization of self. This can lead to schemas that are atypical to the group of one's peers who will later interact sexually. Some of these aspects of sexual identity development are keyed into issues of relationship, and I shall discuss them in that context in the next chapter, along with adolescent sexuality and its role in self-concept formation.

IMITATION AND IDENTIFICATION

Babies and children copy what they perceive. They imitate facial expressions and try to duplicate actions. Seeing that the child is trying to imitate her, the mother says, "Not this way," imitating how the child has done something, and then says, "But this way," showing how to do it in a more desirable way. In the process, the child learns what kind of imitation elicits positive and negative responses from the parent.

Mimicry leads to an action. The repetition of the action leads to an internalized plan for that action. This plan will make it easier to perform that action in the future, so that it can become automatic. Sets of such automatic response plans become aspects of the self-schema. These plans are unconscious. Suppose, for example, a child has a parent who titters nervously when someone else speaks in an angry tone of voice. The child may watch and hear the parent and mimic the response of tittering and, with many repetitions, will acquire this as a habit. Even though unaware of the habit, the child may—when anger is in the air—titter. As a sum total of many such episodes, a child may identify with a particular role and/or a specific person. *Identification,* as discussed in chapter 4, may involve not only this bit-by-bit assembly by observation and mimicry but also the development of a holistic schema of another person and then the use of this schema as a self-view. Identification assimilates aspects of another person into the self; it preserves a continuity of forms of being across generations.

Protection of Coherent Self-Organization by Defensive Maneuvers

The child is often in a weak and passive position. Traumatic situations with adults or older children, which enforce premature recognition of this vulnerability, may result in an excessively weak, defective, or bad self-schema. Protective parents may also be unable to shield the child or prevent harm to themselves. An excessively helpless self-schema may also be developed through identification with and imitation of a helpless parent. Even worse than bad or defective self-schemas, the child may be vulnerable to use only of fragmentary sub-self-schemas. The result may be a felt sense of identity chaos, perhaps manifested by a feeling of flying apart, having bodily emptiness, or frightening disorientation (Winnicott 1962;

Stolorow and Lachmann 1980). Defenses can protect the child from such dangers.

ROLE REVERSAL AND IDENTIFICATION WITH THE AGGRESSOR

Faced with vulnerability to harm in a turbulent, periodically threatening situation, a child may focus on the most powerful figures in the environment. If these people are aggressors and the self is victim, the child may prefer to reverse roles and *identify with the aggressors* because, being strong, they have the best survival potential. Having used this defense mechanism of identifying the self with aggressors, the child may then follow the role of making others victims to avoid the victim role for self. Having made this identification, the child may in later life victimize others.

EXTERNALIZATION

With growth, the child is likely to get into trouble and, hence, to meet frustration. Bad things happen; one gets hurt; others issue threats. The question of *who is to blame* arises. Too much blame activates too much shame, an emotion that may impair a sense of self-coherence. In fact, in states of high shame many people feel smaller or wish to disappear, as in sinking into a hole. Bodily systems are also dysregulated, as in blushing. To protect the sense of integrity of the self, the child seeks to avoid blame and, instead of faithfully analyzing reality, may dislocate blame from self and place it on others. This defensive process within the child's own mind is a manipulation of schemas and is called *externalization.*

Externalization is sometimes taught to children by a parent as a defense against guilt or shame; the parent may spank "the bad toy that hit the baby on the head." A fluid process of *internalization and externalization* is involved in a mechanism that has been called *projective identification* (M. Klein 1948; Kernberg 1984; Masterson 1980; Grotstein 1981). In projective identification, an aspect of the self is removed from the self-schema and placed instead in the working model or schema of another person. This is usually a meaningful person, such as a relative, lover, boss, or physician. In ordinary projection, the other person is then seen as bad, deplored, and rejected. In projective identification, the subject remains close to the person in whom the bad trait is located. That closeness is often marked by hostility toward the other for having the bad traits; and by this hostility, the subject may indeed provoke the other into having the trait (for example, feeling hostile to, or wishing to get away from, the subject). Therein the subject gains some relationship with the other person, even if that relationship has negative emotional expressions, and the existence of the relationship may serve to prop up a flagging self-schema. The rule seems to be that

105

it is better for some people to have an ongoing negative relationship than to feel totally alone.

IDEALIZATION

Some children are in danger of developing self-schemas that depict them as incomplete, damaged, or unworthy. This threat seems to occur more when the closeness, empathy, and emotional support from caregivers is unavailable or given very erratically, or when the child is abused. The child who experiences very deflated self-concepts may enter states of mind that are sour, empty of hope, and full of bitterness or anxious vigilance. As a defense against such deflation, the child may learn irrational degrees of idealization of another to protect against excessive deflation. Excessive idealization of some real or fictional figure in the child's world may bring its own potential for frustrations and deflation when that figure does not perform up to the projected expectations. Hope in the idealized figure may turn to rage, and the child may behave in ways that further impair the situation of interaction, leading to less and less satisfaction for either party (Kernberg 1976).

Since idealization of the self may also be used to protect against deflated and weak self-concepts, the child may develop unusually grandiose self-schemas. These may be associated with ambitions for greatness in excess of one's real potential, demanding more talent and skill than the child possesses or can learn. The need for self-idealization to avoid organization of experience with deflated self-concepts means the child has to engage in processing information in such a way as to be unable to achieve a true approximation of reality. Fantasy more and more will have to replace reality-testing thought, and action itself may be avoided to escape the feedback inherent in its consequences.

In order to prop up grandiose self-schemas, the child may continue to view others as if they were part of the self rather than independent persons with their own wishes and needs. Normally, the child gradually learns that one's inner wishes do not automatically control parents, even though parents are responsive to expressions of need or desire. In defensive maneuvers, the child goes on believing in omnipotent control of the self over others. As mentioned in chapter 5, Heinz Kohut (1972, 1984) used the term *selfobject* to refer to the use of these schemas of others as extensions of the self. The other is expected to read the mind of the self and behave accordingly. One function will be to serve as a distorting mirror, reflecting not so much reality as an inflated view of the attractiveness and accomplishments of the self.

A related mechanism, also noted by Kohut (1977), is pairing off with another person in order to reduce one's vulnerability to deflation of self-esteem. This pairing is often a part of normal early adolescent development, when identity is under major revision, and a solid self-organization has not been established. The boy or the girl finds a peer, each serving the other as a twin, and they become inseparable. Each gains from the reflection of the other, and also from the sense of connection in a strong, bipolar unit. Because it has served a defensive function, loss of the *twinship figure*, as in losses of other selfobjects, may lead to states of depersonalization, hypochondriacal anxiety, or chaotic anxiety at losing identity.

Twinships and selfobjects are an aspect of another, often normal coping strategy used by young children to counter loneliness and threats to self-coherence that can occur on separation from caregivers or loss of their empathetic attention to the self. In this maneuver, one idealizes an object, using a familiar piece of clothing, a security blanket, a stuffed animal, or a pacifier as an ally to self. These valued self-supplements are called _transitional objects_ because one uses them to tolerate separation (Winnicott 1953; Bowlby 1969; Tolpin 1972).

Imaginary companions perform the same role, the child using fantasy rather than an actual object. The imaginary companion may take on functions that the child is developing but has not yet integrated as symbols in self-schemas, such as inner voices of conscience about what acts are right or wrong (Benson and Pryor 1973).

THE SPLITTING OF SELF-SCHEMAS

Because of the danger of such emotional states as separation panic, deflated shame, hopeless depression, and blind rage at frustration, the child may manipulate schemas of self to stabilize those concepts that can maintain less painful states of mind. In the defensive maneuver called *splitting*, the child may handle threats by compartmentalizing subschemas into varied self-schemas in order to organize some states of mind on an all-good self-schema. There are, however, self-perceptions, memories, and fantasies inconsistent with perfect goodness; and these must be placed into another bad self-schema (Freud 1940; Masterson 1979). The splitting of self-schemas thus leads to true and false selves (Winnicott 1962) and to *dissociation* of good and bad memories (M. Klein 1948; Fairbairn 1954; Kernberg 1967, 1976, 1985; Horowitz 1977c; Marmar and Horowitz 1986). Only one set of memories is available to experience at a time. Self-coherence is protected at the expense of developing realistic working models.

Role-relationship models may also be segregated into those that are all-good and those that are all-bad. The purpose seems to be to maintain a sector of conflict-free goodness at the expense of creating a major division in mental schemas and so in states of mind. The shifts in state of mind governed by different good and bad self-schemas are so pronounced, and the states so different, that one can seem like quite a different person from mood to mood. Multiple personalities in one individual often both have a range from very good to very bad and stem from traumatic experiences at crucial stages of early development when the world seemed to turn sharply from good to suddenly, frighteningly, and overwhelmingly bad.

Lifelong Development in Self-Schemas

While there are milestones in the development of the self-organization, the task is never over and does not occur only at specified transition periods. Rather, it is a process of both trait maintenance and change throughout life. Crises at any point may lead to change in self-schematization as a result of mourning and to new learning as in identification. It is important, therefore, to view self-organization and reorganization as a process continuing throughout life (see Emde 1983, Colarusso and Nemiroff 1981, and Levinson 1978 for a review and synthesis).

Daniel Levinson (1978) has defined some of the polarities that are themes in self-reorganization throughout various transitions in life. Based on work by Carl Jung (1933) and Erik Erikson (1959), such polarities include those between *youth* and *age;* the self as *destroyer* and the self as *creator* or *caregiver;* the self as *masculine* or *feminine;* and the self as *connected with* or *separated from* others. Wishes and threats on these themes may be progressively more integrated into harmonies over a lifetime of revised self-organization.

George Vaillant (1977) studied a group of college-educated men over a forty-year period which began during their university years. He found that major modes of defense tended to persist over time, and to be modified into progressively more adaptive forms. At midlife, many men who had been bland in youth became increasingly more zestful and interesting, as they oriented their behavior more clearly to their ideal schemas and recognized what skills they had indeed mastered. Vaillant noted many remarkable changes in self-organization throughout adulthood, heightened during the midlife period.

The aging person who believes that he or she has little effect on others through a diminished social role may feel loss of integrity and states of despair, as Erikson (1982) has suggested. To ward off such states of despair, the person may shift to sadistic, brutal, power-wielding, and potentially destructive role-relationship models and, as a result, harshly bear down on others, especially the young. Destructive aims are often more potently realized than creative ones, and one may bolster a flagging sense of self by embracing them. Renunciation of such coping strategies may build new characteristics and self-concepts, such as wisdom, humor, and a useful, philosophical sense of life as transient (Kohut 1977; Levinson 1978; Colarusso and Nemiroff 1981).

Masculine and feminine characteristics are present in both sexes. In gender stereotyped cultures, the traits associated with the opposite sex are warded off so that the man becomes hypermasculine and nonfeminine, and the woman hyperfeminine and devoid of masculine traits. Normally, as a person matures, the warded-off or undeveloped characteristics associated with the "other sex" may be gradually integrated into the self-organization—an integration that occurs over the entire life cycle, often most prominently in midlife, as outlined by Carl Jung and analytical psychologists (Whitmont 1969). In some Western cultures in midlife, men may become less consumed with efforts to master others in the outer world and more introspectively concerned with self and personal values; they idealize others less and are less inclined to condemn others. At the same time, a woman who has lived in a narrow sphere as family caregiver may now wish to explore creative and competitive mastery of the larger social world. She may extend her leadership capacity from a small group to a work institution.

Summary

Development of self-schemas can be a progressive synthesis of partial schemas into larger, more unified forms. The earliest ingredients may be provided by the genetic makeup of the baby and the course of fetal growth. Then the childhood and adolescent interactions with the human figures in the environment will be crucial in shaping temperament into character. An early phase is probably developing a series of *self-schemas.* Later, these may be gathered into *supraordinate self-schemas.* Eventually a unifying *self-organization* may develop. This eventuality may take a lifetime; it may never be achieved by some, even by late adulthood.

Weakness in self-organization may be understood in several ways. At one level, a weakness may be due to lack of integration of various self-concepts into a relatively unified self-organization. This weakness predisposes a person to relatively choppy changes in state of mind, as where one shifts too fluidly among different self-schemas. Without supraordinate forms, the person cannot tolerate ambivalence well: hatred toward others owing to insults to the self is not modified by recognition that the self is also loving toward them; the need to subordinate the self to the directions of another is not softened by the recognition that in other situations one directs the other in what to do. Ambivalence intensifies, and increases the likelihood of, an angry, aggressive state of mind or a passive, withdrawn, and sulky one, even when the other person is acting in a nice way.

At another level, weakness in self-schematization can be related to development of specifically defective, feeble, worthless, or incompetent self-schemas. When these schemas, rather than more effective ones, organize behavior, one may enter states in which one is especially tense and dependent with worries about abandonment or withdrawn in fantasy. One may feel sad, anxious, and disgusted with the self. Irrationally weak self-schemas, when active, lead to maladaptive behavior patterns because the person, judging self to be defective, does not rise to challenges.

The worst aspects of weakness in self-organization are those states of mind that suggest entry into *identity chaos.* The person may feel catastrophically frightened of self-annihilation. To bolster a flagging sense of self-coherence, the person may use irrational but emotionally effective defensive maneuvers of the type mentioned in this chapter. Other defensive maneuvers are also available for self-protection; and these protective operations will be further discussed in chapter 10. Meanwhile self-organization can be better understood by considering the development of role-relationship models, and the embeddedness of self-concepts in such schemas. That is the topic of our next chapter.

7

The Development of Role-Relationship Models

RECURRENT maladaptive patterns of interpersonal behavior are based in part upon the use of inappropriate but significant role-relationship models in the construction of working models of current situations. Role-relationship models are not genetically determined, insofar as we know, although their development is influenced by a person's temperament, biological endowment, and cultural environment. Role-relationship models develop in the context of interpersonal behavioral patterns and then serve to guide such behavior in the future. Such schemas may be used in a normal way to create adaptive working models, or in an abnormal way to create maladaptive ones.

Role-relationship models originate in childhood. New versions are built on the substrates provided by early schemas. Radically new role-relationship models may, however, develop at any time in life. Traumatic situations are especially important as contexts in which changes occur, both during childhood and at any time later in life, including late adulthood.

In this chapter, I shall review the role-relationship models that organize the more common focus of recurrent maladaptive interpersonal behavioral patterns. Knowledge about these role-relationship models is gained, in large measure, in the context of clinical work in psychotherapy. The recurrent pattern is often enacted in treatment, as an aspect of transference phenomena, as well as in the repeated stories the person tells about past and present relationships. The role-relationship models are inferred from the many repetitions observed by both patient and therapist. The origin of the rigidly used, maladaptive patterns is often traced to childhood transactions, in an effort to help the patient develop a continuous sense of life history and self growth. These interpretations of origin are often reconstructions of what *might* have happened, based on incomplete and possibly biased memories. Of course, childhood memories are often recalled after decades of forgetfulness; but the patient may vary these memories over time in treatment, and any inferences about the cause of childhood patterns drawn from these memories are not necessarily true (Pine 1985).

One important aspect of psychodynamic theory is the integration of the life history of an individual in terms of recurrent themes in self-appraisal, work life, and social life. The irrational elements found in present patterns often seem more rational as schemas for an earlier period, especially for childhood. Many schools of thought, including divergent brands of psychoanalytic and psychodynamic theory, vary in terms of how they relate specific childhood situations to adult forms of personality disorder. In this chapter, I assume that we cannot make these connections with any degree of certainty. Longitudinal research efforts will be necessary before we are able, validly, to link childhood patterns with adult patterns (Block 1971; Emde 1981).

I have chosen to discuss common role-relationship models in a sequence that deals with three sets of complex issues: issues of supplying love and care, issues of power and control, and issues of sexuality and status. These issues are approximately developmental, and follow with some changes the early formulations of Freud about the oral, anal, and genital sequences in psychological growth. Under each of these categories, I aim to provide the reader with details about how normal and abnormal role-relationship models may develop in childhood and then later influence adult behavior.

Early Psychoanalytic Theory

Freud explained patterns he observed in adult patients in terms of theories about transformations of the psychic energy force he called *libido*. This force was seen as an instinctive drive which was channeled through various structures developed from the transactions that occur in a family, in relation to the developing capacities of the mind of the infant and child.

Freud postulated that libidinal energy, derived from the biological unfolding of sexual instincts, is distributed toward objects during three phases of development—the oral, the anal, and the genital zones—each emphasizing a zone of the body where occur transactions with the caregivers (1905). For example, the earliest zone was seen to be the mouth. In sucking milk, the infant might engage the mother in different ways: sucking, biting, expelling the nipple, sealing off the mouth. The mother might give, withhold, remove, or intrude the nipple too far (Erikson 1950). Repetition of a given pattern would form an expectancy pattern, the precursor of a role-relationship model.

As the toddler learns sphincter control, issues around toilet training arise. Who determines by whom, when, and where the feces should be expelled? Power struggles might occur, perhaps elaborating previous power struggles with regard to when feeding will take place, how much is to be fed, and how rapidly.

Still later, the child's efforts to attract the interest of others would involve gender-specific mannerisms and bodily presentations—sexual displays that do emerge clearly in children between two and five years of age. Trauma, overstimulation, excessive gratification, or developmental arrest could, at any phase, cause the relationship pattern emphasized at that stage to prevail over time, instead of giving way to more advanced patterns. In addition, strain at that level of development could lead to a compensatory regression to use of schemas from a previous level. These *fixations* and *regressions* have been inferred in adults undergoing character analyses by psychoanalysts who agree on this point although differing in other theoretical perspectives.

Erik Erikson focused on these transactional issues and mapped out development not only through these early oral, anal, and genital phases but throughout the life cycle. Each transition period in life added new challenges, and so new role-relationship models might be developed. He deemphasized the sole primacy of libido in charging these object-relationship

113

patterns, and emphasized social issues and the pressing importance of personal identity.

In Erikson's view of transformation, the stages classified by Freud (1905) and later by Karl Abraham (1924) as oral, anal, and phallic were considered in social terms as phases in development of the self through a sequence of learning new social transactions. In the earliest transactions involving issues of supplies, as in feeding and the emotional refueling that occurs through holding, the infant acquired the schemas that would lead to traits of trust or mistrust of others. Later, during the phase of learning bowel and bladder control, the toddler acquired schemas that were either self-affirming, in developing a sense of increased autonomy from others, or self-depreciating, in causing shame and doubt about self-regulation.

Still later, on top of and in transformation of such role-relationship models as already developed, the child would learn initiative, competence, a sense of personal identity, and then build toward learning intimacy, the capacity to contribute to larger groups of others, and personal integrity. Each phase of this prototype of a life cycle would also have its down side, the bad or vulnerable views of role-relationship models built on failures to relate well.

Some of the issues at every age during the life cycle are summarized in table 7.1. The approximate ages are derived from developmental observations, and vary from culture to culture to some extent. As mentioned, the psychosocial stages are derived from classical psychoanalytic theory (Freud 1903) and subsequent work (Franz and White 1985; Sullivan 1953). Summary of life-crises, and their implication for personality, is based on the work of Erik Erikson (1950, 1958, 1959, 1980) and others as elaborated on and rearranged by Jerome Singer (1987).

The personality implications presented in table 7.1 accord with both the development of self-organization, as covered in chapter 6, and the development of role-relationship models of attachment to others, as will be discussed in this chapter. At every point a developmental task can become a life-crisis if the person has high internal conflicts, or a deficit in the ability to develop the appropriate new schemas, or is adversely affected by losses and insults or by lack of available teachings from the environment.

However accepted by early psychoanalytic theory, recent theorists have regarded the energy concepts of Freud as outmoded (Appelgarth 1971; Thickstun and Rosenblatt 1977; G. S. Klein 1976; Peterfreund 1971). Yet clinicians have found value in observations of life history and character development of adults as organized roughly by the oral, anal, and phallic model (Fenichel 1945).

In this chapter, I shall discuss early development of role-relationship

TABLE 7.1

Development and the Life Cycle

Age (approximately when task or social expectation first appears or is critical)	Psychosexual Stage	Developmental Task, Life-Crisis, or Societal Expectation	Personality Implication	
			Individuation Pathway	Attachment Pathway
Infancy (to 18 mos.)	Sensory-Oral (Freud)	Achieving secure attachment; giving and receiving affection; learning to walk and beginning to talk	Trust vs. mistrust	Trust vs. mistrust
Early Childhood (2–5)	Muscular-Anal (Freud)	Developing self-control; beginnings of sense of right and wrong; communication skills	Autonomy vs. shame	Object and self-constancy vs. loneliness and helplessness
	Locomotor-Genital (Freud)	Developing capacity for play and imagination	Developing private personality; initiative vs. guilt	Beginning to play with other and to "show off"; playfulness vs. passivity or aggression
Middle Childhood (7–12)	Latency (Freud) School Age (Franz and White) Juvenile Chumship (Sullivan)	Relating to social peers, school groups, forming close friendships, learning new motor skills; developing cognitive skills, accepting or adjusting to one's changing body	Industry vs. inferiority	Empathy and collaboration vs. excessive power or caution

TABLE 7.1 (Continued)

Age (approximately when task or social expectation first appears or is critical)	Psychosexual Stage	Developmental Task, Life-Crisis, or Societal Expectation	Personality Implication	
			Individuation Pathway	Attachment Pathway
Puberty and Early Adolescence (12–15)		Learning psychobiological and social sex roles; developing specific sexual "appetites" (heterosexual or homosexual attractions); confronting issues of group membership, "popularity"; specific athletic, artistic or academic skill development	Identity vs. identity diffusion	Mutuality interdependence vs. alienation
Late Adolescence (16–19)		Learning to understand and control the physical world and the broader social milieu; developing an appropriate symbol system and conceptual abilities; learning creative expression	Identity vs. identity diffusion	Mutuality interdependence vs. alienation

TABLE 7.1 *(Continued)*

Age (approximately when task or social expectation first appears or is critical)	Psychosexual Stage	Developmental Task, Life-Crisis, or Societal Expectation	Personality Implication	
			Individuation Pathway	Attachment Pathway
Young Adulthood (20–30)		Relating to the system of occupations; family formation, citizenship	Career and life-style formation vs. drifting	Intimacy vs. isolation
Adulthood (30–50)		Relating to childrearing and to economic stress and opportunity; responsibility to older and younger generation family; community, citizenship, organizational relations, e.g., union, vocational group, clubs	Life-style consolidation vs. emptiness	Generativity vs. self-absorption
Maturity and Seniority (55 and over)		Relating self to broader world and to universe; confronting retirement; grandparenting or aged parents; civic responsibilities; leadership roles; values as having continuity after death of self	Integrity vs. despair	Active participation vs. isolation and loneliness

SOURCE: J. L. Singer, "Psychoanalytic Theory in the Context of Contemporary Psychology." The Helen Block Lewis Memorial Lecture, American Psychological Association, 1987.

models in terms of three broad and more or less sequential types of situation: those that involve supplies of love and care (what has been called the *oral phase*); those that involve issues of power and control over self and others (or the *anal phase*); and those that involve further expansion of self-organization and interaction with others, including sexuality and gender identification (or, the *genital phase*). In each of these broad and loose categorizations, I shall contrast normal, or ordinarily adaptive, formation of role-relationship models with the development of schemas that lead to recurrent maladaptive interpersonal behavioral patterns and to pathological deflations of self-esteem.

The Issues of Supplying Love and Care

EARLY TRANSACTIONS WITH CAREGIVERS

The mothering figure provides an envelope of safety around the dependent infant. The infant cries; the mother responds. Each regulates the state of the other; the two are to some degree a unified pair. The way in which need and response are repeated becomes a role-relationship model. The schema may be a good one: the sequence saying in effect, "Care is coming when I need it. I am well attached to another who will provide for me."

When the supplies of love and security are consistent with and adequate to the particular child, that child is able to develop good role-relationship models and, hence, character traits of optimism that can sustain the individual through periods of later strain. These would be the securely attached children with resilient self-concepts, as discussed in chapter 6 (Ainsworth 1973; Main 1975; Sroufe 1979). On the other hand, inconsistency, deprivation, or traumatic lapses in care may dispose the child to develop negative role-relationship models and, hence, character traits of pessimism and mistrust (Erikson 1950; Spitz 1960; Bowlby 1969, 1973; Mayman 1968; Blatt and Lerner 1983).

Some caregivers devote themselves so fully to a baby that they give instantly the moment anything is needed, and adore the baby constantly. The child may, as a result, gradually develop a self-schema of being the adorable one, of receiving perfect care and admiration from a loving and ever-present mother. If the mother worships the child even when the child is sullen, demanding, or hostile, then the child will tend to develop role-relationship models of a perfect self, grandly entitled to receive service from a slavelike worshiper. Once the child begins to interact with others beyond the home, one usually replaces such views with more realistic ones. But in circumstances that later threaten self-cohesion, the child may stick to grandiose self-schemas and unrealistically amplify role-relationship models of entitlement. Much more common, however, than oversupply of attention are transactions in which a baby is undersupplied, frustrated, given contradictory responses, or traumatized.

The role relationships of an anxiously attached child may be of a vulnerable boy or girl clinging to an unreliable caregiver. The caregiver is seen as a person who may unpredictably surge toward or away from a nurturing role. The aim of the child is anxious vigilance to see which way the mother is going. The child clings to signal fear, and expects the mother to give more care once she sees the child is frightened of her departure. Adults who repeat these role-relationship models show anxious dependence on another person or on a group. Such adults may, in using peer supports to bolster a sense of safety or personal identity, become vulnerable to peer-group pressure out of fear of ostracism.

If repeated separations have lasted too long for the child, the child may develop a self-schema as an abandoned waif, pining for a neglectful caregiver, whom the child sees as hopelessly gone and as refusing to return. In this sad state, the child may try to elicit care from others, yet can experience that need as shameful and preconsciously develop a self-concept as independent, not needy, and aloof from caregivers, or from peers who are cared for. The role-relationship model may be one of an embittered self, looking hostilely upon a world of unfair people and enviously on those with desired traits (Kernberg 1984). Unnecessary aggressions, challenges that alienate others, and withdrawals in times of stress may become character traits (George and Main 1979).

These untoward role-relationship models, which contain scripts of neglect or abuse of the child, are most likely to develop in situations where the mother or father are depressed, alcoholic, addicted to drugs, distracted by severe social, economic, or wartime strains, and themselves abused or neglected in childhood. In these life situations the child may build a script for better caregiving, and for providing food, shelter, and emotional refueling. For example, the mother whose interest in caregiving is flagging may be revived into concern and care by the child's falling ill or getting injured. If this happens often, and satisfies the child, he or she learns that script: when one's deep need for care is frustrated, one has to suffer and display suffering in order to receive care or pleasure. Thus, suffering becomes, first, a necessary prelude and, then, may be sought as a precursor to satisfying some appetite for care or pleasure.

A triangular relationship model—that is, one with three interacting roles—may develop around the child's wish for love and care. One party may be seen as an unreliable or neglectful caregiver: the bad one. Another party may be seen as a rescuer and supplier: the good one. A variety of dramatic scripts can develop on this basic triad (Karpman 1968). The most frequent type starts when the self displays need; the bad one then aggressively deprives the self; and the good one witnesses the neglect, defeats the aggressor, and rescues the self. The repeated use of such a three-party role-relationship model may lead to situations in which one displays masochistic suffering and encourages two potential caregivers to fight over who will be loved by the subject because he or she gives the best help.

PASSIVE-AGGRESSIVE PATTERNS

A pathological variant of dependent scripts is found in some people, who play the role of the one unable to assume the responsibility for self-care. The display of this role to another provokes that other person to take responsibility for providing care. The subject may at first receive the care with a show of gratitude. But there is a resentment and expectation that care will not be well provided. The subject then tries to show the caregiver up as neglectful, intrusive, or providing the wrong kind of what one wants. Repetitive use of such scripts is called a *passive-aggressive style,* in which one—by seeming "not to do anything"—actually behaves with hostility.

Such was the case of Chet, a typist, who was asked to work with an executive while her secretary was on vacation. He resented leaving his friends in the typing pool—an irritation heightened when the woman demanded high-quality work. Whenever her instructions were not explicit, Chet carried them out incompletely or with slight errors. Even if her instructions were clear and explicit, Chet did his assignment very slowly and without interest. If he was not given exact instructions about what to do after completing a task, he would remain idle instead of taking on other obvious tasks.

The executive became increasingly irritated and, finally, lost her temper about one specific episode. The interdepartmental green stationary had been used for an important outside letter, one that Chet knew should have been done on a white letterhead. In the explosion that followed, she cursed Chet. He then acted as though he was extremely hurt by what she said. He complained widely, saying he had been harshly castigated for a trivial error, and that she had given him poor supervision. In remorse at her intense reaction to Chet, the executive then had to become scrupulously "nice" to him, tolerating his poor performance of his duties and his sullen demeanor.

WHEN NEED MAY BE SEEN AS GREED

In the passive-aggressive script, the goal is to blame the other person rather than the self for a lapse in well-being. In a different role-relationship model, the self may be seen as blamed for being so greedy that the caregiver is harmed. A mother may reinforce such an attitude if she acts as though she were always depleted by the needs of her child.

RIVALRY FOR ATTENTION

Rivalry for limited supplies of care, as when another sibling is born, can lead to envy or jealousy of the attention paid to the other. The repeated wish to get rid of a rival may lead to the self-concept of wishful destroyer of the sibling. A three-party role-relationship model may be based on a proposition that there is only a limited amount of love or nurturance in the world. According to this proposition, when one needy person obtains supplies such as maternal attention, the other needy person is depleted (Beck 1979). When this role-relationship model is active as a working model, one may resent another person for even sincere expressions of need for care, and there may also be guilt or shame for one's own need and for one's resentment of the other.

While usually siblings learn to love and to get along when rivalry occurs, in some children this process is impeded. The parents, and the family as a system, may support the belief that supplies of love and concern are limited in quantity, so that what one person gets another cannot have. Instead of understanding that love grows between persons and that mutual kindness and caregiving increase emotional support for all parties, such persons may later regard life as if it were a "zero-sum" game in which only one person can win. Such people may even fear loving, lest they be personally impoverished by loving another.

DEFENSIVE COMPROMISES AND LATER CHARACTER FORMATION

Conflicts always occur, to some extent, between what the infant or child wants and what the caregiver can and will do. Conflicts develop within the child out of schemas showing both the desired and the dreaded consequences of a wish. For example, the child's desire for food and attention from a caregiver may activate a role-relationship model that can appease that desire. In this model, the self may be seen as a worthy and dependent child, the caregiver as a good, attentive person who will give what is wanted on expression of that desire—the *desired* transaction at the top of figure 7.1. The same child may have a *dreaded* role-relationship model in which the caregiver may be unavailable or likely to abandon the child. The child may pine in vain for such a caregiver, as shown in the dreaded transaction beneath the desired one in figure 7.1.

Having both the desired and the dreaded role-relationship models, the child may be unable to sustain the idea of the caregiver's possible criticism should the child signal his or her desires. The caregiver might scold the child for wanting too much or too often, and then abandon the child. To avoid this outcome, the child may develop a sequence: express need; then, if criticized, efface the self before the controlling caregiver. This role-relationship model is the problematic transaction of figure 7.1 because it leads to submissive self-abnegation.

To continue with this situation, the child may find a way to compromise with this type of controlling caregiver in order to get attention and avoid criticism. Instead of exploring the world in a zestful way, the child may become obedient and passive to the parent. All actions conform to what the parent wants, in order to obtain some gratification and avoid abandonment. The child allows the parent to become an overly dominant caregiver, one who structures all the child's time, and who receives total obedience out of fear. This may lead to a situation that seems quiet, nonturbulent, and devoid of interpersonal conflicts, since the child is predictably compliant. But the very safety of this *compromise* role-relationship model sets the child up for a life of dependency and conformity instead of optimal self-development through curiosity about and adventurous explorations of the world. This defensive transaction is shown at the bottom of figure 7.1.

The Issue of Power and Control

CONTROL OF ACTIONS

The infant learns to crawl, then to stand, and finally to walk—an increased control of muscles made possible by development of the nervous system, which also makes voluntary excretion possible. The unpleasant task of changing soiled diapers and wet bedding enhances parents' interest in having the child learn bladder and bowel control as quickly as possible. Many transactions with the caregivers occur in respect to this crucial stage of socialization.

For the child, it is convenient and tension relieving to excrete whenever

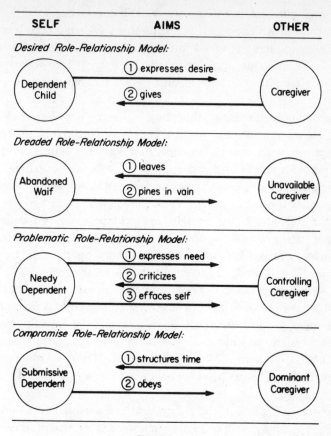

Figure 7.1

Dynamic Analysis of Relationship Model about Supplies

an urge occurs; but it is also exciting and interesting to attain mastery over the body and gain the pleased enthusiasm of parents by the display of such new abilities as excretion in the toilet. In addition to the interests of the baby and parents, the culture and environmental ecology determine when and how these transactions over bowel and bladder will take place. Some societies require strict control at an early age; others do not. Parents teach children to conform with the rules of society. Sanctions within and outside the family thus determine how the child will be socialized. After the child has learned to control the excretion of feces and urine, parents usually cease to reward the child and instead punish him or her when there is "an accident."

Children perceive many new facts about their bodies as they come to understand excretory products and the organs of elimination. What was inside comes out and is thrown away. What was part of "my" body is now flushed down the toilet. Has something valuable been lost? What makes these products appear? Who controls the elimination? Who says when and where? While these questions are not put into words as such, they are answered in some way, leading to new schematization during this period.

The desired outcome during this phase is a sense of will, responsibility, and competence. An adaptive result is a sense of personal control over the body, its movements, and its products in a way that brings one securely into accord with the family and society. Maladaptive outcomes can be found in patterns that make the person feel shame and self-doubt. Adaptive schemas will most likely involve a parent who fosters in the child a sense of the ability to do things right, to be competent in self-control, and to have self-esteem for taking on social responsibilities; while maladaptive schemas may be more likely when a parent diminishes the child by making it feel bad, dirty, flawed, or incompetent as a total person.

These attitudes are based not only on transactions over elimination, but on the wide range of acts now possible for a mobile child. Without knowing the danger, a child may pull down a lamp or stick a finger into an electric socket. The parents teach the child to accept instructions from a distance, calling out a firm "No no," for example. The child must learn that these signals mean "Stop," but that they are not a sign that he or she is bad and unloved.

In response to the will of the parent, and to a personal set of intentions as well, the child may wish to comply in order to gain attention and praise, and in order to avoid punishment or further threats. At the same time, the child may also want to act without restraint and to have power over self, others, and objects. The child learns that, although parents can punish and reward, they can be made miserable and also can be controlled.

The parents may have conflicting motives during this phase. While they want the child to conform to desired patterns, they may have different value schemas about what is desired. Mother may differ with father over what is the greater good. Moreover, conflicts may exist within each parent between the ways he or she was brought up and would prefer to have been brought up.

Schemas were developed in each parent during childhood. These schemas had self as child, the other as parent; but role-relationship models are always reversible: the self has also learned the role of the other. Now, with parenthood, these child-parent role-relationship schemas are reactivated. The parent will always have a tendency to enact automatically some roles of his or her own parents however much that treatment was disliked at the time. One may, in so repeating history, deeply dislike these tendencies in oneself—as did Sharon in respect to her little girl, Annie, now three years old. One day she was standing on a stool as Sharon was putting papers together into a looseleaf notebook at a counter. The little girl imitated her mother, putting pages together—but not in order. Sharon asked her to stop, saying, "Mommy will be done soon. Just wait a minute." When Annie persisted, Sharon repeated her remark more firmly. Annie kept on sorting the papers. Sharon slapped her in the face, then felt searing remorse, cried, and hugged Annie very hard.

Sharon's mother had often slapped her in the face when she disobeyed her—and did so until Sharon was a teenager, when she threatened to hit her mother back if she did not stop it. Sharon always hated this sudden surge of temper in her mother, and had vowed to her own dolls, in play, that it would never happen to them, and of course never to her own real children. Then, faced with work pressures and a deadline that was hard to meet, she did almost reflexively act as had her mother. The schema was there and worked automatically when the situation triggered it. Sharon had to work on restraining this automatic response tendency.

Sharon had another response that she became aware of and learned to control. It was not a pattern she liked, and it certainly did not conform to her current values. In this pattern she found herself becoming resentful of Annie when she herself had been very kind and giving to her daughter. Annie did appreciate and love Sharon, but at such times this did not seem to be enough of a reward. Actually, what Sharon was resenting was not consciously clear to her for some time. Then she realized that she resented the fact that Annie was having a better childhood with a better mother than had been the case for Sharon herself. The child self-concept in Sharon wanted this good loving caregiver that she, Sharon, was being for Annie, and felt a rivalry with Annie for having more of what she was denied.

While rivalry and envy are normal in the development of children, heightened rivalry and vengeful envy can lead to an excessive competitor-rival role-relationship model. Such schemas may be established more decisively if and when parents do enter into rivalry with their child, as in being jealous of the child's joys and privileges. A parent who had bad, inadequate, or absent parents may even manifest jealous envy of the child for having good parents.

The conflicts that occur in struggles between parents and an assertive child create ambivalence in most parents. They want the child to obey and do good things; they also do not want to break the child's spirit, make him or her overly conformistic, or guilty. Relative strength and weakness of will are also issues in this phase of development. Even the act of deliberately evacuating the bowels in a specified place can be seen as being strong or weak. Because this act is praised by the parents, correctly, as growth and mastery, it feels strong: "Doing it like the big people." But it also can be devalued by the self as weak, since it gives in to parents, gives up a spontaneous pleasure, and may even be seen as magically depleting the body by letting its valued products disappear. Similarly, defecation in bed may be viewed as a weak and shame-filled act. One who does that is just a baby. But it may also be a strong act, that of an aggressively self-assertive if not revengeful child, who punishes neglectful parents by making them clean up the mess.

In such ways, the child learns that by compliance or defiance, parents can be manipulated in the same way that they manipulate and control the child. As the parents recognize the force of the willful child, they increase the control used as a countermeasure. Stamina may be an important factor in how these power struggles are resolved. With parents who are fatigued, overburdened, anxious, or depressed, a child who is strong-willed may be able simply to wear down the mother or father in these difficult negotiations over power and control and so lead to a role-relationship schema in which the self-concept is that of a *stubborn soiler* in relation to a *degraded powerless parent*. Later in adulthood, such a role-relationship model might lead to a behavioral pattern of willful neglect of duties flaunted before a supervisor.

THE UNCONTROLLED CHILD IN RELATION TO THE UNCARING CAREGIVER

Sometimes a parent seems to be unavailable and uncaring just at times when the child feels most out of control. The child may soil himself, wet his pants, or urinate in bed and expect that the parent will perhaps scold him, but also will set matters right by cleaning him up. If the parent does not come, or comes and lets the child stay in this mess "to teach him a lesson," then the hope for control from the parent is dashed. Repeated transactions of this sort can be internalized as a role-relationship model in which the child schematizes himself as defectively uncontrolled and the parent as insufficiently caring to help him with self-regulation.

This role-relationship model between the uncontrolled child and the uncaring caregiver may contain many aims, one of the most prominent of which is hostility for frustration of wishes. The child gets angry at the parent, and lashes out in some way—perhaps just verbally, perhaps by some physical act. The child may have even struggled to gain his way, and won as the parent gave up a fight. Even in this condition of victory, the child may be beset with self-doubts. The child has been strong, but strength in the child cannot be a stable situation in relation to parents, because the child is in fact dependent and small. The child wonders why the parents let him win, let him be obstinate or hostile. The child may feel too powerful for his own self-regulatory capacity, reinforcing the dangerously uncontrolled view of self and, paradoxically, a resentment toward the parents for not being strong enough to stop his bad behavior.

THE ROLE-RELATIONSHIP MODEL OF A DEGRADED SELF IN RELATION TO A HARSH CRITIC

Inevitably, some of the child's actions will be criticized. There are many ways to criticize a child. One is to carefully criticize a specific behavior while avoiding disparagement of the child as a person. At another extreme, the parent may ridicule and shame the child as an individual. Moreover, a parent who struggles to avoid self-disgust and social shame may obscure his or her own role as a participant during troubled times. By blaming the child, the parent can feel superior. There may even be pleasure in harshly criticizing the child. Repeated transactions of this sort will lead the child to develop a degraded self-concept and the expectation that whenever the self fails to please, the other will express intense scorn.

Sometimes a child is expected to do something that she cannot do correctly all the time. When the child makes a mistake, the parent accuses the child of being stubborn or having bad intentions. Both parties are confused about whether the child *can* do it right but *will* not, or whether the child *cannot* do it right at the moment even though she *wants to.* For example, the child may learn to excrete in a toilet but have an occasional involuntary accident. In addition, there may be episodes of deliberate soiling in order to punish the parent for some frustration. The presence of the willful soiling may lead the child to believe she is "always in control" and thus always responsible for her mistakes. A perfectionistic attitude may develop, in which the ideal of always "doing it right" is regarded as really attainable. This is a set-up for self-doubt and, with repetition of failure and harsh criticism, for self-degradation. The degraded self-concept has to be warded off, and one way to do that is to put someone else in the role. The role-relationship model can be reversed: the self can become the harsh critic and debase someone else who can be found to have fallen short of some perfectionistic ideal. The character trait of habitual fault finding in others, as well as the self, can be the result of this kind of hypervigilance directed toward whomever is to blame for imperfections.

These character traits of perfectionism and fault finding are often associated with self-doubting ruminations, the kind of unproductive review of situations and choices that actually prevent clear decisions (Shapiro 1981). The situations that lead to episodes of rumination are usually those in which there is some ambivalence about complying or not complying with the wishes or rules set by others. The ambivalent person cannot ever be clear about whether she *can* comply but will not, or whether she *cannot* comply. If she can comply but will not, then she is *strong;* if she cannot comply, then she is *weak.* If she is strong, that may be *good;* she will be independent of the control of others. It may be *bad;* she will be a willful soiler or spoiler of cooperative enterprises, or even harm the others by defeating their purposes. If she is weak, that may be *good* because it means that closeness through dependence and submission is all right, or *bad* because the submission is dangerous to personal purposes. With all these alternatives, no decision can be reached because thought becomes convoluted, cloudy, and confusing! Real interactions are disrupted because the person moves toward and away from true independence.

DOMINANCE AND SUBMISSION

In society there are usually hierarchies of many types. To adapt well, one needs to learn to take directions and follow some rules without feeling weak, bad, or degraded by the submission. One also needs to be capable of responsibly giving instructions and enforcing important principles without degrading others or becoming overly controlling of their identity. It is possible to develop a character structure where the role-relationship models of submission and dominance are each present, important but dreaded.

In some personalities, often called *obsessional, compulsive,* or *rigidly overcontrolled,* neither position feels safe. Constant undoing of one role with another may be a defense. Personalities who want power but fear its consequences often cannot enjoy a dominant position. They also cannot feel satisfied when they are under the jurisdiction of another person. Thus, when they submit they do so ungracefully, attempting to undo the rules that are imposed. When in power, such persons may become corruptly selfish, sadistically harsh toward others, or disorganized because they feel suddenly weak and want to escape from feeling vulnerable.

Anger and fear are important emotional components of this configuration. Yet persons with such personality structures may have learned to fear any intensely emotional state of mind. The roles of dominance and submission may switch so rapidly, the views of strength and weakness oscillate so quickly, that no emotion has time to build. A mildly depressed mood may set in instead as a consequence of paralysis of action. The case of Bert, a dental student in danger of flunking out of school, is an example of the activity of such role-relationship model configurations in adult life.

Although Bert was able to perform well in basic science courses, he had difficulty with faculty authority figures in clinical dentistry. He did not remain in any relationship for long, even with his peers and girlfriends, because he would engage in a power struggle over what to do next which the other person found irritating. Bert was now in danger of flunking out of school. He was criticized by his supervisor because he had not filled out insurance-payment reports about patients he was responsible for treating. All the students complained about doing these forms, but Bert was seen as a rebellious leader raising tension between students and supervisors over this issue.

Realizing he was close to losing his career, and having been advised his personality was an issue, Bert sought psychotherapy. He told his therapist that he sometimes felt that doing the reports was irrelevant to either providing client service or gaining instruction for himself. He rationally knew that it was necessary for the survival of the clinic that payment for services be obtained through the insurance reports, but when he sat down to fill out the documents, he felt as if he were weakly submitting to the authority of his supervisor, and wasting his own time.

When asked by the supervisor to bring the forms up to date, Bert would sometimes comply submissively and at other times be stubbornly neglectful, belligerent, and sour. In the latter case, he would immediately feel that he had gone too far, and apologize obsequiously. The instructor was irritated with both his resistance and his obsequious submission: neither was true cooperation.

Bert would try to make himself do the reports, setting up times and schedules for this task. Seated before his desk, pencil above the forms, his thoughts would shift in a confusing manner. He would sometimes see himself as capitulating meekly to a lousy system, slavishly filling in diagnoses and procedures. At other moments, he felt he was being too strong because his categorization of his patients according to gum-and-tooth disease seemed cold and inhuman. He then felt as if he did not care enough about their problems, but was only obtaining money for the clinic.

Shifting between these positions about *doing* the forms as being too weak or too strong, Bert procrastinated, allowing a great many reports to pile up. He also saw *not* doing the forms as being too weak or too strong. In avoiding routine paperwork, he viewed himself as an idealist moving decisively ahead without submitting to bureaucratic nonsense. On the other hand, he could also see his refusal to fill out the forms as a sign of his weakness; he was unsure of his ability to make correct formal diagnoses, and would soon be exposed as a child playing at being a dentist. As these do/do not, strong/weak thoughts went back and forth, Bert was paralyzed and could not act.

It is very likely that he learned to undo one relationship schema with an opposite role-relationship model from his parents during his childhood. The child, in challenging a parent, needs to learn a clear way to succeed in assertion, to cooperate in new decisions, and to submit to superior judgment, in order to organize flexible behavior from any of these relationship models, schemas, or scripts. Bert as a child may have been harshly controlled by a parent, and then seen that parent be upset at such behavior and back down, letting Bert gain control, and then say that was bad and wrest control back again. Thus he had learned the script of doing and undoing, and of reversing who is in the power role.

The Issues of Sexuality and Status

The next phase of personal-interpersonal development—the phallic or genital phase of psychoanalytic theory—involves the self in a wider range of actions involving the family and playmates. These actions can lead to a pleasing sense of purposefulness or to a sense of guilt for "going too far"—attitudes of purposefulness or guilty hesitancy that can become later adult character traits. Sexual drives are a vital feature of evolution and survival, and the ways they are handled in reproductive and pleasure-seeking behavior are vital patterns in society and in individual personality.

As the scope of action widens, one continues earlier efforts to find the nature of the bodily self, including knowledge of genital organs, orifices, and sexualized contacts with others. Earlier, especially during the second and third years of life, one has made the pleasurable discovery of one's erogenous zones through self-stimulation. Similarly, visual observation and tactile exploration of the bodies and movements of significant persons in one's home yields knowledge about gender and role differences.

While the baby may touch anything, the growing child may be forbidden to touch or even look at certain parts of the body, such as the breast and crotch of the mother. More rules about right and wrong bodily behavior are now taught to the child: genitalia of parents are not to be touched; one may not examine one's own genitals in public; the groin is to be kept covered; and one may not enter the rectal orifice even with one's own fingers.

These rules and taboos are taught both consciously and unconsciously by the parents as the child tries various forms of behavior, seeking admiration or mutual interest, and sometimes getting a negative response such as a scolding. Parents, siblings, strangers, and television are also teaching not only the ways of society and subcultures but how far one is expected to observe the rules. Schemas include knowledge of rigidity or fluidity in minding the rules or compromising with values.

Killing is also an aspect of value formation. There are rules about what it is good to kill (bad germs) and what it is bad to kill (pets).

The child sees and touches dead plants, insects, animals, and sometimes people and may kill insects or small animals. Thus is added to the menu of danger a basic fear: the danger of personal death, whether conceived of as paralysis of action, a long sleep, a severance of connection to others, or a permanent end to life.

The idea of death leads to intense fear of annihilation of the self. The child seeks reassurance from parents and peers to cope with this fear. Beliefs in an afterlife or in reincarnation can readily be inculcated at this age. The child also speculates about the causes of death. An irrational notion of the cause of death may be dormant when one later as an adult develops an understanding of death, but be activated by some traumatic threat and then evoke an irrational emotional reaction. If, for example, the child believes that loud shouting can cause death because a grandfather was felled by a heart attack during an argument, then that child as an adult may have the character trait of hating to be involved in loud disputes. When driven to use an angry tone of voice, one may later feel inexplicably very guilty: the irrational childhood view continues unconsciously even though it may seem silly if consciously recognized.

New beliefs are also developed about courtship, sex, and reproduction. Sexual anatomy is of special interest and may lead to playful explorations of the body of a child of the opposite sex. This activity may take the form of the "doctor game" ("If you show me yours, I'll show you mine"), examining dolls to look at the bottom, or exploring all orifices of pet animals. As part of general bodily comparison, the child may press his or her palm against that of a parent, looking for differences in size. This recognition of size differences may make the child feel small and want to be big. The child also notes the size of sexual body parts and wants to become an adult in this sense as well. Boys may worry about having a smaller penis than men; girls, about having no breasts. A boy may also fear that he will lose his penis and scrotum; a girl may develop a fear that she had such organs but that they were taken from her. Persistently irrational fear of loss of body parts in general, or of male genitals in particular, is called *castration anxiety.* As in speculations about the causes of death, a child may develop, and unconsciously retain, beliefs about what kind of interpersonal transactions might lead to such losses.

SEXUAL IDENTITY

A person who is biologically male will usually form a psychological gender identification as masculine and find a sexual interest in women. A person who is biologically female will usually form a feminine gender identification and find a sexual interest in men. Sexual biology, gender identification, and psychological sexual interest are usually coordinated but not inevitably so. Other developmental lines may occur. A person who is biologically male may have a gender identification as female and a sexual interest in either males or females. Every combination is possible (see Green 1987; Stoller 1985*a*).

There may be multiple interacting influences on sexual preferences, including: the genetic endowment of the child; the play of hormones and other influences such as toxins, from fetal to adult development, which affect the unfolding of genetic properties; an individual's history of repeated or traumatic sexual experiences leading to role-relationship models and scripts; and the sexual practices encouraged or suppressed by a particular society.

A female child, for example, learns from observation that she is anatomically similar to her mother, sister, and other little girls and different from her father, brothers and other men. Her shape is not exactly that of adult women, for she is a child and uncertain of what she can become during adolescence. Gender identification is already present to some degree by a year and a half of age. Between ages three to five, the little girl may show off her body in a flirtatious way. How she does this will depend on what she has seen, which often is how her mother uses her body in relation to her father or other men. The little girl will practice what she has seen with her father, brothers, or boyfriends.

The girl, being a child, is usually not a major rival of the mother's in obtaining the father's sexual interest: that is, in a "good" triadic situation, the child is not a real threat to the mother's sexual bond to the father. Instead, the mother will be pleased to observe the little girl's trial flirtatious behavior, as she attempts to attract gender-specific or sexual interest. The father will also enjoy this trial behavior, unless he has his own anxieties about the matter. In the ideal situation, both father and mother are to a certain extent pleased by the little girl's pleasure in her own body, and her efforts to show it off to get their attention and interest. Their reactions to the little girl's trial behavior are, of course, limited by taboos against incest.

By temperament, the child may lean toward the opposite gender, and the outcome of a child's wish to dress as the opposite gender may be determined in part by the parental response. A boy may want to wear dresses, play women's roles; and a girl may want to wear boy's clothes, play rough-and-tumble sports, and enact men's roles. These desires, normal in a child, receive some social judgment for or against their continuance.

Parental response will rest on many factors, including the sex of child desired by a parent, the security of a parent's self-concept, and the position of a parent in regard to social proprieties. When, for example, a little boy wants to be like a girl, his development will depend both on the persistence and strength of these wishes and on the reactions of parents to them. Some such boys may become feminine; others may have warded-off but dynamically active strivings for femininity. Of the feminine boys, some may later prefer homosexual erotic encounters; others, heterosexual or bisexual ones. Since such variations may occur even in identical twins, they probably have other causes than genetic codes and are heavily influenced by child and parent interactions (Green 1987).

If a boy wants to be a girl, and if a girl wants to be a boy, there will probably be anxiety and conflict about these desires within the family and peer groups. While normal self-schemas and role-relationship models can be developed in these circumstances, the conflict between anatomy and psychology, and between social attitudes toward both, will make development of self-organization more stressful. The result may be a courageous, resilient character formation or a susceptibility to neurotic problems, or sometimes a combination of both.

It is normal for any person to contain schemas of self as either sex—probably as part of the evolutionary flexibility of our species. Almost any kind of learning seems possible. Social attitudes are incorporated in the child as enduring attitudes. Current wishes are assessed against such values. In some cultures, certain wishes must be repudiated in terms of anatomy and gender: "No, I must not, that is too masculine," or too feminine. As a general rule, the more mature a person gets, the more flexibly one can accept having traits seen socially as being of either sex—an aspect of schematic integration called earlier the development of supraordinate self-schema (see page 102).

INITIATE AND MENTOR ROLE-RELATIONSHIP MODELS

A good role-relationship model to develop during this phase of learning attractive gender characteristics is that between initiate and mentor. The usual mentor for gender identification is the parent or other adult figure of the same sex; the initiate is the child learning to behave in the ways that the adult uses with the opposite sex. Mimicry, imitation, and enactment of the role in play are trial actions that develop gender-specific self-schematizations. The pleased response of the mentor encourages the bold learning efforts of the child. An envious response by the mentor figure can halt learning because it causes anxiety over loss of love and fear of retaliation for usurping a private, unsharable role. A critical response from the mentor can lead to shame over once-bold learning efforts.

AGGRESSOR AND VICTIM ROLE-RELATIONSHIP MODELS

As an extreme form of bodily intimacy, sexuality involves both issues of threat and strong drives to overcome the fears engendered by that threat. For the child, early understanding of sexual-reproduction behavior may be accompanied by worry. The boy wonders, will insertion of the penis mean that it might be nipped off or lost? The girl wonders, will penetration mean pain, will pregnancy mean rupture of the stomach?

Children often get their first information about sexuality by seeing copulation in humans or animals, which is then explained to them. Also, children often hear and sometimes see their parents having intercourse. Seeing sexual intercourse for the first time, the very young child may think that the actively moving person is doing something hurtful to the more passive receptive person; or the guttural sounds and fast movements may make the child think that both parents are fighting. If the child sees the father penetrating the mother, the act may seem to be an attack rather than a mutual pleasure; and moans of pleasure may be mistaken by the child for pain.

From repeated or single shocking perceptions of sexuality, the child may develop an aggressor-victim role-relationship model of erotic encounters—especially if such role-relationship models have developed around other themes. The child who has been abused in terms of violence or of overcontrol—by frequent unnecessary enemas, for example—may have a victim self-concept, with others as aggressors. Medical illness, especially when involving repeated hospitalization or painful procedures, may also lead to such schemas of the child as victim and others as aggressors.

In the phase of expansion of role-relationship models, the child can also learn a self-schema as aggressor. The child learns what can make the parent uncomfortable. If sexual display makes the parent uncomfortable, the child may undress and exhibit genital organs or masturbate in public, not just to gain autoerotic or exhibitionistic pleasure but to hurt the parent deliberately, as perhaps a revenge against some real or imagined frustration. Similarly, the child may steal coins or other personal items from the parents in order to get even with them. At such times, especially if undetected, the child comes to conceptualize the self as aggressor, the other as a victim.

The most troublesome role-relationship models are those developed when the child is used by an adult as an instrument of sexual, and some-times of sadistic, pleasure. Some transactions are seductive; others, forceful assaults. All leave the child with self-schemas that may have elements of confusion about sexuality.

Forceful assaults, where the child feels frightened or hurt, can leave behind a role-relationship model in which the child is the victim. Later, adult sexuality could be hampered by organization of the state of mind with a role-relationship model in which the self is a sexually unready child and the other an overpowering figure.

When the sexual molester is a parent, even worse consequences may occur. Suppose a father uses his daughter sexually. The girl may develop a role-relationship model in which the father is a selfish molester penetrat-ing an unwilling and hurt victim. Other transactions with the father may be kindly, and a good parent-to-child role-relationship model also devel-ops. The child may find it hard to schematize the selfish molester and the trustworthy daddy as one and the same person—a traumatic strain that makes it hard for the child to view herself as one and the same person.

There may be a dissociation between self-schemas and between differ-ent role-relationship models containing different self-schemas. Supraordi-nate schemas may not develop, so that one has difficulty understanding that a frustrating person is kind at times, that the hostile self loves at times. Instead, emotional reactions are exaggerated, and there may be sudden shifts in state of mind. Later in life, the person may be vulnerable to shifting "personalities," as seen in extreme form in multiple-personality disorders. There are thus at least three consequences of such trauma to the child: the child learns a role as victim and expects its repetition; the child learns the reciprocal, aggressor role by identification and may enact it in later life; and the child finds it hard to coordinate onto one concept of the parent extremely different roles, which may impair relationship schemas and self-integration into supraordinate self-schemas.

In parental seductions without sadistic or overt sexual components, the child may not recognize at the time that something morally wrong is taking place. The parent may seem pleased; the child's body may feel pleasant and strangely exciting. Later the child learns that such interactions are bad, and the memory becomes shocking. The child may then repeat the memory with horror, and develop the victim, bad child, or self as identified with aggressor roles already mentioned, as well as defensive processes to ward off recollection of the memory and the association of self with such pat-terns of action. Later inhibition of sexuality may result.

The consequence of dissociation between what was done and what ought to have been done includes failures to integrate schemas for sexual desire with schemas for moral living. Moreover, revengeful motives may get interwoven with sexual schemas, leading to role-relationship models in which transactions are both sensually exciting and hostile. Hence, incestuous liaisons, especially those involving children and adolescents, can lead to later sadistic or masochistic perversions, impaired capacity for love, inhibition of capacity for pleasure in normal sexual intercourse, and impairment in fulfilling parental roles (Steele and Alexander 1981; Eisnitz 1984–85; Shengold 1979).

COMPETITOR-RIVAL ROLE-RELATIONSHIP MODELS

The child is strongly motivated for connection. When witnessing a connection between two other people, one may envy the bond and feel left out. One will also envy attributes that attract attention. The little girl wants to be capable of bearing children like a mother, and of having breasts or pubic hair like her mother, if these traits are seen as attractive. She may want to have a penis like her father or brother. The little boy may envy women because they can bear babies and have breasts. He may wish to have a large penis like his father, pubic hair, the biggest chair at the table, or the most food on his plate.

THE OEDIPUS COMPLEX

Parents cannot be perfect. While it is desirable to respond to a child with empathy, pride, and teaching, a parent inevitably sometimes misunderstands, envies, or responds too flirtatiously or hostilely. These responses can be well tolerated in a matrix of affection and love. Nonetheless, parents who excessively stimulate, distort, or repudiate the child's sexual approaches to them—as part of both learning gender identity and exploring sensual pleasures—may foster unusual interests and rivalries within what Freud called the *Oedipus complex,* from the tragedy *Oedipus Rex* by Sophocles, one of the great dramatists of ancient Greece.

In this play, Laius, king of Thebes, is warned by an oracle that his unborn son will slay him. When Jocasta, the queen, gives birth to Oedipus, Laius orders that the baby be carried away to a deserted mountain to die of exposure. A shepherd, however, discovers and rescues Oedipus, who is then raised in the court of a neighboring kingdom. As a grown man, Oedipus encounters Laius at a crossroads. Neither knows the other's true identity. In a fight over who has the right of way, Oedipus kills Laius and goes on to marry Jocasta and become king. But when the kingdom is afflicted by plague, an oracle reveals that the gods will continue to vex the kingdom until the murderer of Laius is found. Oedipus dedicates himself to unraveling this mystery and, upon doing so, finds that he is guilty of his father's murder and of incest. Stricken with horror and remorse, Jocasta hangs herself, and Oedipus blinds himself.

In usually unconscious fantasies, sometimes conscious as dreams or creative products, the child may repeat this story of killing the rival parent and having sexual possession of the desired parent, only to be punished for two wrongs. If there are such fantasies, it is normal to give them up and plan to find an appropiate partner as an adult.

One form of oedipal configuration emphasizes the theme of the son's aim to establish an erotic connection with his mother, competing for her with the father. This is a *positive oedipal configuration.* In females it revolves around an erotic striving toward the father, competing for him with the mother.

In a *negative oedipal configuration,* the son wishes to establish an erotic connection with his father while competing with or attempting to get rid of his mother. Similarly, the negative oedipal configuration in the daughter contains the wish to establish an erotic connection with the mother, while competing with or hoping to get rid of her father. Both positive and negative oedipal configurations can involve brothers and sisters in the same way as mothers and fathers.

If the child develops an oedipal configuration, and represses its aims rather than giving them up, there may continue to be unconscious guilt and a fear of surpassing or competing with figures who symbolize the rival parent, or of loving and getting close to figures who symbolize the more desired parent in the triangular role-relationship model of an oedipal con- figuration. Children with threats to self-esteem and stability of self- organization may become excessively preoccupied with oedipal fantasies as a way of bolstering self-schemas by imagined victories. Giving up such usually transient fantasies may be harder because the alternative is to feel insignificant.

SELF-CRITICISM

The oedipal configuration is not simply triangular but may be conceived of as a four-party situation. In addition to the desire for another person and the competition with a third, there is the fear of criticism from a fourth person or "audience." In the Greek plays, this took the form of the gods, the Greek chorus, the implied rules of society. In intrapsychic schematiza- tion, it can be called the *critic* role. The critic role assigns blame and also gives permission for various strivings. It regulates the degree to which one can attempt to gain what one wants within the family or outside of it, and the degree to which otherwise natural drives have to be restrained because of social demands and priorities.

In early psychoanalytic theory, the development of *conscience* and the *ego ideal,* derivatives of the critic role, were said to be the result of a resolution of the Oedipus complex (Freud 1912). We now believe that value schemas are formed even sooner and continue to evolve in every phase of life, as an important aspect of self-development (Loevinger 1976*a*). One successfully regulates strivings so as not to be too meek (so as to be able to obtain knowledge, sex, and power in the outside world) and not too bold (and does not break incest, power, hierarchy, territory, and rage taboos within the immediate circle). Failure fully to schematize a set of values—that is, to establish an appropriate and self-owned critic role—can lead to turbulent mood changes and to ambiguous assignment of blame and praise.

One aspect of such unself-owned criticism involves an introject, a conscious concept based on a schema of someone else. An *introject* is a critical "figure" who seems to speak in the mind in the role of someone else. Visual images may represent that person's face; or auditory images, his or her voice. Patricia, for example, was a young married woman who complained of a recurrent unbidden image of her mother's scowling face. During sexual intercourse with her husband, this image occurred at the moment of vaginal penetration. The vivid image of her mother's scowling face appeared before her, as if it were several feet over the bed, but she knew that it was generated in her own mind. The first time it occurred, Patricia reacted by crying and feeling frightened. Later, even though she knew the image would occur, she found that she could not prevent or dispel it. The image of the scowling face dissipated of its own accord in a minute or less. This symptom persisted for a long time. Even when she got used to the image, she still experienced disgust, shame, and anxiety when it appeared. As the image faded, she could suppress her disgust, re-establish genital arousal and reach a sexual climax "in spite of her mother!"

By piecing together material from psychotherapeutic work, Patricia and her therapist were able to get some idea of the unconscious thought processes that led to the development of the unbidden image. Role-relationship models of herself as a bad girl, of her father as a bad but exciting man, and of her mother as an injured and critical party organized a set of warded-off ideas and feelings. While she never consciously experienced these thoughts in just this way, they can be approximated:

I am sexually excited by my husband. But whenever I think of my husband, I am reminded of my father, toward whom I had sexual feelings. I felt that sexual feelings toward my father were wicked and dangerous. I might be caught doing or thinking something bad, or he might hurt me with his big penis. Mother made me miserable when I flirted with father. After all, she told me sex was disgusting, but if you wanted children your duty was to put up with it. What I want is wrong, and I had better not allow myself to get excited. Maybe if I think of how bad she would make me feel if she were to catch me thinking erotically, that would scare the sexual feelings out of me. Just imagine her seeing me! That makes me feel disgust, shame, and anxiety.

BISEXUALITY

Boys and girls develop both masculine and feminine schemas. Carl Jung (1959) saw these identifications in either sex as separate forces he called the *anima* and the *animus,* respectively; Freud called this identification *bisexuality* (1905). Thus, by adulthood, each individual includes in his or her repertoire of self-concepts one that is gender identified as the opposite sex. These self-concepts may emerge in dreams or manifest themselves as an interest in cross-dressing (a common theme in movies, plays, and operas) or in masturbatory practices. In some cultures, these opposite-sexed self-concepts have such negative codings that conscious recognition of their presence is abhorrent; and behavior organized by that cross-sexed self-concept must be totally disavowed.

Research has indicated that basic male or female gender identification is usually firmly established by age two to three, and that modification thereafter is difficult or conflictual (Stoller 1968; Money and Ehrhardt 1972). Preferable to total inhibition of feminine self-concepts in a boy, or to masculine ones in a girl, is an acceptance of such self-schemas within supraordinate self-organization that emphasizes one's biological gender as boy or girl without disowning other useful feminine or masculine interests. Both Jungian and Freudian psychoanalysis, for example, seek to aid people to accept the "bisexual" or "anima and animus" components of their personalities.

LATENCY

The term *latency* was developed in psychoanalytic theory to refer to the period from about age six to the onset of adolescence, at about age twelve (Sarnoff 1976). The word *latency* is not a particularly apt description for this period of immense learning; it was used in classical psychoanalytic theory because of its emphasis on sexual drives. By about age six, most early childhood sexual aims have shown themselves; and in Western society, the intensity of sexuality surges again in adolescence. Different societies influence their six-to-twelve-year-olds variously, and sexual preoccupations and activities are not foreign to this age group. Sexual abuse of these children is also not rare and will affect role-relationship model schematizations.

The mind at about six years of age has a surge in capacity as learning is enhanced by the ability to reason about how the self might be in the role of others. Reasoning enhances what one has previously copied through mimicry. Since one can also imagine changes in situations, one can anticipate cause-and-effect sequences (Piaget 1951; Inhelder and Piaget 1958; Flavel 1963).

The child may be amazed by his or her own new capacity for thoughtfulness. A new kind of communication may delight parents. Enhanced self-confidence emerges, and children at this level are ready for school. They begin to imagine and learn about their potential place in their society. The anticipated future is schematized and affects motivation. The child uses games to practice roles and rules, and play becomes a trial run of social transactions.

One learns and contrasts value schemas. The new social matrices allow the child to affiliate away from the earlier primary caregivers. The child may embrace values other than those of his or her parents. Learning secrecy, for example, means both fidelity to peers and the ability to hold parts of the self independent from mother or father (Meares 1978).

Schemas of self in a group develop, and the child may even tolerate suffering to keep such ties. Organizing facts, collecting things, memorizing sports standings or song lyrics are all aspects of the surge of effort to bring order to, schematize, and become part of the world.

Comparison of self with other children becomes conceptually clearer, and the relative status of self to others emerges in play, at school, and at family gatherings. Social cruelty is common; and one learns of the existence of ethnic slurs and other injustices. Peers may say one is stupid, ugly, clumsy, or weak, and one must learn when these traits are *not* an aspect of self while sorting out and learning acceptance of and how to use one's real attributes. Unable to develop larger role-relationship models of self in peer groups, some children may schematize themselves as loners.

As the child spends more time beyond the family circle—at school, with peers, with lessons, roaming the environment alone—schemas of the surrounding world are further developed. Capabilities are enhanced, measured, tested. Social rules about courtesy, hierarchy, and territory are learned consciously, but mostly without awareness. If they are available, the child assumes the precursors of social and work roles at home, at school, and in the working environment. Schemas of leadership and group membership are developed. If there is sufficient support in the environment, maladaptive self-schemas and role-relationship models developed in the family may be modified by learning adaptive ones in the peer group and with teachers (Sarnoff 1976).

ADOLESCENCE

The growth during adolescence of sexual characteristics, intellectual capacity, and the ability to generalize more fully allows the boy or the girl consciously to contemplate self more clearly. Supraordinate self-schemas may be elaborated, and one may be able to generalize an "I" experience as having continuity across multiple self-concepts. For the first time, more fixed personality characteristics are apparent (Offer and Offer 1975).

The increased ability, size, and expectations of the adolescent will lead to modifications during the replay of role-relationship models already developed in childhood. In addition, one has increased ability to analyze the motives of oneself and others, and to understand ideals and values in terms of hierarchies of relative importance (Mussen, Conger, and Kagan 1980; Blos 1979). Cultures vary in their rites of passage, which, in effect, tell the adolescent about values, change in status, and the responsibilities of learning and having different kinds of prowess (V. Turner 1969). Adolescents may, as a peer group process, develop counter rituals rather than accept those of the older group (T. S. Turner 1978). These function to establish group schemas and value systems. During the growth and consolidation of identity during adolescence, one rearranges and reinforces role-relationship models—as did fifteen-year-old Joe, who was proud of his growing competence at school, at play, and with the girls he was just beginning to date. One night he had several of his friends over to play basketball, using the hoop over the garage door beside the family house. He had been taught by his father how to dribble, shoot, and defend during many early evening games between the two of them. His father had been quite proud of being a good teacher for Joe.

Now, however, Joe was taller than his father and wanted to play a very competitive game with his friends. His father, Bruce, came out and watched the game for a time. After Joe missed a shot, Bruce said scornfully that this was no way to lay up for that particular shot at the basket. Uninvited, he plunged into the game, showing all the boys the proper form. He was, after all, a former college letterman in basketball even though he was short.

Joe felt irritated when his father horned in and showed off, and moved out of the court to sit on the grass to watch what was happening. His friends were polite to Bruce, thanking him for showing them how to make that shot, and saying they were tired now.

After the friends had left, without coming in for soft drinks as Joe had expected, he told his father that he felt humiliated by what he had done. Bruce angrily said that Joe was an ungrateful son, that he, Bruce, was only trying to be helpful to him and his friends. Joe walked abruptly away to his room. Later after dinner, when Bruce asked Joe to take out the garbage, the boy said airily and sarcastically that he was too busy with his homework. Then, after only a moment at his desk, he went downtown to hang out, even though his parents told him not to.

This type of transaction was repeated between Joe and Bruce. The underlying issue had as much to do with the father as with the son. Bruce was also changing, aging physically. He worked at a job that required heavy labor and good physical coordination, and felt that his strength, stamina, and reflexes were on the decline. He tended to be ashamed of this, although it was slight, and part of a normal aging process. His vulnerability to shame led him to want to bolster his own self-concept as mentor to Joe in initiating him to the ways of basketball, sports, and life in general. This attitude did not mesh well with Joe's current peer attachments, especially in a group where he, having identified in part with his father, was taking on a leadership role as their mentor.

Bruce was not only being a mentor, showing Joe and his friends the "right way"; he was also being competitive, putting them down by showing he could do it better than they could—and thus reversing his experience at work, where the younger men now seemed to be stronger than he. Bruce was forcing Joe into a degraded position where Joe felt shame. Shame is one of the most difficult emotions for adolescents to experience, because of their great insecurity about personal identity in relation to idealized hopes and demeaning fears; and Joe had to cope with it by moving even further away from Bruce, becoming not only more independent but more rebellious.

Thus, the rebellious young man striving for independence from the controlling and critical father became a role-relationship model because of such repeated transactions. It was not a new arrival in terms of schemas, for it was built up out of earlier role-relationship models which had to do with subordination and domination, independence of aims and purposes, and dependence on others for structuring of action.

It was important for Joe to be able to rebel, and to tell his father off for his intrusion on the peer group—and to do so in a way that did not seem to destroy the father as father or capable man. If Joe believed that he had crushed his father's spirit by telling him not to intrude in the games, by being angry, or by being rebellious and going to hang out, then he might be vulnerable to feeling remorse, guilt, or shame. If Joe were very fearful of his own power to harm Bruce, he might have had to swallow his indignation, and weakly cave in, leading to his own shame. If Joe was terrified of ever following the lead of his father, however, he might become so rebellious that he would lose the benefits of the continued good teaching and emotional support that his father could provide during Joe's adolescent and young adult years. He might take on negative choices that did not suit his own values and aims, but were simply contrary to the directions his father urged upon him.

These excessively rebellious and dependent alternatives would each be rigid structures of character that would limit Joe's adult personality. Fortunately, both he and Bruce were capable of multiple role-relationship models, using the more compatible and mutual ones to soften reactions to the minor episode in which each felt hurt by the other.

ADULTHOOD

Role-relationship models continue to develop throughout adulthood (for a review, see Levinson 1978; and Colarusso and Nemiroff 1981). The processes are much the same as in childhood, except that there is more emphasis in childhood on building new kinds of schemas, more emphasis in adolescence on combining schemas into supraordinate structures, and more emphasis in adulthood on revising and updating existing schemas. Some new schemas and new integrations of schemas are formed throughout life. Life-crises—including desired ones, such as pregnancy and birth—bring about an increased rate of change in schemas as the individual practices new ways of adapting.

Raising children allows a recapitulation of many of the role-relationship models that the adult developed as infant and child. This recapitulation allows a review of the feelings and ideas organized by the role-relationship models, not only with an adult mind but with a reversed role—that of parent. The parent is, unconsciously, also a child again; and some primitive schemas are now modified, leading to increased sagacity and wisdom. Matters that were once painful, like frictions between child and parent, may now seem more bearable, even humorous, in the sense meant by the classic phrase the "human comedy."

On the other hand, certain preoccupations of childhood, while evolving somewhat, also continue a morbid repetition in adulthood—as happened with Frank, an accountant with a specialized practice, involving firms that had become financially insolvent. His childhood had been filled with fantasies and worries about death. He had disliked and felt cheated by his father, who had a belligerent attitude toward the children wanted by his wife, Frank's mother. She was chronically depressed, and Frank also felt cheated by her lifelessness, although she made what he saw as pathetic

143

attempts to play with him. He had fantasies that these were not his real parents, that they would die and the real, loving ones would show up.

In childhood, Frank had states of mind like those of his mother and father. Sometimes he was sullen and belligerent; at other times, apathetic and listless. He used these states, however, to get attention: teachers often wanted to cajole him out of his sullen stance; and in adolescence, girls tried to rouse him from his lethargy. Despite everything, he had gained an ability to invite others to rescue him, in the ways he felt his parents did not.

Frank wanted his father to give him the loving attention, including caresses that he did not obtain from his mother. Because the caresses seemed incestuous, homosexually dangerous, Frank avoided manifestations of these wishes by behaving in a detached manner. He began to pride himself on being a lone wolf. He also wanted the same thing from his mother; but when these wishes frustrated him too much, he used a different compromise. He became preoccupied with other women, and was able to turn on a charming, wooing, and winning state. When he won the interest of a woman, however, his mood turned sour, because she then seemed to be the wrong kind of woman for him.

At such times, he was preoccupied with suicidal thoughts, which were, finally, his motive to seek treatment. In that treatment, he developed a transference reaction in which he believed that his therapist was depressed and lifeless. Frank then acted belligerent and remote, with a chip-on-the-shoulder attitude toward the therapist. He also at times had transference feelings that the therapist was, like him, turning to other patients, male and female at different times, with a sexual interest. Then he would fantasize how these rival patients, whom he sometimes saw before and after hours, would have a fatal accident. This would punish them for having the attention of the therapist.

As a child, Frank developed a role-relationship model in which he was a weak child, vulnerable to death and unprotected by his uninterested parents. His career was adaptive: he would save moribund business firms by careful attention to and nurturing of their income and expense flows. Yet he felt he could not expect nurturing from others. He perceived any woman interested in him as being interested in the wrong way. Although he found the therapist attentive in a working model, his enduring role-relationship models were so morbid that they challenged any realistic view of the therapeutic alliance that was being created. He misperceived the therapist as uninterested, as lifeless, or as becoming more interested in other patients. The extraordinary, if maladaptive, repetitiveness of the childhood substrates of his schemas became apparent in this way.

Perverse Role-Relationship Models in Adult Sexuality

The sexuality that begins in childhood, and takes on potency and relationship to new objects in adolescence, solidifies in adulthood. Partners continue commitment for long periods, for a lifetime or at least for years. The intense pleasure of mutually enjoyed sexuality is a powerful reinforcement for the schemas that lead to the satisfying actions. In spite of such powerful reinforcement, mutually satisfying sexuality is difficult to achieve because many other aspects of intimacy with another person are required as a relationship continues over time. Some persons are unable to develop the required role-relationship models and supraordinate schemas.

Human sexuality is not a pure urge toward reproductive behavior and gratification in the acts involved. Sexuality commingles with many acts that seem perverse in isolation. Foreplay, variations on intercourse, and afterplay take on many forms that are not abnormal and add excitement, provided they are conducted in a setting of mutual pleasure. Some people have recurrent maladaptive patterns that are outside this range of normal polymorphous, or multiform, sexuality. These perversion patterns are also based on role-relationship models that often contain an important aspect of hostile aggressiveness directed at either the self or others (Stoller 1979).

While the role-relationship models that involve perverse sexual aims are developed in childhood, they are capable of modification in adolescence and early adulthood. Since the operation of these perverse sexual role-relationship models is associated with intense pleasure and relief of sexual tensions, they tend to recur, engrained in schemas. They are thus difficult to change because it is hard to learn new, more mutual role-relationship models. I shall briefly describe some of these perverse role-relationship models.

SADISM AND MASOCHISM

In *sadism,* one derives sexual pleasure from assuming an aggressive role in injuring or degrading another person. Part of the gratification may come from feelings of power over the degraded other, even to having the power to force that person to experience sexual excitement. In some milder sadistic sexual practices, the pain of the other is only feigned, to arrive at arousal perhaps for both the sadistic and the masochistic partners.

The masochistic role is to submit to the will of the powerful other.

145

Sometimes the fear of being under that power adds excitement to the state of mind in the erotic situation. Sometimes the fear or pain are part of a script that begins with these negative aspects but leads to future pleasure. The fear or pain may, in that script, be a kind of necessary prepayment to expiate guilt, or to gain the attention of the other, to deserve the subsequent sexual satisfaction. In addition, the passive role as slave of the sadistic other declares the self to be in bondage, and so not vulnerable to criticism for the acts conducted.

Sexuality that is neither sadistic nor masochistic may be more frightening than sadomasochistic sexuality, even though sadomasochism threatens pain and/or degradation. But for some people, normal sexuality threatens a dangerous merger with the partner, a feeling common at the height of joint sexual excitement. Taking turns in having an orgasm, and having very different roles may reduce the fear of cohesion, of loss of the sense of self. More often, however, normal sexual practices are associated with boredom, or lack of erotic excitement; and one seeks the thrill of aggression and fear in the sadomasochistic role-relationship models, as a route to the kind of excitement necessary before a pleasurable orgasm can occur.

Sadistic sexual role-relationship models are also reinforced by the absence of sexual schemas that contain scripts for mutually loving and gratifying sexual transactions. Some people never have shared sexual satisfaction and never hope to achieve it. Their basic sexual role-relationship model may be one in which they signal erotic interest, and the other then rejects them as uninteresting or even repulsive. The response of the self in that type of role-relationship model is usually a mixture of shame, fear, and rage. The sadistic attack on another, fueled by the rage at expected rejection and personal frustration, reduces shame and fear. This sadism involves organization of behavior and conscious experience by a self-schema that is stronger than the other, a self-schema that represses the schemas of fearful or shameful states of mind where the role-relationship model may be that of the flawed self rejected by a stronger person. The sadistic assault on another by the self may take the form of rape, and serve, in part, as revenge on the other for the lack of desired interest in the self. Erotic excitement in the rapist is fueled by the pleasure of degrading the other person.

VOYEURISM AND EXHIBITIONISM

The type of hostility just mentioned can lead to other ways of forcing the self upon a sexual object that is seen as rejecting the self. The role of the self can be as looker, seeing the nakedness of the other against the latter's will. Looking, a normal component of sexuality, becomes the major vehicle for voyeurs or peepers, and the sexual object is victimized by being observed against his or her will, while undressing or engaging sexually with someone else.

Another component of sexuality is that of exhibiting the sexual self to show off and solicit interest. This act of a sexual script also can be isolated so that it carries the whole weight of sexual behavior in a schema repeated again and again. The person then may "flash" or exhibit the nude self, or just the unclothed sexual organs, in a variety of flashing behavior where the victim is a person who is forced to look. Thus, normal looking and showing can be perverted to voyeurism or exhibitionism.

FETISHES AND RELATED PERVERSIONS

A *fetish* is a sexual fascination with an object or activity that is often associated with absence of more normal excitements. Articles of underwear, shiny skinlike material, and shoes are common fetishes. The fetish object has come to symbolize an erotic person, and an erotic fragment of that person's body or pattern of activity. A shoe may be exciting because it symbolizes a container, like a vagina, into which something, a foot or a penis, is inserted. The shoe is, at the same time, a phallic symbol, so that a woman's shoe can seem to be both penis and vagina to the fetishist. Sometimes the fetish is not so much a concrete object but a particular activity, as in the case of Larry, who experienced sexual pleasure and orgasm only if he was crawling through a window into a house, in which he had at some previous time seen a woman whom he did not know. The risk involved in possibly being discovered making an illegal entry added to the excitement; eluding such discovery was part of the story line. He always selected a time to enter a window when no one was at home, in order to reduce the risk. To him, as he imagined the woman, the window symbolized her vulva, her sexual opening. In entering the house through the window, he was forcing her to submit to his desire in symbolic form.

Why did Larry achieve orgasm when he acted his story out in this dangerous way? Why did he not simply masturbate in his own room using a fantasy that followed the script of this role-relationship model? For him, fantasy during masturbation was not sufficiently "real." Why, then, did he not seek out a woman for a normal sexual relationship? For him, a relationship with a woman was too frightening. He assumed that he would be rejected by a real woman; or, if not, that he might be engulfed into her identity and purposes. He needed just the right amount of reality (crawling through a real window into the house of a real woman), just the right absence of reality (no woman present and no male rivals for her attention), and just the right combination of danger and safety to evoke sexual excitement.

The self in various perversions often has an active, strong, and wicked or dirty role in relation to a defective or weak other person. This view serves to ward off a self-concept that is passive, weak, and pathetically clinging because of sexual inability. The evoked state of mind is one of dangerous excitement rather than humiliation or lonely deprivation.

A warded-off role-relationship model may be one where the parents have good sex organs and are bonded with each other, while the self is considered to be without adequate sex organs. The aim is to have the good sex organs and enjoyable sexual object, and also to be revenged for the imagined deprivation. The perverse script contains an act of hostility to gain revenge—an act that says in effect, "I—*not* you—am the one with the good sex organs" (for example, "I am the one who has the fetish object, or who is engaged in the activity"). There is also a defiance of others: "You have to accept what I do, whether or not it upsets you" (Stoller 1985*b*).

The establishment of such perverse role-relationship models often occurs at that state of development when the child is highly envious of gender differences and sexual intimacy between the parents. If the parents or other adult figures assault the child, even if they only overstimulate and then enrage the child by frustration, the child may be propelled toward reversing roles from victim to victor, by invention of the perverse story line. Even excessive tickling and physical teasing can lead to these effects. Underlying the wish for sexual excitement is the fear of the consequences of lack of relationship. What is perverted is the direction taken by drives for relationships and sexuality with others.

The adult develops new schemas from experience and repetition of working models based on experience. These new schemas evolve from the substrates of childhood schemas. Nonetheless, childhood schemas remain in the mind, and their activity may, in part, determine mood. The results may be puzzling because access of childhood schemas to conscious reflection seems very limited. One may wonder why one has an emotion and be unable to figure out any reason for it. To understand such puzzles, I now turn from a fairly exclusive focus on schemas of self and others to a discussion of how sequences of conscious experience are formed.

PART II

Conscious and Unconscious Mental Processes

8

Consciousness

INTERACTION among persons within the primitive tribe of *Homo sapiens* gradually developed into communication. In a sense, consciousness in its present form is a mentalistic communication and probably evolved along with communicative capacities (Hilgard 1977). Instead of actual signals between persons, signals within the mind could be used for trials of action and to prepare for the future. In contrast to communication within a tribe, conscious thought was a private matter, and allowed for gradual evolution of a capacity for individuality.

It is not surprising that conscious experience, springing from this evolutionary basis, uses as its elements words as well as pictorial and gestural symbols—the modes of human communication. These allow for an awareness of perceptions, thoughts, feelings, and, usually but not always, a sense of the self as an agent of that awareness. This chapter, which deals with those verbal, sensory, and motoric elements, begins a discussion, to be elaborated in later chapters, of how conflicting goals for thought may affect conscious representation and disrupt the usual synthesis of several modes of representation into a harmonizing stream of consciousness.

Conscious trains of thought are partly under voluntary control and partly under the control of unconscious processes. Sometimes mysterious elements intrude into one's consciousness despite one's lack of intention to think them, or even one's conscious intention to avoid thinking of them. These intrusive episodes increase in states of stress, as described in the first chapter of this book, and may signal the activity of unconscious processes.

Such an experience can occur when a consciously directed stream of thought bends suddenly in an unintended direction.

Clara reported in a psychoanalytic session a daydream that began intentionally and ended with intrusions into consciousness of elements she did not want and found hard to dispel. During this phase of her analytic work, she was attempting to become fully aware of and master ambivalent feelings toward her father and her husband. She had recurrent fantasies and dreams in which there were two male figures: one, an enemy she hated and fled from; and another, for whom she pined because he might love and cherish but not use or manipulate her. Her father and her husband could occupy each role.

At the onset of this particular daydream, Clara was making a dress for herself. It was late evening, her children were asleep, and her husband was working late at a meeting. She was sewing stitches that required only repetition. She began a pleasant visual daydream of the dress as completed. She imagined wearing it to a cocktail party, seeing in her mind's eye how its vivid yellow brought out the warm tones in her bronze skin. She imagined the glowing admiration of the socially prominent hostess. Then she imagined a gentle, handsome man coming over to meet her because she looked so appealing. Then, as her daydream continued, they went for an increasingly intimate walk in the garden.

The daydream, initiated deliberately, was spontaneous, Clara having no consciousness of planning the next step. In the unfolding scenario, the hostess came rushing out to the garden. Clara wondered why. The hostess said there was a phone call. Clara then was on the phone. She imagined the voice on the phone saying her husband had just been killed in a car crash on the highway. At this point, her visual and auditory images ceased, and she stopped sewing to do some more mentally occupying task because she felt upset at the idea of imagining her husband's death as part of a daydream.

When one falls into a daydream, one tends to doff the usual commitments or restraints, saying to oneself in effect, "What if I were free to do the following?" But Clara's daydream led her to the frightening desire to be free of her husband. The prospect of the handy elimination of the major obstacle to a romantic encounter was too close to the reality of Clara's rushes of anger at her husband, and to her recent impulses, which she had been restraining, to find a new source of romantic and mutual interest. The idea of her husband being hurt and eliminated from her life was not an incidental "what if" prelude to a fanciful story, but was connected to a real, but inadmissible wish. Hence, she experienced this conscious representation as intrusive and hard to dispel.

Clara's fantasy was organized by a role-relationship model of herself as a sexually attractive woman, showing herself to advantage, and receiving admiration and courtship interest to which she reacted in kind. The intrusive ideas were organized not only by an association in thought ("What if I were free to do this?") but by a different role-relationship model of harming her husband. This invested the auto accident with too much emotion, and with emotion about emotion ("How terrible to think that!") to tolerate, and she had to break off the flow of reverie.

Clara's daydream was formed in visual images. These images changed in time, and she was also aware of herself watching the story. The phone message was experienced in auditory images. Clara experienced the content of these auditory images as unwanted thoughts. She deliberately shifted her attention and stopped the intrusive contents by deciding consciously to think of a different theme. Yet she herself had, unconsciously, generated both the intrusive images and the decisions to replace them. If neurological capacities are in good order, what, then, are the unconscious psychological reasons for such intrusions as the news of her husband's crash in Clara's daydream? Why is consciousness not under full conscious control?

Conscious Thought: A Special Tool

The brain has evolved as a specialized organ for processing information from sensory perception and organizing the plans to be followed by other bodily organs including the muscles. Animals can react with marvelous swiftness; the human athlete moves precisely at enormous speed in directions computed from numerous inputs. Unconscious brain functions accomplish most of this activity without consciousness. In fact, consciousness proceeds too slowly for swift response to stimuli.

Because conscious thought is slower than unconscious information processing it can, in a sense, be more careful. Consciousness allows one to make careful and rational choice between opposing alternatives. One can compare incompatible purposes and plan how to act. In such acts of choice and will, one can sometimes merge discrepant views and contradictory goals as well as make compromises. Complex aims can be organized into a series of steps that will be carried out when circumstances warrant, and in a determined order. Motivation can be enhanced by anticipating incentives or imagining feared consequences of failures to act. New modes of reaction can be decided upon and then practiced with conscious care, until enough repetition has occurred to form a schema. Then one may act with less active awareness, by unconscious habit.

Consciousness also provides a system for restoration, compensation, and incentives for action, as through daydreaming or dreaming (Tomkins 1962; Singer 1966, 1984). Clara's daydream was, at its start, a restoration of morale. A person practicing the piano in a way that has become tedious may, as an incentive and self-stimulation, have a reverie composed of visual images of the self performing a concerto brilliantly and receiving a thunderous ovation.

Different modes for consciously representing ideas and feelings each have special properties. Complex concepts can be seen in multiple modes. Consciousness allows the combination of all these different ways of organizing information, and blends them into a synergistic whole. It may operate as a kind of shared workspace for blending diverse information, and allowing interaction of subordinate modules for information processing (Baars 1987). Consciousness heightens a sense of self as an agent of initiatives, as a subject having enduring mindfulness over time. Self-monitoring is also heightened by conscious awareness, and decisions may be made about what of consciousness to express to others and what to conceal (G. Mandler 1975, 1985; Ekman 1984).

This view of consciousness as only a part of a vast amount of information processing is relatively recent. Philosophers once regarded conscious thought as the center of man. Descartes said, *Cogito ergo sum* ("I think, therefore I am"). Greek philosophers believed that thought proceeded by establishing inner replicas, images, of external objects. These units were then connected by associations into sequences of thought. In psychology, words were believed to be the prime units of conscious mentation, with sensory perception simply reporting the outside world (see J. M. Mandler and G. Mandler 1964, for a review).

Freud (1915) believed that, in childhood, images are the primary mode of representation, giving way gradually as words become dominant for conscious thinking. He always emphasized visual imagery as a road to unconscious domains (Freud 1900). Jean Piaget (1930) and Heinz Werner (1957) charted the developments of early to later phases of thinking, emphasizing different organizing properties of images and words. Jerome Bruner (1964) charted the evolution from very concrete, enactive representations through the use of signs and symbols in iconic representation, and then the more abstract properties of symbolic representations. I describe the enactive, the image, and the lexical modes of conscious representation and believe them to be directly homologous to communication through movements, depicted sensory images, and verbal expressions (Horowitz 1970, 1983).

Modes of Representation

Each of these modes of representation has its own infrastructure for codings and schemas. The mode selected for a given set of ideas may be the system that has the most appropriate organizational properties. As the same theme (set of ideas and feelings) is translated from one mode to another, the patterning of the information may change. In addition, to these modular components (as reviewed by Jerry Fodor [1983]), some high-level schemas, such as role-relationship models, may organize information across all modes for conscious representation, leading to the seamless subjective experience of many states of mind. Some of the intrinsic properties of each mode of representation are outlined in table 8.1. A visual diagram of the modes is shown in figure 8.1.

In figure 8.1, cross-modal consciousness is shown as the center of the "circle of consciousness." In a harmonious state of mind, there are no distinguishable separations of mode: that is, in normal states, the average person uses many modes of representation simultaneously, without clear-cut division. Enactions blur into image representations in the form of kinesthetic, vestibular (and visceral), or somesthetic images. With many cultural variations, people use their hands to draw in the air aspects of the pictorial scene they are describing. Image representation blends with lexical representation in the form of faint auditory, kinesthetic, or visual images of words. Words and enactive modes merge through subvocal speech. *What is represented in one system is freely and effortlessly translated into other modes of representation. But when one has unconscious defensive aims, inhibition may block one or another form of representation, and cause one to have a subjective sense of cleavage between systems.* Of course, inhibition can block all modes of representation, in which case the warded-off contents are regarded as repressed. *Despite inhibitory regulations, intrusive episodes can break through to conscious awareness.*

THE ENACTIVE MODE

Facial expressions and bodily gestures are the communicative form of enactive representation. Muscle tensions also affect inner thought, as conscious experience (Zajonc 1980). Any muscle tension can be involved, not just the striated muscles that control the skeleton and skin movements.

TABLE 8.1
Modes of Representation

Mode	Subsystems	Sample Organizational Tendencies	Sample Statement	Sample of Complex Units of Represented Information
Enactive	Skeletal neuromusculature Visceral neuromusculature	By directionality and force; by operational end products	"X does this."	Gestures Facial expressions Postures
Image	Tactile–kinesthetic Olfactory–gustatory Visual Auditory	By simultaneous occurrence, spatial relationships, concrete categorization of similarities and differences	"X is like this." "X is like Y." "X is here, and Y is there." "X and Y happen together." "X does this to Y."	Body images Relationship between self and others
Lexical	Different languages	By sequentiality and linear structure; by abstract categorization	"If X and Y then Z because X + Y = Z.	Phrases or sentences Lists Logical deductions

Source: M. J. Horowitz, *Image Formation and Psychotherapy*, rev. ed. (New York: Jason Aronson, 1983).

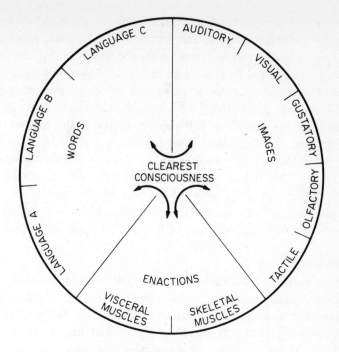

Figure 8.1
Circle of Conscious Representation

The bowel and blood vessels as well as the heart have their own muscles, as do various glands: these are called the *smooth muscles* of viscera.

Tensions of smooth and striated muscles have many effects. Emotional feeling is one prominent result of these tensions. The gut and throat may constrict first, leading to sensory images, and only then to verbalized emotion, as in the thought, "I must be scared of something."

Four brief examples of enactive thought will clarify these concepts:

1. A little boy wants some candy that he has been emphatically told not to touch. As he tentatively reaches for it with one hand, he makes a stern reproving face and grasps his reaching hand with his other hand.

2. A woman, while conversing, seeks to use the expression, "He likes to pin people down"—but has, for the moment, apparently repressed the phrase. While attempting to recall it, she makes a hand gesture of pinning something down, thus representing, or acting out, the desired thought. Then the words she is seeking enter awareness, and she is able to say them.

3. While imagining a coming tennis match, a man notes that he anticipates making various strokes by very slight muscle tensions and
micromovements. If he closes his eyes to imagine the game, his eyes
may go back and forth beneath his eyelids, as if following the ball
(an association of visual imagery and enactive representation).

4. A woman in psychotherapy is beginning to become aware of and to
describe her unrealistic self-concept as physically and spiritually
degraded and ugly. She pauses in silence as she gropes for words.
During this pause, she grimaces, a peculiar tension making one
corner of her mouth gape. Next she becomes aware of this facial
contortion and of the feeling of disgust that accompanies it, and only
then realizes that this facial expression resembles, in form, an injury
that had disfigured the face of her mother (Horowitz 1983).

THE IMAGE MODE

There are various types of image representation, each in a sensory organizing system: visual, auditory, tactile, olfactory (smell), gustatory (taste),
and kinesthetic sensations of movement and position. The most common
image experience is the "garden variety" visual image, which is experienced by about 95 percent of all persons, although some have visual
thought images that are fleeting and of only partial or dim sensory quality,
while others experience conscious thought as a series of detailed, colored,
intense images (Singer 1966).

Image formation allows one to review information for new meanings, to
contemplate objects in their absence, and to seek new similarities and
differences. This is a constructive process by which one combines, compares, and recombines sets of information from perception, memory, schemas, and fantasy. Just as certain microtensings of muscles can be called
"thought by trial action," images may be called "thought by trial perception." Skill at conceptual manipulation by formation of visual images is
useful to architects, painters, and surgeons. Skill at auditory image formation is useful in poetry and music; kinesthetic imagery, in dance; olfactory
and gustatory imagery, in cooking.

Images may enter awareness in a spontaneous flow which seems mys-
teriously unintentional. Auditory images may play and replay a tune in
spite of one's efforts to stop it. In some persons, this process, sometimes
called *automatic imagery*, occurs continuously during everyday waking
thought. Others experience such "inner movies" only during hallucinatory
states, hypnagogic reveries, or dreams. In some persons, censorship oper-
ates less keenly over image formation than over lexical representation,
allowing warded-off ideas to emerge. Analysts, including Joseph Breuer

and Sigmund Freud (1895), Carl Jung (1959), and Laurence Kubie (1943), have attempted to use visual images to skirt defensive processes and gain access to usually unconscious fantasies and repressed memories. They have told patients to think in pictures rather than words and to report whatever images then formed. Furthermore, emotional responses to images may be greater than those to purely verbal representations (Jung 1939, 1959; Ferenczi 1950).

Because visual images can evoke intense emotion, one can, by forming specific images, modify or transform an existing emotional state. A sense of danger can be activated by formation of threatening images; sexual desire, increased by erotic images; anger, fostered by images of insult and outrage. A person may form anger-provoking images in order to become angry and thereby ward off the experience of more threatening emotional states, such as fear or guilt (Jones 1929). This effect of imagery is used methodically in experimental psychology in order to study the mood-related associations of certain memories (Bower 1981).

The image-representation systems have an overlapping and dual input from external and internal sources: that is, a consciously perceived visual image may be a combination of stimuli coming from the retina and from aroused internal schemas. Visualizing a two-dimensional drawing as being a three-dimensional room is one example; so also is an *illusion,* where one may see a stranger's face as if it were the face of a person one was pining to see.

Such phenomena as illusions and hallucinations indicate that the image systems of conscious representation have at least a dual input of information. Perceptual stimuli enter these systems from sense organs, and internal information is added by schemas and networks of memory. In some experiences, the stimuli of perception are fused with internally derived elements, and one does not know consciously which aspects of the experience are really in the outside world, and which come from the inside.

This multiple input into the image systems of conscious representation can be illustrated for visual thought images (see figure 8.2). To the left of the figure are internal and external perceptual stimuli. External sensations are what one usually thinks about when talking of perceptual stimuli, but the eye itself can contribute stimuli from, say, the debris floating in the fluid of the eyeball and from the shadow of small blood vessels lying between light from the pupil and the photosensitive nerves of the retina. These internal and external sensations may, to varying degrees in different states of mind, form conscious impressions in the gridlike matrix used in the figure to depict the system for forming conscious visual images (Horowitz 1970). Stephen Kosslyn (1981) calls this the *visual workspace.*

Into that same matrix may flow information from other sources. One, shown at the top of the figure, is from memory of image codings now to be repeated. This form of active memory allows a later digestion of a set of perceived information. That set, a *percept,* is repeated in a conscious representation, and new forms of it can be tried. The same percept can be refigured through organization by alternate schemas, permitting revaluations of what percepts mean, and of how to cope with that meaning. The tendency to repeat stressful and perplexing percepts consciously, even intrusively, may be due to the functions and effects of such active memory.

On the right of figure 8.2 is schematic input. The schemas referred to here are usually the smaller-order ones that allow a person to decipher the external world by organizing it into meaningful small wholes, which are then articulated into larger meanings. The sequence and regulation of this internal input may then be organized by larger schemas of people, objects, and environment. Both primitive and mature rules for associating concepts may be used to relate external input to internal memory. *Primary process* refers to primitive rules, logic, and types of association of meanings; *secondary process* is a later, more refined, and more logical development (see pages 180–81).

At the bottom of figure 8.2 is another source of input from other modes of representation. Other image systems such as auditory image representation may contain information that can be cross-translated into an image version. Verbal systems may influence visual image formation, and enactive conscious representations can also be transformed into visualizations. One can feel a shape by moving one's fingers around it, and translated that action through kinesthetic images to a visualization. Some persons may have color hearing: when they hear certain tones, they see certain colors—a translation called *synesthesia.* Other people may color numbers: when they read a number, it seems to have a certain hue.

Thus, a consciously experienced visual image may contain elements from what is seen outside; it is organized by internal schemas and influenced by active memories and conscious representations in other modalities. The conscious experience is a synthesis or best-fitting composite of diverse inputs. The calculations involved in this image formation are not themselves conscious. Similar diverse inputs are involved in other systems for forming conscious representations.

THE MODE OF LEXICAL THOUGHT

In the course of individual development, the relationship between words and what they signify is established. At first, sounds and words are used in communication, as in babbling to the mother and maintaining a loving contact by taking turns in expressions to one another. Later, the child

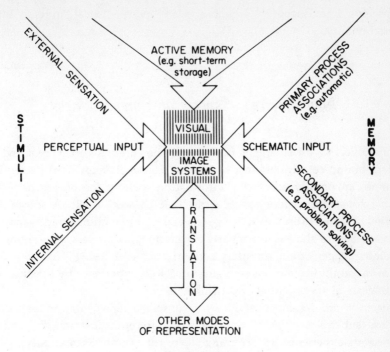

Figure 8.2

Model of Input into the Image Systems

Reprinted from M. J. Horowitz, *Image Formation and Psychotherapy* (New York: Jason Aronson, 1983).

moves beyond the interpretation of sounds, inflections, and tonalities to use words as a means of representing and thinking in the absence both of real objects and also of intense images of objects. The acquisition of lexical representation allows progression to new levels of conceptualization, abstraction, and reasoning.

The lexical system is a development from the earlier modes of enactive and image representation. Lots of phrases are metaphors, as in "get the point" or "pin him down" (Lakoff and Johnson 1980). Construction of meaning in word sequences requires temporal ordering, just as visual representation requires spatial ordering. The enactive and image modes also continue development *fostered* by the acquisition of lexical capacity and temporal-ordering capacity. Impairment in such sequential ordering capacity will lead to retardation in language use in communications. Recognition of being less capable than peers may affect self-schema formation.

"Pure" lexical representation is conceptualized as actionless (no subvocal speech) and imageless (no auditory, visual, or kinesthetic accompaniments). As I shall discuss, such "purity" is seldom found; rather, there are conscious experiences that are more or less "purely lexical" in representational quality.

Neurological Aspects of Consciousness

Consciousness, an emergent function of the cerebral cortex, requires an intact brain. Yet, the brain may respond electrochemically to perceptual stimuli, apparently processing information without the person having a direct conscious experience (Shevrin 1988; Marcel 1988). A substantial period of time of cerebral activity—several hundred milliseconds—may be needed before the person reports a conscious awareness of wanting or deciding to perform a voluntary action (Libet et al. 1983). This time may allow a modification of an emerging conscious experience by unconscious appraisals of its potential effect (Libet 1987).

Each of the systems described for conscious representation rests on a neural substrate. Relative activation of different substrates may affect conscious experience. In dreaming sleep, for example, conscious experiences occur that are predominantly in visual imagery, and the substrates of visual imagery show more electrical activation than do those for lexical thought during such periods.

Disruption of neural substrates may impair conscious representations, and that will affect psychodynamic processes. The person may fill in what is missing with some internal meaning structure, or explain the conceptual loss in terms of psychological rather than neurological causes. A paralysis of the left side of the body may result from disruption of the right cortex of the brain, and the person may lose a conscious sense of the functions of that side of the body in a symptom called *anosognosia.* A person with a lesion in a part of the cortex called the *parietal lobe* may disown, in conscious experience, the opposite side of the body, the side affected by the signs of motor and sensory loss. When asked why the given arm, say, does not move, one may make up a story—perhaps that it is very tired and wants to rest now. The making up of a psychological story to explain the experience is itself a symptom called *confabulation.*

Loss of neural function can impair the ability to form visual or other images in consciousness. As with loss of motor ability, the person may psychologically fill in the defect, even hallucinating to replace a blind area.

Loss of neural connections between the two cerebral hemispheres can also affect conscious experiences. Sperry (1966, 1969) found that splitting the hemispheres led to what was in effect two forms of noncommunicating consciousness. Stimuli presented selectively to the receptive systems of either right or left brain might be processed differently by the two hemispheres. The dominant hemisphere processed word stimuli better than did the nondominant one; the nondominant brain was superior in visual and spatial thinking. Gazzaniga and Le Doux (1978) have suggested that, in normal, unbisected brains, there is a crossing over so that consciousness is achieved as a result of models developed by a synthesis of different recursive models, in which each hemisphere duplicates information from the other hemisphere. The frontal lobes are believed to play an important role in this construction of conscious thought from rapidly processed, unconscious forms constructed in parallel times and channels.

Many disturbances in lexical consciousness, called *aphasias,* are based on insults or injuries to the brain. Aphasias include problems in translation from one mode of coding, or representing meaning, to another. In some aphasias, one cannot decide on the word meaning of auditory images; in others, one cannot enactively form words although one consciously knows the lexical meaning of auditory images.

Neurological damage affecting emotion is found in a set of symptoms called *approsodias* or *dysprosodias.* As with aphasias or dysphasias, there are various forms of the inability to have a complete conscious representation of what others mean by emotional tones in the voice, say, or to convey emotion in one's own vocal communications. While this text focuses on the psychodynamics that affect the capable brain, the disabled brain will produce changes in thought and emotion and alter psychodynamics.

The Conscious Representation of Complex Emotions

Complex emotions are aroused by a configuration of ideas, self-concepts, and views of others. For example, anger is a simpler emotion than envy, which contains elements of anger. How might we model a complex and familiar experience such as a feeling of envy in terms of modes of conscious representation? One example is provided by the case of Judy. She was in psychotherapy for a variety of reasons, one of which was a tendency to feel intense envy of women, and to ward this off by feigning indifference. The compromise of indifference did not work; she still wanted to be close to other women and so she felt lonely and rejected. Analysis of many small, insignificant episodes of envy was one route taken to help her gradually to master this trait.

Though a senior in college, Judy was still shy around men her own age. She was in a class with a man whom she found appealing, and hoped he might seek to get better acquainted with her. While he looked at her with interest, he also seemed shy about making the first move. Karen, another woman classmate, sat next to him one day, introduced herself, and got into an animated conversation. Judy envied Karen her poise, good looks, and courage.

Let us break down the envy experience into its components in order to illustrate how this complex emotion was consciously represented, to show the linkage and overlap between the concepts of *ideas* and *emotions*. I emphasize this linkage and overlap because the two concepts are usually discussed separately.

Envy existed as a relationship between Judy and Karen. The attributes of Karen were consciously represented, after the actual perception, by memory images of it. Judy could, in her mind's eye, see Karen behaving in a way that she later called "poised, good-looking, courageous." The imaged actions could even be emulated in enactive representation, as Judy showed a posture and facial expression imitating Karen's patterns.

Judy's envy of Karen also involved self-reflection. She visually represented her own face and compared it with Karen's, finding her own face less appealing in her imagination. She lexically labeled Karen as "prettier" than she. Judy also had an imaginary image of herself in Karen's place, beside the man, and felt a flush of anger that Karen had usurped her in this position. She experienced this anger as bodily sensations. First there was an enactive representation through change in the muscles surrounding blood vessels in her face. This was then consciously represented as sensory cutaneous images of heat in her face.

There was an additional consciously represented component to the flare of envy. Judy also had forecast in words the idea that she would never be able to summon up for herself the courage and poise she noted in Karen. That view made her feel more frustrated, angry, and sad about the experience. The sadness came as lexical ideas that things would never go well for her, and as an enactment of sadness leading to sensory cutaneous perceptions, of feeling a slackness in her face following the flushed, hot, angry feeling also localized in her face. Judy experienced not just envy but such a dislike of feeling envy that, immediately upon the conscious experience, she tried to put the complex emotion out of mind. She did so by consciously speaking to herself in words and auditory imagery, in her imagination saying, "He was not really very interesting." She then instructed herself to have visual images of a photograph in which she was attractively groomed and dressed for a prom, and together with her smiling high school boyfriend. These deliberate representations were her conscious ways of ending the state of mind in which she felt so envious. *The complex felt emotions during that state of mind were all consciously experienced as representations in one mode or another. Ideas were also represented in some mode. In the flow of conscious experience, felt emotions and ideas were commingled.*

Learning cross-modal representation of ideas and feelings enhances one's self-regulatory capacity and sense of personal mastery. Words are especially helpful in gaining control over emotions and impulses. For example, when adolescents have difficulty communicating ideas and feelings, they may act them out. To improve coping, it may be useful for one to learn to translate these acted-out ideas into verbal communication, as did fifteen-year-old Paul, who had recently begun conspicuously to steal, drink, and cut class at high school. Eventually he was placed in an adolescent specialty unit of a psychiatric hospital because his problems seemed to spring from psychological conflicts rather than criminal intent. At first tactful and cooperative, Paul then began to break the rules. He brought a bottle of wine onto the ward, lied to the staff, and was generally provocative.

Repetitions of these provocations made it clear that Paul was acting out the role of a rebel, particularly attempting to provoke women staff members into reacting angrily toward him. His hostile taunts of women elicited relationships in which these women felt either helplessly enraged or reacted in a harshly authoritarian manner. At the same time, he attempted to set up an alliance with male staff members in which he idealized and imitated them. Paul worked to enhance any hostility he might find between the male and female staff members so that they would distrust each other. If a woman had scolded and restricted him, he went to a man and tried to show her up as unfairly overreacting.

Paul's ward pattern recapitulated his family pattern. His mother oscillated between overcontrolling, harshly punitive efforts and a fluttering helplessness in which she demanded that Paul's father punish him. His father vacillated weakly between allying with Paul and with the mother. Underlying Paul's wish for alliance with men and his manifest toughness, he had a weak self-concept. He was angry with his father for being a weak role model.

The psychiatric staff recognized and discussed Paul's pattern of provocation and attempted to empathize with his inner feelings. They developed a consistent approach to dealing with his behavior. They patiently called Paul's actions to his attention by labeling them and asked him calmly and repeatedly what these acts might mean. This dialogue, geared as it was toward establishing verbal meaning and communication, surprised Paul. He felt increasingly uneasy. He tested the staff to see how far he could go before they would retaliate by abusing or rejecting him. Then he developed various positive and intense feelings toward individual members of the ward staff. He began to speak about his sense of being weak, his angry feelings toward his parents, and his fear of growing up and having to leave his home.

He gained conceptual skills as he learned not only to analyze his actions for intention, but to allow his aims to become a conscious part of his thought, as images and words rather than sets of behavior. He learned to communicate his emotions, especially his urgent, angry sense of frustration, verbally rather than behaviorally, and so felt more in control. His increased sense of capacity for this type of "adult" behavior helped him bolster a competent self-concept.

Thus, lexical representation allowed Paul to modulate his expression of his ideas and emotions. In dynamic psychotherapy, verbal communication is encouraged for this reason. When, however, emotion is flat rather than intense, image representation may be encouraged, by asking for dream reports, accounts of current fantasies, spontaneous drawing, or guided daydreams (Horowitz 1983; Pope and Singer 1978).

Dreams

Dreams are a form of consciousness during a state of sleeping. In dreaming sleep, for biological reasons, most conscious representation is in the mode of visual imagery. Muscles are relatively inhibited during dreaming sleep. Any verbal representations are usually pictures of words or auditory images.

During dreaming, there may also be a change in which schemas are operative, including those for channeling wishes and fears and for defending against "bad" thoughts. The sequence of ideas and feelings in dream pictures is much different from that during daytime visual reveries; and more childhood memories, primitive wishes, and magical thinking may occur. This is the reason Freud called dreams "the royal road to the unconscious" (1900).

Some dreams stand out as having very special, if mysterious, *symbolic properties.* For example, a man dreamed of a giraffe lying on the ground, its long neck looking like a limp snake. In the dream, he had an idea that the neck looked vulnerable, as though someone might step on it. The dream occurred the night before a panel discussion in which the dreamer was to participate at a public meeting. The dream images were a complex visual way of making a self-admonition or warning: "Don't stick your neck out." Dreams that give such appraisals of states of danger to the self have been called *self-state dreams* (Kohut 1977; Ornstein 1986).

These symbols often take a perception received during the day—the *day residue*—and use it as the core of a visual image to which many current concerns are attached. For example, the dreamer may have seen a red car driving fast during the day, then dream of a red car that is driving too fast. The dream may symbolize a fear that the self is going out of control in impetuously pursuing some goal. The same dreamer might go on to dream of trying to close a door upon a dirty room or of walking an unruly dog that tugs at its leash—all depicting action against a threat, a warning to stay in control (Eisnitz 1986).

Dreams contain symbols from the cultural heritage of times past. Even though most of us in the free world now live in a democracy, dreams contain kings, queens, princes, princesses, trolls, and other figures from childhood stories and myths. The fascination with certain symbolic figures beyond everyday experience in ordinary waking life has led to discussions of archetypes and prototypes of human dream life (Jung 1959). Formed from unconscious mental processes, the contents of dreams may often surprise the sleeper, and the mystery of their source has still to be penetrated by our waking understanding.

Most people dream at times of falling, of houses catching fire, of being menaced by monsters, of being too paralyzed or too slow to escape. In some of these anxiety dreams, there is a translation from enactive representation to imagery, for the sleeper's muscles are indeed paralysed during dreaming as a result of neuronal inhibition in the brain. Even so, the images may also symbolize one's inability to master some current daytime threat.

Nightmares are an extreme form of anxiety dream. While almost everyone has an occasional nightmare, some have recurrent bad dreams. Five percent of people seeking a medical consultation complain of difficult nightmares (Bixler, Kales, and Soldatos 1979). Some nightmares have a recurrent theme that takes different variations. Severe nightmares occur to persons who seem to have heightened problems with feeling resentment or expecting and fearing hostility from others (Hartmann 1984; Vela-Bueno, Soldatos, and Julius 1987). Fatigue, drugs, drug withdrawal, and other biological factors may also increase the likelihood of nightmares.

Dreams thus range from pleasing wish fulfillments to terrifying scenarios of threat. Both wishes and fears may be presented in the visual representations that characterize dreams. Many dreams are also apparently banal, having no clear manifest intensity of emotional meaning. Many unconscious formative and regulatory processes are going on to produce these fascinating states of consciousness. The creative symbols sometimes found in dreams, and their often long and complex story lines indicate a tremendous scope to such unconscious integrations and recombinations of meanings.

Compared with the scope of unconscious mental processes, consciousness is relatively limited. It is slow and relatively singular in attention as compared with unconscious information processing. To get this slow, careful processing for the most important issues and choices in life, the portals to representational systems must be regulated so that only some information gets in. The best-fitting, most useful schematic organization may be used for information that is consciously represented, and less salient organizations and codings may be usefully omitted from conscious representation.

From a study of the phenomena of consciousness, including intrusions of unwanted representations and omissions of wanted ones, we must conclude that unconscious judgments are being made. As these seem to include self-appraisal of the ability to cope with incipient representations of ideas and feelings, I shall now turn to what goes on in unconscious thought and the precursors of felt emotion.

9

Unconscious Processes

A Personal Case

ONCE, when I was a medical student, I was making rounds with my teacher, a resident on a medical ward. We entered the room of one of his patients whom I was to examine. As we stood by the bedside, I felt my pulse suddenly quicken. I entered a state of anxious hypervigilance, and wondered why I had "the jitters." I was aware simultaneously of the odor of a rarely used antiseptic, but attached no immediate significance to it. I also had a sense of *déjà vu*, the uncanny feeling of having been before in just this same kind of situation, although I had never been in that hospital room nor seen that patient.

I concealed my fear and examined the patient as I had been taught. My jittery state of mind did not subside until we left the room to continue our rounds. Later I analyzed my reaction, associating to all the elements of the memory. Only then, and only gradually, could I reconstruct a much earlier memory associated with the peculiar smell of that antiseptic.

As a child, I had throat surgery for an infected abscess. I shared a room with a flyer whose face had been badly burned in war. He had undergone major plastic surgery to reconstruct his mouth, and the surgical wound became infected. I also had a complication, a post-operative hemorrhage, and became terrified that I would become as badly disfigured or near to death as I saw this man to be. The smell of the anesthetic in that childhood hospital room was the same as the odor that triggered my reactions in the

169

later situation, and had been associated with the traumatic fear I experienced as a child. This had happened long ago, and I had not thought of this flyer and his disfigured face until the memory was activated by the specific odor of the antiseptic. Yet an unconscious thought process had associated the odor to that memory and triggered fear.

My first conscious representation as an adult medical student in that hospital room was of my own bodily reaction of alarm. The meaning of the odor to me personally was not consciously represented until much later in time, although the emotion-evoking processes based on unconscious associations were virtually instantaneous.

This type of association of an emotional reaction (in my case, the alarm emotion of fear) with a stimulus that occurs along with a state of mind, has been called *conditioning*—in particular, *classical conditioning* (Pavlov 1928; Skinner 1953). The smell of the antiseptic was not a threat to me; the image of myself as facially disfigured or dying was what had terrified me. But the smell had occurred at the same time as my distraught state of mind, and was now part of a schema that, when operative, aroused fear. The felt emotion, through enactive and image representations, became the only first access of the schema to my consciousness.

The shift in state of mind from calm to jitters through unconscious thought, as in my case, is not uncommon. Making the associations conscious is part of the routine procedure in psychotherapy. The conscious reflection does not erase the unconscious associations that lead to emotion and mood changes, but the understanding, and hence the expansion of meanings, enhances one's sense of self-mastery. In this chapter, I will use my own experience to model further the unconscious processes leading from a calm to an alarmed state.

As I entered the hospital room, I was organizing my perception of the situation, and my actions within the situation, according to a role-relationship model in which I was a competent medical student, mentored by a competent doctor, and in which we were coping together with cooperative patients who needed and received medical care. My state of mind was calm and attentive. I was unaware of any sensations of pulse, heart beat, knotted stomach, or muscle tension. Like other stimuli, my perception of the antiseptic odor was fitted into the calm schema I have just described as I entered the room. While the antiseptic smell was not inconsistent with a hospital schema, it was also associated in an important way with elements in another schema.

This other schema coordinated memories from a traumatic event in my past. That schema also involved hospital rooms, patients, doctors, this particular odor, and myself in a junior position. A working model containing these elements could also be developed from this enduring schema from the earlier traumatic events. In that model, I was a vulnerable child, facing harm or death in relation to others who were perhaps not competent enough to protect me. That working model would be associated with the state of "the jitters."

The association of the odor to the vulnerable-child schema set off an unconscious alarm reaction, a sudden alerting response in preparation for the possible repetition of a danger situation. The alarm reaction led to bodily changes and then to my conscious sensations of rapid pulse, tightened stomach, and muscle tension. This whole pattern was a transition from the state of calm to "the jitters." The resulting hypervigilance led me quickly to check all my surroundings for danger—a check that tended to confirm the working model in which I was a competent medical student, as well as the facts that the patient was not me, and the resident was my competent mentor. I suppressed the actions of tension and rapid gazing about associated with the interruptive jittery state, focused on my tasks with the patient, and inhibited trains of thought until I might later contemplate why my pulse had raced and I had had the jitters.

The odor—in its context of hospital room, patient, doctors, and myself in a junior position—was interpreted by networks of unconscious associations. Patterns of associations could be assembled according to various schemas. The question was, Which schemas were the best fit and gave the best interpretation? These would become working models of my situation.

In the hospital room as an adult medical student, there occurred in my mind parallel processing of the ongoing perceptions of the situation according to at least two contradictory schemas. My conscious experience was being affected by two working models: one based on a childhood schema, and the other on a more recently developed adult schema. Most of my conscious representations were organized according to the adult schema, but intrusive representations of bodily feeling from the alarm reaction were processing the same perceptual information according to the childhood schema.

The working model based on recent adult experiences contained a self-concept as a competent medical student working with a physician mentor and a cooperative patient. The working model based on childhood traumatic experiences contained a much weaker self-concept: that of a sick, vulnerable child, one unprotected by doctors and in danger of becoming like a terribly injured patient. The potential threat as organized by the childhood schema was important enough to arouse alarm systems and to interrupt my conscious focus on examining the patient. I used conscious thought to reappraise the situation and decided to oppose that interruption

171

at the time by an act of conscious will *(suppression)*. Later I deliberately recalled the interrupted train of thought and allowed its meanings to unfold consciously.

My conscious reason for postponement was lack of time, the decision made in terms of what to do when. Continuing rounds seemed more pressing. A quick look to recheck the situation had shown no real signs of danger. I did not know why I should feel jittery; and this train of thought marked by the feelings of alarm was stored in a form of memory that tends to return later as unfinished business. Such *active memory storage* has usually been called *short-term memory* and contrasted with *long-term memory* (Broadbent 1971). The word *active* is used because the information stored in this manner has a tendency to repeated representation and, if important, will continue to be coded for more than a short time.

The repeated representation allows secondary appraisals (Lazarus 1966). This review and reinterpretation by new working models is desirable because the information has not yet been well meshed with schemas, but has been marked as potentially high in personal relevance. Since active memory storage has limited coding capacity, only a limited number of memories can be held in this way. The most important memories, assessed by preconscious processing, tend to be the ones retained. Emotional activation is one sign or marker of such importance.

The Activation of Emotion

The pang of fear that I felt upon smelling the peculiar odor of the unusual antiseptic was determined unconsciously by association of that odor to a memory of fear and a schema that included a concept of my personal vulnerability. My *conscious sensation* of my heart racing followed *the preconscious processes* that had activated the sympathetic nervous system as an alarm response (Crook 1980; Dixon 1981). My conscious recognition of these physical sensations as those of alarm operated as a further motivation for me to interrupt my existing conscious plans and to look around me for potential threats. Last in the sequence was a conscious, lexically represented analysis of why I had reacted emotionally in an unexpected way.

Conscious emotions can be unpleasant, especially negative ones associated with undermodulated states. Certainly, I did not want to feel jittery when I was about to examine a patient in the presence of my mentor. In order to reduce conscious experience of emotion, one can control the emoting processes that lead toward conscious representation, and can do so after some conscious representation has occurred. I was thus able to mask my anxious state of mind, experiencing the internal conscious representations, but composing my face, voice and actions as if I were not anxious but calm. Such control operations can also operate unconsciously. The unconscious mind is looking ahead, modeling potential consequences, and making regulatory adjustments as a result of such anticipations. In my case, I was probably thinking unconsciously that I did not want to display fearful tension to the patient and resident, lest they think less of me.

EMOTION AS FEEDBACK

Emotional systems, once activated, operate on their own schemas to generate signals that inform the self and others about how a situation is going. The judgments that activate emotional systems and then also evaluate emotional responses are based in part on the associations among ideas.

When a situation is experienced, the mind quickly forms reactive ideas, which associate it to all kinds of possible meanings. Each reactive idea is also associated with other ideas, in a network of potential meanings. One form of association is a matching operation in which a current idea is compared with an enduring attitude. The comparison of the ideas responding to a situation with enduring attitudes of what is wanted or dreaded, or what should be, tells the person how things are going, for better or worse, and so informs one what to approach or avoid.

Matching ideas with propositions about what is wanted or dreaded may lead to activation of emotional systems. This emoting response is most likely in mismatches, when one's views of a situation discord with one's desires or ideas about what is right, standard, or enduring. Emotional activation can lead, in turn, to consciousness of felt emotion. To regulate excitement and tension and to prevent dreaded states of mind, various control processes may be activated as a feedback loop. These controls may inhibit the ideas and matching operations, which then reduces emotional arousal.

CONTROL OF EMOTION

A person caught up in a neurotic level of mental disorder, or one with a hyperactive fear-arousal system, might not have been able to suppress the surge of anxiety I felt in that hospital room. Instead, one might be disposed to having a full-fledged panic disorder, with an irresistible desire to flee the scene—an action that, in these circumstances, would be followed by intense shame. That result might reinforce a fear of hospital rooms, making it more general than before, and leading perhaps to a phobia for such environments. Matters would now be in a vicious cycle, for acting on that phobic behavior would be incompatible with being a medical student. The eventual outcome could become quite bad: leaving school, becoming depressed over failure, having an impaired self-concept with deflated self-esteem and a timid withdrawal from challenges to self-competence. The difference between this terrible outcome and a variety of less maladaptive ones involves many factors, of which an important one is control over ideas and feelings.

I used the word *control* here in a very general way. What is regulated may be the preconscious processing of ideas, the entry into emoting systems, the schemas that are used to organize an overall state of mind, and the various modes for consciously representing ideas and feelings, or planning to express them in action. The control processes may not only be inhibition but may also *facilitate* reduction of usual inhibition, or *dysinhibition.* Several control processes may occur at the same time in organized or disorganized ways. If emotion is getting too intense to serve as an adaptive motivator, or if expression of feeling to others is a threat, then the processes leading to the activation of emoting systems can be inhibited. In the next chapter, I will examine the variety of such controls for use in situations of mounting stress or conflict. Here it is useful to focus on conscious and unconscious aspects of control.

Unconscious control processes are ever active to a greater or lesser extent. Deliberate conscious efforts can often counteract these unconscious controls. It is not always possible, however, to know consciously that an unconscious control is operating. A disjunction between the aims and activities of conscious and unconscious controls can be further illustrated by a case history in which a woman's feeling of erotic arousal was commingled with a level of tension that prevented her from satisfying her current wish for sexual gratification.

Ruth, a woman in her twenties, complained of her inability to have an orgasm, although she was attracted to her husband, often sexually aroused, and lovingly involved with him. During her psychotherapy, she mentioned that she experienced an inexplicable visual image of the color green when closing her eyes during sexual foreplay. Before describing this phenomenon to the therapist, Ruth had mentioned in passing that she tended to enter a state of tense, erotic nervousness when she dressed in green clothes. She made this comment after she purchased a green dress, wore it to therapy, and, to her considerable embarrassment, entered that state of tense, erotic nervousness during the therapy session. Only later, in another therapy session, did Ruth note that, when she was having sexual intercourse and becoming excited, she developed a visual image of green luminosity. She would then get tense, fail to maintain arousal, and not have an orgasm.

In associating to the specific green color of her mental image, she recovered a previously repressed memory. Her father, an alcoholic, frequently drank at home. When Ruth was twelve years old, she was sitting on a couch with him watching TV and fell asleep. She awoke and was petrified when she felt him rubbing her genitals through her dress. She felt paralyzed and could not just get up and leave. She remained motionless and began to enjoy the sensations. She averted her face from him, looking in the opposite direction, seeing only the luminous green through the lampshade of the table lamp. She felt depersonalized, as if she were in the lampshade and not in her physical body. Ruth was in conflict between a desire to escape and a desire to stay so as not to offend her father.

It was possible in therapy to discover the warded-off themes that led to the unwanted tension, and thus to help Ruth to enter more satisfying states of erotic arousal. With recollection, she gained insight into the meanings of the specific green color. Choosing and wearing a green dress was a repetition of a traumatic sexually seductive event in her childhood which had involved strain and conflict. Conscious contemplation of these associations led her to review her complex past relationship with her father and her current relationships with both the therapist and her husband. By this consciously reflective thinking, she could emphasize the distinction between the schemas of incestuous, fearful sexuality with her father, and the developing schemas of adult, permitted, unincestuous, appropriate routes to sexual feelings with her husband. Her sexual feelings for the therapist were like a transition, because he was both an older, fatherlike figure and a person she had come to trust who would neither criticize what she felt nor react in a sexual way.

As just one aspect of her conscious choices on this theme, she gave away her new green dress. This action followed her decision that a preferable route to erotic feeling was *not* to wear green, but to dress instead in some new color to be associated with new trials of a sensuous state of mind, not with the past conflict. At the same time, she was able to see that her act of buying the green dress was, in a paradoxical way, part of a bold effort to become a sexually mature woman. She had unconsciously viewed getting "green" as part of a schema for feeling sexy.

Now, by conscious reflection, it was possible for her to plan ways of feeling sexy that were less likely to co-exist in the incestuous schema of memories; thus, she reduced her fear and sense of depersonalization during sexual activity. The therapist was able to encourage Ruth to use conscious reflection and self-calming to continue on in a threateningly novel situation and to endure some fear, rather than quickly to avert fear through inhibition. By such means Ruth learned to see what might happen, and she gradually developed more realistic working models, which allowed her more poise and a sense of personal choice in sexuality.

REVISION OF SCHEMAS

New working models develop as a consequence of processing the information contained in novel situations. A repetition of these new working models leads to changes in such schemas as role-relationship models. Some elements may be retained, others modified, during these processes of schematic change.

New working models of familiar situations can also be developed as these situations are experienced differently. Heightening conscious representation of a situation by carefully observing its elements can lead to new working models which, in turn, allow better observation and so on in cycles of feedback.

When one notes an important incongruence between the news in a novel situation and existing schemas, one can change either the news or the schema (Piaget 1970). The news can be reappraised, especially after one has acted to find more information, or even change the situation. Stories can be made up that give an apparent explanation (Dennet 1986). The schemas can be revised by making new working models during waking mentation, and possibly during sleep mentation in the review of memories during dreaming. Indeed, the integration of active memories from residues of the day with more enduring schemas may be one of the functions of dreaming sleep (Breger, Hunter, and Lane 1971; Hartmann 1964; Winson 1985; M. Reiser 1984).

The processes of reappraisal and revision of memories and working models may not require conscious representation at all, although they affect conscious representation. If reality tests out as remaining unmatched with schemas, revision of schemas is necessary for maximum internal modeling of external reality, as shown in figure 9.1.

The processing of coded units stored in active memory may be completed either by decay of that memory over time or by successful relating of the news contained in this unit with existing schemas. When the news is really new, the working models or the activated schemas must be revised, thus completing the train of thought initiated by the representation of the new information. When incongruities are involved, conscious thought may be especially useful as an aspect of solving the problem of what the news "really" means.

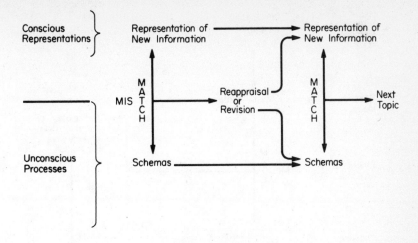

Figure 9.1

The Revision of Schemas

Important incongruences lead to reappraisal and revision: congruence means that thinking can proceed to the next topic.

In either conscious or unconscious thought, the person may not always use the most adaptive choice between reappraisal or revision. The importance of the news can be dampened by a variety of controls—as happened in the case of Steve, who used several controls of ideas and feelings to prevent a dreaded state of mind.

Steve was a surgical resident at a crucial level of training, one that would dictate his future career. During this training year, the faculty surgeon with whom he worked gave Steve feedback on several occasions about how he was not meeting required standards of skill in performing operations. These conversations, if fully absorbed, would be bad news because they conflicted with his goal of becoming a great surgeon.

The discrepancy between the new information—that he had only mediocre skills in key areas—and the enduring attitude—"I must have great skills in surgery"—threatened to bring on a painful emotional realization. He unconsciously anticipated the danger of entering a dreaded state of mind, and, in order to avoid it, activated controls that tended to dampen his realization of the implication of the faculty surgeon's remarks. The surgical resident paid *selective inattention* to cues from his mentor, *forgot* to contemplate the conversations later when he was alone, and also *depreciated* the opinions of the chief when speaking to other trainees.

Steve's inhibitory maneuvers, chosen at a level below clear conscious awareness, were defensive compromises. His mood was stabilized at a

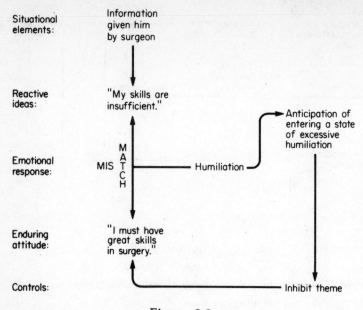

Figure 9.2

Controls as Feedback: Anticipation of Emotion and the Inhibition of Ideas

tolerably positive level at the expense of exercising maladaptive avoidances of useful information about his social reality. The feedback loop of ideas, emotions, and controls is modeled in figure 9.2.

Fear of entry into an excessively humiliated state of mind is a defensive motive for inhibitions of the distressing theme. Such fearful anticipations are often called *signal anxiety* (Freud 1911) in psychodynamic writings. The largely unconscious anticipations produce a smaller emotional response than might fully conscious representations. This small increment of emotional response is not just of humiliation; it is a fear or anxiety about entering a state colored by a massive experience of shame. That small amount of fear signals danger, and the danger anticipated can be reduced by some type of control operation.

While emoting systems are not stifled by the prevention of conscious representation, such control operations do reduce felt emotion, and thus may prevent the amplification of emoting processes (Tomkins 1962). In this manner, the emotional consequences of processing certain types of information can be modulated. The results may be adaptive—processing emotionally evocative information in a dose-by-dose manner for example; or they may be maladaptive, failing adequately to adapt to situations because of inattention to how to cope with them.

178

FELT EMOTION

In order consciously to feel an emotion, one's regulatory systems must allow some type of representation as enactions, images, or words. In the previous chapter, I noted that anger can be experienced in terms of hostile movements such as bared teeth and clenched fists, visual images of knives and guns, verbal declarations such as "Drop dead!" The idea that one's skills are insufficient for a surgeon could be represented by such words as "I'm no good," by images of the self leaving the floor of the training program, by motoric facial expressions characteristic of shame, and/or by bodily postures of self-concealment.

The fullest conscious experience would contain representations in these different lexical, image, and enactive modes, using each to advantage. Enactive representations would inform observing others and the self how intensely one was feeling anger or shame. Images would reveal hostile aims or self-abasement in the relationship between self and other, and words would tell a story and give a rationale for the anger or shame and indicate what its consequences might be.

Unconscious and Preconscious Processing

MULTIPLE CHANNELS

The progression of a theme of thought in its course to conscious representation can be modified by a variety of primary- and secondary-process organizations of information, which may proceed, for a time, in separate but temporally parallel channels. The output of these different parallel processes may be different, and may even compete for access to consciousness. The themes progressing toward representation may be activated by externally or internally derived stimuli or motives.

A new set of stimuli can be processed simultaneously along multiple routes. Only some of these parallel-processing channels can have potential access to conscious representation because conscious information processing is limited in its capacity. If the contents are accessible to consciousness, they are considered to be *preconscious* rather than unconscious (not directly accessible).

Before conscious representation can occur, some choice may be made about which parts of the information being processed will be selected for first attention. This choice is made on the basis of many factors which mediate between sensory inflow, schemas activated by inner needs, current intentions, and priming of memory forms by association to conscious representations (Dixon 1981). Moreover, different rules of organization can be followed. Historically, Freud (1911) referred to multiple forms of thinking by dividing the formative organizing principles into primary and secondary process.

Primary process rules for forming thought were regarded as the earliest form in which desires channel themselves into actions. In the associational sequencing rules of the primary process, highest priority is given to immediate and direct gratification of wishes; hence, to memories of prior sources of satisfaction of the appetite or drive currently surging as a forming wish (Freud 1900). Magical, irrational connections of ideas may be used to imagine that such satisfaction can now occur again. Thinking in this form, when manifestly represented in conscious derivatives such as vividly intense images of what is desired, may seem irrational and creative. The thought products include fluid displacements of attributes of one object or person to another. Symbols are prominent as a result of condensations, as are magical assumptions about meaning. Dreams may contain visual stories organized by primary process.

Freud assumed that the rules of *secondary-process* thinking develop from the matrix provided by primary process. Logical rules for rational reasoning are the main additions. Piaget (1930, 1937), Inhelder and Piaget (1958), Flavel (1968) explored the sequential acquisition of reasoning capacities. Like primary process, secondary-process thinking is motivated by wishes and fears, but with added attention to the opportunities assessed in processing inflow, to values, and to other current intentions. Secondary process also adds rules about time; and the ability to expect the future and plan for it permits delays in impulses toward immediate gratification in favor of long-range purposes and values.

Rational reasoning in consciousness was regarded by Freud as the highest derivative of secondary-process constructions; he hoped to increase its power by promotion of insight into usually unconscious fantasies. Development of secondary-process thinking includes acquiring the ability to restrain intense emotional expressions when they appear unwise. Freud saw some of this wariness as caused by the frustrating or bitter experiences of life. He saw dreams as a means of safe regression to primary-process rules for organizing thought, and delusions and hallucinations as a less safe regression compelled by loss of secondary-process capacities.

In primary process, there is a tendency to make associational linkages by sheer resemblance, by clanging rhymes or color similarity. There is also a tendency to make great unifications, forging powerful symbols. The logic of rational probabilities of what can happen in time and space does not always apply to this, the realm of *magical thinking*. Instead, the rule of magic, personal and cultural, may organize the associative connection of one element with another. One has a tendency to think in terms of the metaphors and allegories depicted for us consciously in mythology, fairy and folk tales, and some forms of poetry and art. Heroes, witches, royalty, ghosts, demons, and animals are common roles, just as birthing, killing, mating, and seizing territory or objects are the common actions of these stories (Jung 1964). (For a review of primary- and secondary-process organization of thought, see McKellar 1957; Rapaport 1967*b*; Gill 1967*b*; Holt 1967; and Noy 1969; and Freud, on the two principles of mental functioning [1911].)

The division of two types of thought sequence into primary- and secondary-process thinking is probably incomplete theory. The division does serve to remind us that rational conscious thought is not all there is to mental life, even though it dominates reflective self-awareness.

DRIVES FROM WITHIN

How can we conceptualize the drives arising within the mind?

There are many unconscious aspects of information processing. Some are computational: for example, placing the body in space to figure out coordinated plans; constructing words into grammatical sentences, elemental forms into pictures; and assembling tones in melodies or harmonies (Olson and Bialystok 1983; Jackendoff 1987). Some unconscious processes involve a high order of planning alternatives or highly imaginative and creative new solutions to problems or contradictions (Rothenberg 1979; Gardner 1982; Weiss and Sampson 1986). Other aspects of unconscious information processing stem from long-standing intentions organized into unconscious fantasies, such as a goal to master in adult life traumas suffered as a child or to consummate previously thwarted desires (Arlow 1969). Spurs to unconscious processing and conscious thought also spring, as raw urges, from the depths of the person.

These raw but powerful urges are called *instinctive drives*. Reproductive drives, for example, are a combination of *built-in programs* for action and a triggering into activity of such programs by biochemical levels of such messengers as *hormones* and *neurotransmitters*. With a surge of sexual hormones, anatomy, physiology, thought, and emotions all may change. The built-in programs are genetically carried schemas, and the surge of hormones can affect the activity of these schemas.

In the course of development, the *genetically provided schemas* interlace with the *learned schemas* from perception and psychosocial interaction. A surge of sexual hormones will activate the schemas for organizing sexual behavior derived from nature and nurture. These schemas then organize conscious thought and feeling. The resulting conscious experiences, attitudes about them, and conscious and unconscious reasoning about their possible outcome have, in turn, a feedback effect on the activities both of various schemas and of various areas of the brain, including those brain systems of the limbic system, reticular formation, thalmus, hypothalmus, and pituitary gland that control hormone production and bodily arousal levels. Schemas are in the middle of the transactive system by which the body influences the mind and the mind influences the body.

Sexual hormones may wax and wane depending on many factors, including external social situations as well as biological givens. Social sexual stimulation increases sexual hormones and, thus, drives. The level of such circulating hormones may determine the activation of role-relationship models related to possible sexual satisfaction. There may also be drives for self-aggrandizement for social position in a hierarchy, for territory, for security, and possibly for aggressivity. These are less well understood in terms of instinctive, genetically preprogrammed origins, or hormonal influences.

An emergent drive may lead to organization and execution of an action. Between its onset and outcome, the information and the motive force of the drive will be transmuted according to what schemas are used as organizing forms. Any schema once associated with satisfaction of the specific drive will tend to be activated into a working model as a response to a repeated surge of that drive or motive.

Recent, mature schemas may be preferentially activated because they are more appropriate socially and because they give the most differentiated forms of satisfaction of the aroused appetites. Yet primitive schemas that relate to the drive may also be activated. These other, less mature, less differentiated schemas will then also process the information inherent in the drive; and the outcome of this processing may compete with the outcome from recent and mature schemas at the portals of representation.

While such parallel processing might occur, the mature schemas would tend to keep the primitive schemas in check just as more advanced brain systems keep primitive spinal reflexes in check. With any reduction in use of higher-order schemas, the lower-order forms might gain primacy in organizing responses to a drive. Instead of using well-differentiated role-relationship models for expressing sexual desire or aggressivity, the person may organize experience and action by primitive schemas for expressing lust and rage. If higher-order schemas cannot satisfy a drive, the person may, in response to mounting tension, regress to lower-order schemas.

Lower-order schemas may lead to actions that seem uncivilized, brutal, and foreign to the person. These aspects of unconscious processes, which George Groddek (1950 reprint) called "the it" as opposed to "the I," led to Freud's concept of the id as opposed to the ego. The raw, lustful forms are experienced as alien to the self, or ego.

INTENTIONS AND ACTION PLANS

The direction of association from the starting point of any idea is determined in part by a person's existing intentions. *Intentions* are one's existing purposes as derived from wishes and fears and include a loose form of schemas called *action plans.* While not necessarily conscious, intentions and action plans are stored as working models. They are lined up in order of priority, to be selectively released when a situation warrants it (Newell 1978; Kuhl and Beckmann 1985).

While some intentions and action plans are unconscious, the release of intentions and action plans can be influenced by conscious *acts of will,* by conscious *decisions* made as a result of contemplation. Conscious thought can override both unconscious associations of a stimulus to an emotional response and unconscious plans to act out the transaction sequences contained in a role-relationship model. Nonetheless, intentions and action plans are also influenced by *unconsciously made choices* and by *contagion* from the emotions and purposes of others. There is both a top-down and a bottom-up interaction of conscious and unconscious thinking.

Some neurotic personality patterns are not consciously recognized by the person who repeats the pattern. Conscious intentions may be rationalizations that mask unconscious intentions. Because the conscious intentions may seem sensible to the subject, he or she does not change the recurrent maladaptive interpersonal pattern.

Other people may observe the form of the pattern because it is repetitive. More readily than the subject, such observers may be able to infer the unconscious intentions that also feed into the pattern. By providing the subject with insight into the unconscious intentions, such observers may help the subject to revise his or her conscious intentions.

The revised conscious plans can then override the unconscious plans. Through repetition of new ways of acting, the conscious intentions can become more automatic. What the subject first feels as an artificial change will come to feel more natural as schemas develop, since such schemas allow more automatic functioning.

Translation of insight into change requires many repetitions of awareness and efforts at reflection. Even more so, to arrive at smooth and automatic use of new patterns requires many trials and efforts that at first feel awkward and even risky. As a result, the insight psychotherapies that use psychodynamic theory may take a long time if the focus is on modifying maladaptive personality patterns.

REVERIE AND FREE ASSOCIATION

Intentions govern the flow of thought processes. In alert states of mind, one's conscious goal is often to solve problems. But one can consciously decide to change this goal and seek to establish a reverie or meditative state. This switch in mental set is a way of either clearing the mind for relaxation or of getting in touch with extended meanings of a stimulus by allowing a broader network of associations and organization by multiple, diverse schemas.

One of the changes in a state of mind that can be caused by conscious choice is the shift from alert problem-solving thought to an undirected "empty mind state." This shift is practiced in meditative techniques. Another kind of shift is from goal-directed logic to a free-association state—a shift practiced as a dynamic psychotherapy and psychoanalytic technique. The mental set seems to be non-intentional. One not only experiences whatever "comes to mind," in any mode of representation, but also observes and reports it to the therapist. The therapist notes the sequences, while the person who is free-associating goes on to whatever comes next. While the sequence of ideas may feel random, it is actually determined by unconscious intentions and schemas for processing information. (Crook 1980; Dixon 1981). The observing self or the observing therapist can notice repeated patterns and infer reasons for certain associations.

In observing free associations, one can sometimes note the ebb and flow in communicative openness and reluctance which suggests unconscious conflict in intentions to either reveal or conceal. The person may both long to confess some guilty thought or past act and, at the same time, try to stifle this disclosure. The result is a halting process of revelation, of clarity and obscurity, of emotional expression and backtracking.

JOKES

Jokes are a relief and also a barometer of tensions between unconscious urges and moral prohibitions against raw discharge of these urges (Freud 1927a). Laughter at jokes is such a pleasure that social groups thrive on humor, and professional comedians are paid to perform. Yet a joke can turn sour for any person caught up in excessive conflict about the conscious and unconscious themes activated in response to what is supposedly humorous. For a sharp laugh to occur, a surprising change and association is necessary, and also a sudden change in tension level. Sometimes the sudden change involves a switch from one schema to another—a shift, that is, in one's unconscious interpretation of the consciously understood story.

For example, with a cartoon, one first looks at the picture, then the caption. This sequence is itself the consequence of a learned schematic script. Upon looking at the picture, one's conscious reflection is of the drawing itself. Less consciously or unconsciously, this picture activates several possible schemas into potential working models of how to understand it. One of the prominent schemas is then altered when one reads the punch line: the issue pictured may, by the caption, become suddenly less threatening. For example, under a cartoon of the hooded figure of death in a doorway, a figure much shorter than the person answering the door, the caption could read, "Don't worry, I'm just a small cold," or "Don't worry, I've just come for your toaster." The picture activates a working model of the catastrophic bad news that death has arrived for the self. The caption, a minor script of a safe illness or trivial loss, allows a relief from the tension of that activated threat of death.

In addition to the schema shift, the motives aroused that lead to laughter are complex. The tension that builds up before the laugh may be from the threat of too much fear, excessive personal relish of hostility, degradation of others, sexuality, dirtiness, or that there is a fear of shame if one's base urges are socially revealed. The punch line of a joke suddenly reduces or relieves threat, perhaps even giving a sense of triumph over danger (as in the cartoon example), or successful and acceptable rebellion against a limitation. The joke may allow, for example, the self to feel superior over another, without feeling that one is inflicting excessive degradation. Humor becomes "sick" and sour when excessive degradation of another is used to achieve this sense of self-supremacy, and the action of joking is not taken as play by both humorist and audience.

SLIPS OF THE TONGUE

Slips of the tongue can also stem from unconscious mental processes. Many are based on phonetic factors and processing errors. Others occur because of conflicts in meaning. In the latter slips, elements of the consciously intended theme of discourse relate too closely to some other motivated schema than the working model being mainly used for the organization of the current speech episode. A word from the emergent schema replaces one to be placed in the expected sentence. The speaker may be unaware of the warded-off motives and not understand the slip, or may have been aware but unwilling to communicate the subjective ideas. This is what is now called a *Freudian slip* rather than a simple error of word choice and articulation (Motley, Camden, and Baars 1979).

The Freudian slip can be an intrusion in spite of defenses. It is an aspect of what Freud called the psychopathology of everyday life (Freud 1901). The stress that occurs because of urges opposed by defenses creates a dynamic situation where either consciousness may be punctured by intrusion, or salient omissions may occur. The slip involves both the intruded word and the omitted intended one. Sometimes there are reasons for both the intrusion and the omission (Brenner 1982).

Stress is even greater after serious life events, as noted in chapter 1. Defenses increase, as do intrusions and omissions larger than a word. A more thorough review of control processes and defensive outcomes can now be undertaken.

10

The Mechanisms
of Defense

COMPETING AIMS influence what becomes conscious: one wants, on the one hand, to master threats and stressors and, on the other, to avoid painful states of mind such as may occur when one realizes the emotional implications of a serious event . Some avoidance is healthy, permitting a kind of dose-by-dose working-through process with periods of restoration between other periods of high turbulence. At other times, avoidance of consciousness can be so defensive that it has maladaptive consequences —as in the case of Marilyn. I shall use only a segment from this case (discussed in more detail in Horowitz et al. 1984) to illustrate some of the transitions between a person's states of mind in regard to the theme of sadness after a death—in this case, Marilyn's mother's.

After the death of her mother, Marilyn had a variety of states of mind during the mourning process, states ranging from frightening sadness to giddy excitement in which she impulsively sought out almost any relationship with a man. Of course, she was frequently hurt by the outcome of these relationships, and would swing back into a mood so depressed that she attempted suicide.

Her mother had died quite suddenly, when Marilyn was in a troubled relationship with a man. Her sorrowful reaction to bereavement strained that relationship, and he left her. Marilyn told herself that things would never get better, that she would now be alone forever. These reactive ideas to her two losses were associated with the belief that she would be worthless, and would fall apart if she did not have someone to relate to at all times. She therefore felt despairing fear and entered a distraught state of mind. These experiences were organized by a role-relationship model in which she was a waif, pining unsuccessfully for another person who was lost or would not pay attention to her.

This role-relationship model of a waif pining and searching in vain for a lost caregiver organized a severely distraught state of mind in which Marilyn felt frightening sadness. This state was unbearable so there were motives for defenses against it. The control processes set in motion to prevent entry into this state, or continuance of it, shifted her state of mind into one of giddy excitement in which she risked harm to herself by impulsively flinging herself at men.

These control processes were unconscious but purposive. Of Marilyn, one can say that she had a defensive *purpose,* which was to avoid the state of distraught fear and despair. And, she had defensive *processes*—the ways in which the fear-evoking theme was inhibited. The defensive *outcomes* were, then, the repression and suppression of this theme as well as her use of the giddily excited state as a compromise parodying her wishes and masking her fears.

The defensive processes I have mentioned could have inhibited unconscious mental processes at several levels. The memories of her mother and boyfriend could be inhibited from recollection. Reactive ideas about the memory of the loss could be inhibited: she could *not* think that she was now alone; or if she did, she could *not* associate this idea with the next that things would never get better. Marilyn might also inhibit the role-relationship model of the dreaded state, the one in which she was an abandoned waif.

At the same time that some schemas, associational networks, and memories may be inhibited, others may be facilitated to take their place in the flow and organization of information. That facilitation can also involve a reciprocal inhibition of what she aimed to avoid. Marilyn could facilitate a self-schema of herself as a star, one certain to get admiration from some new and interesting figure. This was the role-relationship model that organized many experiences in her giddily excited state of mind. Marilyn could focus on her own real sexual attractiveness, think of going out to bars, and then be caught up in the many perceptual stimuli of the encounters that ensued.

The control processes inhibited both conscious representation of ideas around the theme of sadness for the loss of her mother and her lover, and the role-relationship model as a waif abandoned by a caregiver, and facili-

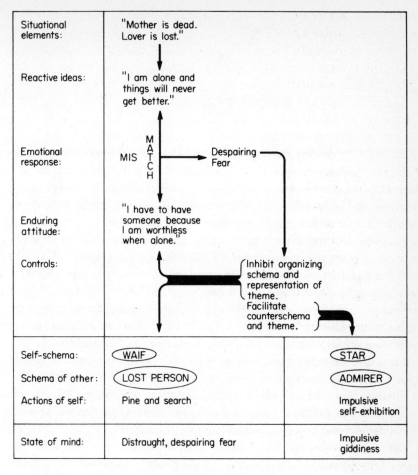

Figure 10.1
The Interaction of Various Types of Control

tated the role-relationship model of a sexy star admired by a man. The excited giddy state was associated with a defensive outcome called *acting out*, the engagement in actions without conscious reflection about their consequences or the reasons for undertaking them. Though maladaptive behavior, acting out was also a defense against another type of maladaptive behavior—the contemplation of suicide to get out of her severely distraught, frighteningly sad state. The interaction of various types of control, those over the representation of ideas and those over the choice of schema for organizing ideas and a state of mind, are shown in figure 10.1.

I shall return to a discussion of how controls work. First there will a review of the history.

Background

An early study of defense was made by Breuer and Freud (1895) in one of the first psychoanalytic works. The defensive outcome described was repression; the process was inhibition of traumatic memories. The purpose, as in the case of Marilyn, was to avoid overwhelming emotional experiences from the conflict involved in recollecting such memories. Freud went on to describe other defense mechanisms. (For a readable history of these early discoveries, see Freud's *Introductory Lectures on Psychoanalysis* [1914–17].)

The first major classification of mechanisms of defense was provided by Anna Freud in *The Ego and the Mechanisms of Defense* (1936). Later, Heinz Hartmann, Ernst Kris, and Rudolph Loewenstein (1964) focused more on coping with reality as aspects of defense, in addition to defense against instinctual drives such as sexual and aggressive aims. Norma Haan (1977), building also on work by Theodore Kroeber (1963), developed a clearer classification of defenses and demonstrated that defensive outcomes can be reliably classified by judges making independent ratings of behavior. George Vaillant (1975) developed a defense-classification system according to developmental level, from primitive to mature.

Vaillant describes eighteen mechanisms as divided into four sets. The first set of primitive, pathological, or narcissistic mechanisms includes delusional projection, psychotic denial, and distortion. I will define these mechanisms in the "Common Defense Mechanisms" section beginning on page 191. The second set of immature defenses includes projection, schizoid fantasy, hypochondriasis, passive-aggressive behavior, and acting out. The third set, at neurotic levels of development, includes intellectualization, repression, displacement, reaction formation, and association. Finally, the fourth set of mature mechanisms includes altruism, humor, suppression, anticipation, and sublimation.

In several extensive studies of men over a long span of adult life, Vaillant found that there was consistency in the styles of defense each man used. He also found that some defensive styles worked better than others in accomplishing long-range adaptation to life stress. These more adaptative styles of defense became the more mature mechanisms in his classification system. For example, before his work, suppression was regarded as a pathological defense mechanism that might result in a "bottling up of the emotions" and in psychophysiological symptoms. In Vaillant's studies, this deliberate conscious effort to put out of mind unpleasant and unsolvable problems and stresses was useful rather than maladaptive. On the other hand, recent studies suggest that repressive styles may be associated with increasing rates of physical ill health (Singer 1987). A specific defensive operation may have both adaptive and maladaptive outcomes.

Common Defense Mechanisms

Before discussing various control processes, let me define some common defense mechanisms, many of which were discussed in earlier chapters. The mechanisms are listed in alphabetical order.

ACTING OUT

Acting out consists of impulsive action without reflection or conscious thought of the consequences, whether good or bad. The suddenness of action may reduce time that would otherwise be spent tensely considering what to do in terms of both desires and feared consequences. In acting out, feelings are sometimes displaced from one arena to another. A teenager angry at home may engage in delinquent acts rather than express hostility directly to his or her parents.

ALTRUISM

In altruism, one deals with emotional conflicts, or internal or external stress, by dedicating oneself to fulfilling the needs of others instead of one's own.

CONVERSION OF PASSIVE TO ACTIVE

To defend against the threat of a weak and vulnerable position, the person may conceptually place self in the active role. Identification with an aggressor is one form of this defense.

DENIAL

The most frequent defense is denial: the avoidance of awareness of some painful external reality. It is accomplished by withholding conscious understanding of the meaning and implications of what is perceived—especially by refusing to take in the extended significance of new information.

Magical thinking ("Pay no attention and it will go away") also plays a powerful role in denial. Within limits, denial is a normal process used to slow down the response to bad news. Persons with myocardial infarctions treated in coronary care units persist in telling themselves and others that their pain is due to "indigestion." Physicians may ignore the early warning signs of cancer in themselves on the grounds that "it means nothing." While denial is considered a "normal" defense, since it may allow a graded acceptance of bad news, it is maladaptive if it interferes with rational action.

DEVALUATION

In devaluation, one deals with emotional conflicts, or internal or external stress, by attributing exaggerated negative qualities to self or others.

DISAVOWAL

To avoid stressful news or its implications, the person may assert that the situation does not matter to him or her; and to cover over unwanted inner fears, wishes, or feelings, the person may say that these emotions are not important to the self.

DISPLACEMENT

In displacement, the avoided ideas and feelings are transferred to some other person, situation, or object. For example, hypochondriacal patients may displace worry and ward off a concern that their minds are failing, and focus concern instead on a body part.

DISSOCIATION

In dissociation, one deals with emotional conflicts, or internal or external stress, by a temporary alteration in the integrative functions of consciousness or identity.

DISTORTION

Various forms of altering meanings and sliding evaluations can be used to distort a stressful topic. Devaluation, disavowal, exaggeration, and minimization are all forms of distortion.

EXAGGERATION

In order to protect self-esteem or emotional balance, certain meanings can be given exaggerated value. For example, personal strength can be appraised in an exaggerated way to avoid fear before a fight.

HUMOR

One may deal with emotional conflicts, or internal or external stress, by using humor and emphasizing the amusing or ironic aspects of the conflict or stress.

IDEALIZATION

In idealization, one deals with emotional conflicts, or internal or external stress, by attributing exaggerated positive qualities to self or others.

INTELLECTUALIZATION

In intellectualization the person avoids the emotional implications of a topic by dealing with it on a purely ideational level. In a related defense, *generalization,* the person deals with the topic at an abstract rather than a personal level to avoid excessive emotion.

ISOLATION

The process of isolation consists of splitting of ideas and feelings, as in having the obsessive idea or image of "killing" without feeling anger or hostility toward the object. This defense leads to flatness of affect or seeming indifference.

MINIMIZATION

As a maneuver to reduce stress, the person undervalues a topic. For example, the degree to which the self was to blame for an accident could be minimized to avoid shame and guilt.

OMNIPOTENT CONTROL

In using omnipotent control to defend against the stress of having others abandon or fail to attend properly to the self, the person acts from an attitude of having total control of the object. Sometimes, when the stress is fear that the environment will be overwhelming, the defense of omnipotent control includes attitudes of an irrational nature, in which the person believes that wishes, rituals, or incantations will bend environmental forces to his or her will.

PASSIVE AGGRESSION

In passive aggression, one deals with emotional conflicts, or internal or external stress, by indirectly and unassertively expressing aggression toward others.

PROJECTION

In projection, a warded-off impulse or idea is attributed to the external world. For example, people who struggle with their own hatred may develop a delusion that others are out to get them. This gives one an acceptable rationale for hating, and allows one to avoid recognition of one's own destructive impulses.

PROJECTIVE IDENTIFICATION

In projective identification, an aspect of the self that one does not wish to acknowledge is placed not in the working model of the self but in that of another to whom the self is closely related. Although the other is then seen as having a bad attribute, the self remains closely affiliated with the other. Instead of distancing the self from the other, who may now be viewed as being angry at the self (rather than vice versa), one may provoke the other person to behave in a hostile manner—thus providing a reality basis for locating the anger of the self as if it were in the other person.

RATIONALIZATION

Rationalization consists of proclaiming logical reasons for actions actually performed for other reasons, usually to avoid stress or self-blame. Rationalization is also used to justify avoiding unpleasant duties.

REACTION FORMATION

In reaction formation, a warded-off idea or feeling is replaced by an unconsciously derived but consciously felt emphasis on its opposite. For example, an older boy is jealous of a baby brother and has a fantasy that if the baby were to die, he would again be the center of his parents' attention. Having such a fantasy, he realizes, is "bad," because he has been "ordered" to love the baby. Reaction formation consists of replacing the wish to be rid of the brother with an exaggerated concern for the baby's welfare. If the defense works adaptively, he cares for his brother even though he wishes, occasionally, for the restoration of his only-child status. If the conflict is intense, the reaction formation may lead to symptoms. For instance, such a boy might have a compulsion to check up on the baby to make sure it is all right, not suffocated or kidnaped.

REGRESSION

Regression consists of turning back the maturational clock and returning to earlier modes of dealing with the world. Some persons confronted with the stress and environmental cues of hospitalization become, for example, "regressively" childlike in terms of demands, demeanor, and dependence on others.

REPRESSION

Repression consists of withholding from conscious awareness an idea or a feeling. Conscious expulsion of thoughts from the mind is *suppression.* Repression differs from suppression in being an involuntary rather than a voluntary process. It may operate to exclude from awareness what was once experienced as inability to remember an important but traumatic event (for example, amnesia) or to curb ideas and feelings that have not yet reached consciousness but would emerge were it not for the defensive process. For example, one may repress the awareness of erotic arousal by a person inappropriate for sexual love, or may repress hatred for someone one "ought to love."

SOMATIZATION

In somatization, one deals with emotional conflicts, or internal or external stress, by preoccupation with physical symptoms disproportionate to any actual physical disturbance.

SPLITTING

In splitting, one deals with emotional conflicts, or internal or external stress, by viewing oneself or others as all good or all bad, failing to integrate the positive and negative qualities of self and others into cohesive images; often the same person will be alternately idealized and devalued.

SUBLIMATION

Sublimation is the process whereby one replaces an unacceptable wish with a course of action that is similar to the wish but does not conflict with one's value system. For example, aggressive wishes may be sublimated into working hard to fight against and solve social problems.

SUPPRESSION

In suppression, one deals with emotional conflicts, or internal or external stress, by intentionally avoiding thinking about disturbing problems, wishes, feelings, or experiences.

TURNING AGAINST THE SELF

In the defense of turning against the self, an inappropriate impulse directed outward is redirected at the self. The guilt that would follow from aggression against an object of hatred can be avoided by hurting oneself (as by self-mutilation).

UNDOING

Undoing expresses both the impulse and its opposite, as in being very domineering one minute and then offering obsequiously to defer to another. In rapid repetition, undoing may lead to indecisiveness.

The Processes of Control

One way to regulate emotion is to control the rate of processing of themes and to choose which topics to think about or communicate. The processes of control can work at different levels. I shall consider here the control of mental set, of person schemas, and of conscious representation and sequences of ideas. By varying how these regulatory processes are used one may accomplish the various defensive maneuvers just listed.

REGULATION OF MENTAL SET

First are those controls that regulate the big picture, or mental set. These control processes act on the decision about what theme will be the next topic for consciousness. A person cannot think about all his or her unfinished business at once. Some kind of choice, consciously and unconsciously made, determines which conceptual area to contemplate.

Suppose a person has several topics stored in active memory. These themes await further information processing. Control systems inhibit and facilitate these options so that only some of them gain representation. Control systems also help determine whether conscious representation will be a blend of words, pictures, or enactions, or whether one mode will predominate.

The processes of choosing a theme and the modes for contemplating it can have several outcomes, as outlined in table 10.1. One of these outcomes is *adaptive regulation.* Take inhibition of a theme, for example. Since a person in threatening circumstances could become exhausted or confused by thinking continuously about the threat, it might be more adaptive to have usefully paced periods of thinking and not thinking about it, which would provide moments of needed rest. On the other hand, total avoidance of the conceptual area might mean the person was unprepared to handle relevant life issues. In such *defensive regulation,* while the inhibition of the topic reduces emotional response, it does not succeed as well as modulated use of this control. Finally, the person may be unable adequately to use this kind of control. We might then expect states of mind marked by daze, confusion, or chaotic jumbles of emotion. We would judge these to be signs of *dysregulation:* that is, that the person was succumbing to stress.

The most important kinds of topic and mental-set control are those affecting intentions, temporal set, sequential set, representational set, attentional set, and activation (see table 10.1). *The adaptive regulation outcomes are marked by flexibility, including use of both reality-based and fantasy-based modes of thinking; the defensive regulatory outcomes are marked by rigidity; the dysregulatory outcomes are marked by loss of volition.*

Note also that the purposes for control may vary and must also relate to other motives, as for expression. A given control process, such as inhibiting a theme, may be adaptive to the purpose of reducing emotional arousal and maladaptive to the purpose of letting others know how upset and in need of help one is. In analyzing any configuration or episode, it is useful to disentangle the purposes, processes, and outcomes of mental controls.

As a brief illustration, consider an architect at work planning the construction design of a building. She may think of the immediate design problem at hand, of her need for the fee she can collect only when the blueprints are approved, or about some topic even more remote from the task at hand—perhaps of how a recent flood destroyed her car, garage, and garden and created a financial strain on her family. For the architect to cope with this situation effectively, it may be best to spend time concentrating on the design problem, and to think later about the implications of the flood disaster and about how to repair the damage to her home.

Were she to think intrusively about the flood, she might be unable to work well on the building plans. Were she never to think about the flood, she would in effect be denying that something important had happened. When thinking about the flood deliberately, the architect might think in terms of its short-range or long-range implications, using controls for temporal set to organize associations into the appropriate sequence. For short-range planning, she might think through what she needed to do in terms of immediate repairs. In terms of long-range plans, she could relate this set of intentions to other intentions—that is, to her plans for a longer stretch of time. In the period of intense planning of repair details, she could usefully pause and restore her morale at a time of dismay with a fantasy of how nice the house will look when it is fixed up.

TABLE 10.1
Regulation of Topics and Mental Set

Processes	Outcomes		
	Regulation		
Types of Control	Adaptive	Maladaptive	Dysregulation
Intentional Hierarchy: Selection of next topic for thought	Dosing (periods of time on and off stressful topic)	Forgetting of stressful topics	
Temporal Set: Short or long orientation	Looking at only one step at a time, relating the event to a lifespan	Denial of urgency of threat, disavowal of long-range implications of changes	
Sequential Set: Problem solving or reverie	Thinking only about what to do next, restorative fantasies	Work obsession during relaxation (a form of undoing); autistic fantasy	Chaotic intrusion of stressful topics; distraught states such as panic, confusion, exhaustion
Representational Set: Words, images, enactions in isolation or with cross translation	Intellectual analysis: Solving problems in words because images evoke too many emotions	Numbing of emotional responses by words without images, images without words; isolation	
Locus of attention toward external or internal sources of information	Restorative changes between activity and contemplation	Compulsive action to avoid thought; remembrance and fantasy to avoid action	
Activation Level: Regulating rate of information flow in various systems of representation	Excitation and rest cycles	Hypervigilance; avoidant sleeping	

REGULATION OF PERSON SCHEMAS

As already discussed, percepts may be simultaneously constructed into meanings by multiple person schemas that may compete for primacy before conscious representations or actions are organized. Defensive purposes may also influence the selection of which person schemas achieve that primacy. The concept of variable control of person schemas such as role-relationship models can be clarified by considering how a person will work through a stressful life experience such as the death of a loved one.

Memories of the life and death of the person as related to the self are reviewed during mourning. Different states of mind occur during this passage through grief. Sometimes one views the death as a loss: a desired person who wanted to stay has been taken away by illness or accident. At other times, one views the death as abandonment, according to a role-relationship model in which the self is needy, the other a deliberate deserter. At still other times, one does not recognize that the deceased is dead, and organizes current life plans in expectation of reunion. The latter role-relationship model produces a mood of hope that can protect against the former ones of sad despair or anger, just as anger can protect against sadness, and vice versa.

The same life event, the death, has different meanings in different states of mind according to which working models are applied to its interpretation. When one interpretation leads to excessive painful and out-of-control emotional response, one can achieve another interpretation by shifting the mood-organizing person schemas.

By use of the "right" self-schema, the person may have a heightened sense of identity and self-efficacy. For example, the person who has a usual state of mind organized by a view of the self as an ordinary person may face an extraordinary challenge, which causes him or her to organize responses by a stronger, more competent self-concept than the ordinary one. The sense of mastery and the mood organized by this resilient self-concept may allow the excitement of the stressful events and the stress response to have a positive aspect.

To defend against the threat of feeling overwhelmed, the person may activate a grandiose self-schema, leading to reassuring but risky beliefs in nonvulnerability to threat. This constitutes a defensive outcome. Similarly, regression to a view that one is a protected child who does not need to remain alert to threat would be a defensive outcome since stabilization of an effective, adult self-schema would be more adaptive. If only fragmentary self-schemas are available for organizing experience, the outcome may

199

be the experience of a sense of losing identity associated with either panic or depersonalization.

The closer an active schema is to actual reality, the more adaptive may be the outcome of the control processes that determine whether it will become a part of the working model. In a time of rapidly changing stress, different schemas may have to be used in succession to achieve the most adaptive outcomes. Persons who rigidly control and maintain the same working model may be too static in response—a defensive outcome.

As certain inner working models threaten to create displeasure, the person may change the schemas in use to reduce this threat. Emotions and intentions that have been related to the self may be shifted in schematic location to be properties of someone else. The irrationality of these dislocations is maladaptive even though the control processes reduce emotional pain and prevent identity crises—a defensive outcome. Such defensive outcomes include the well-known classical positions of *role reversal; projection* of disavowed emotions and traits of self into the inner view of others; and *displacement,* where dangerous wishes toward another person are shifted to some safer object.

A stressful, conflictual situation demands somewhat novel and resilient changes. The person may have to try different inner schemas such as role-relationship models until the right one, or the right new combination, is found. When an adaptive outcome is not possible, the person may nonetheless use such control processes to arrive at a defensive outcome. A conversion of self as passive to self as active by identifying with the stronger, aggressive person has already been defined as an example of such defensive levels of regulation. These control processes that affect person schemas are summarized in table 10.2.

REGULATION OF CONSCIOUS REPRESENTATION AND SEQUENCES OF IDEAS

Many psychodynamic insights come from close observation of the sequence of a patient's stream of consciousness. Whether a person is directly telling a therapist about a stressful event or saying whatever comes to mind in free association, the linear flow of ideas is seldom as well organized as words in print or a planned speech. The topic jumps about; the ideas about it halt and restart; the meanings take new and divergent routes and then circle back. Inferences can be drawn about the reasons for each variation from an intended line of discourse. These inferences often concern controls that are instituted for defensive purposes, to avoid embarrassing disclosures or to reduce the threat of unwanted emotional states of mind. These controls of conscious representation, expression, and sequences of ideas are summarized in table 10.3.

TABLE 10.2

Regulation of Person Schemas

Processes	Outcomes		
	Regulation		Dysregulation
Types of Control	Adaptive	Maladaptive	
Altering the self-schemas used in forming an inner model of a situation	Heightened sense of identity and self-efficacy	Omnipotent disregard of personal vulnerability; "as if" self-concepts; regression to earlier self-concepts; unrealistic avoidance of responsibility; dissociation	Depersonalization; derealization; chaotic lapse of identity; annihilation anxiety; panic upon separations
Altering the role-relationship models used in forming an inner model of a situation	Resilient changes to maintain coherence between working model and actual situation; sublimation; altruism	Role reversals; identification with aggressor; projective identification; dissociations and splitting; altruistic surrender; use of others as self-extensions; idealization; passive-aggression; displacement	

Table 10.3 lists some processes that may control the sequence of re-presentations—processes that begin with the linkage between representations, that then revise working models to accord with new information, and that end with practicing new forms until they become new schemas.

Let us consider these controls of thinking about a topic in relation to a stressful new experience.

A person uses associational networks and schemas to seek information from memory in order to understand a stressful situation and in order to mobilize skills for mastering it. This process includes anticipating what is likely to occur in the future and how to meet future demands. Emotional

TABLE 10.3

Regulation of Conscious Representations and Sequencing

Processes	Outcomes		
	Regulation		Dysregulation
Types of Control	Adaptive	Maladaptive	
Representing next ideas			
Facilitation of associations	Contemplation of implications	Rumination and doubting	
Inhibition of associations	Dosing; selective inattention; careful choice of what is expressed; suppression	Denial; disavowal; repression; isolation; numbing; communicative reluctance; somatization; acting out	
Sequencing ideas			
Seeking information	Understanding; learning new skills	Intellectualization	
Switching concepts	Emotional balancing	Undoing; reaction formation; displacement	Intrusion of ideas; emotional flooding; indecision; paralysis of action
Sliding meanings and valuations	Humor, wisdom	Exaggeration; minimization; devaluation; reaction formation	
Arranging information into decision trees	Problem solving	Rationalization	
Revising working models	Learning; identifications; acceptance	Externalization; introjection	
Practicing new modes of thinking and acting	Replace previous automatic reactions with new ways of responding	Counterphobic behavioral patterns	

arousal can become too intense, making thinking difficult. From time to time, inhibitions of the representation of ideas and feelings may be needed to restore enough equilibrium to proceed on the topic.

The theme may need to be examined in tolerable doses, one dose at a time, to avoid overload. Switching attitudes about a topic may restore emotional balance. By playing around with the evaluation of different elements in a theme, one may achieve restorative moments of humor or come to inevitable consequences with an appropriate degree of wisdom. By rearranging the information, one can accurately appraise the possibilities, solve problems, and create new solutions. By practicing a new working model, one is gradually desensitized to fear and other painful emotions associated with the stressful new experience; and outmoded ways of doing things gradually become dormant, although never completely erased.

The previous paragraph describes some adaptive outcomes of control processes. Such processes can also lead to the common defensive mechanisms listed earlier in this chapter. The most important of these are unconscious but purposive forgetting (repression), the avoidance of evaluating perceptions (denial, disavowal), the numbing of emotional responsivity to a topic (intellectualization, isolation), persisting vagueness or distortion about what is happening (including rationalization, exaggeration, and minimization), and reaching comforting but irrational decisions (magical undoing, reaction formation).

Three control processes—inhibition, switching concepts, and sliding meaning—can now be illustrated by the case history of Harry (derived from a case report, Horowitz 1974, and also detailed in Horowitz 1986): One night this forty-year-old truck dispatcher took a run himself because he was shorthanded. The load consisted of steel pipe carried in an old truck that had armor between the load bed and the driver's side of the compartment but did not protect the passenger's side. Late that night, Harry passed an attractive and solitary woman hitchhiking on a lonely stretch of highway. Making an impulsive decision to violate the company rule against passengers of any sort, he picked her up.

A short time later, a car veered across the divider line and entered his lane, threatening a head-on collision. Harry pulled across the shoulder of the road into an area that seemed clear, but crashed abruptly into a pile of gravel. The pipe shifted, penetrated the cab of the truck on the passenger's side, and impaled the woman. Harry crashed into the steering wheel and windshield and was briefly unconscious. Regaining consciousness, he was met with the grisly sight of his dead companion.

After the highway patrol arrived Harry was taken by ambulance to a hospital emergency room. No fractures were found, his lacerations were sutured, and he remained overnight for observation. His wife, who sat up with him, found him anxious and dazed that night, talking of the events in a fragmentary and incoherent way so that the story was not clear.

The next day he was released. Against his doctor's recommendations for rest, and his wife's wishes, he returned to work. From then on, for several days, he continued his regular work as if nothing had happened. There was an immediate session with his superiors and with legal advisers; and while severely reprimanded, he was not fired. Thereafter Harry thought about the accident from time to time but was surprised to find how little it seemed to affect him emotionally. He was responsible and well ordered in his work, but his wife reported that he thrashed around in his sleep, ground his teeth, and seemed more tense and irritable than usual.

Four weeks after the accident, he had a nightmare in which mangled bodies appeared, and he awoke in panic. Throughout the following days, he had recurrent intense and intrusive images of the dead woman's body. These images, together with ruminations about her, were accompanied by anxiety attacks of growing severity. He developed a phobia about driving to and from work. From his regular habit of weekend drinking he went to nightly use of growing quantities of alcohol. He had temper outbursts over minor frustrations and experienced difficulty concentrating at work and even while watching television. Harry tried unsuccessfully to dispel his guilty feelings about the accident. As a result of his complaints of insomnia, irritability, and increased alcohol consumption, his doctor referred him for psychiatric treatment.

In the psychotherapy of Harry, various important themes, which were inhibited at times during the stress response period, were worked through. These themes included guilt over being part of the cause of the woman's death, guilt over the sexual fantasies about her he had had before the accident, guilt that he felt glad to be alive when he realized that she had died, and fear and anger that he had been involved in an accident and in her death. The fear was that the accident might be repeated; the anger was at destiny, the other driver, and everyone associated with the accident, including the police who investigated afterward. He also revealed an episodic magical belief that the woman had "caused" the accident by her hitchhiking, and some of his anger was directed toward her. Being angry with her led him back to feeling guilty.

These themes were not activated by the terrible accident and death alone. Friction and lack of sexual interest in his life had led to fantasies about having sexual affairs with other women and to flirtations in bars that had caused him to feel guilty before the accident. He was angry with his wife before the accident, and that anger became associated with the anger at the woman hitchhiker after the accident. The accident and all the associations to it formed a thematic complex sharply incongruent with Harry's wishes to remain bodily whole and unharmed, with his wish to view himself as a moral man who did well and did not harm others, and with his wish to share fairly with other human beings the good and bad things that happen in life.

The violence involved in the accident can be conceptually organized by role-relationship models with victim and aggressor roles. For three of the themes already mentioned, the self can be placed in the aggressor role; and for another three, the self can be placed in the victim role. Self-as-aggressor views might lead to guilt that a victim, the woman hitchhiker, died; while self-as-victim roles are more likely to be associated with fear or anger.

Of the three themes related to the self-concept as aggressor, the first is often called *survivor guilt*. Harry felt relief that he was alive when "someone had to die." The idea "someone had to die" was part of a magical belief that fate has to take some victims. It was like the idea of a bullet having, or not having, "my name on it" during battle. Recollection of this idea and of his relief elicited a sense of guilt in him at being the survivor.

He also felt as if he had caused the woman to die, because both of the fantasies that had led him to pick her up in the first place, and of the magical belief that if he had not picked her up, she would have lived. This belief was part of the idea that had he not picked her up there would have been no accident: in other words, that he had the magical power to choose the victim destined for death, and had somehow chosen her through his own desire to survive. This second theme involving strong self-schemas is an irrational train of ideas that is typical of the many topics of reflection that occur after a traumatic event and that are a part of working through to completion the active memories of and associations to the event.

The third theme in a set of self-concepts as strong and aggressively assertive concerned Harry's sexual fantasies about the woman before the crash. When recalled afterward, these fantasies were incongruent with his sense of moral fidelity to his wife. Recollection of this theme about the accident led to guilty feelings.

Of three themes involving the set of self-schema of victim, one was the apprehension that he could have been in the woman's place. Harry was appalled by the vivid memory images of the gory damage to her body and the possibility that his body could have had similar rips, tears, and breakages. The vivid image of his body sundered and the memories of her injuries and contorted body position interfered with his usual attitude of personal invulnerability. The result was a state of fearful dread and tension.

Harry could also become fearful when he thought of how he would be accused by the company of breaking the rules. He might be fired, losing both financial security and a good work identity. In this second self-as-victim theme, he would have to think through all the possible consequences.

The third victim theme was also organized by a self-schema as victim in a relationship in which the young woman was in an aggressor role. This role-relationship model organized a train of thought about how *she* made the accident happen by appearing on the highway in a tempting or needy manner. Of course, thinking in this way would not mesh with Harry's own sense of what was realistic, as the accident was in no way her fault. As he was having this train of thought, he would first feel angry and then guilty for being angry with her.

Each of these six themes could cause intrusive ideas and pangs of intense feelings that Harry wished to ward off. At first he controlled his mental set rigidly so that the topic of the accident did not gain conscious representation. Then he entered into phases in which active memory of the traumatic events did lead to conscious representation. He had the nightmare of mangled bodies and the daytime recurrent unbidden images of the woman's body. The themes of fear of bodily injury and of survivor guilt were the first to be consciously represented.

It is now possible to analyze a theme in terms of how different controls of conscious representation and sequencing might operate once the controls of mental set permit some contemplation of the warded-off topic. I shall thus in the next section examine, in respect to Harry's theme of survivor guilt, the control processes of inhibition of associations, switching of concepts, and sliding of meanings.

Analysis of a Theme: Survivor Guilt

As part of the trauma he remembered, Harry perceived the dead woman's body and his own bodily sensations of being alive, and immediately associated the presence of death with the fear of finding himself dead. The difference between the expectation of finding himself dead, and the realization that someone else and not he was dead, led to a momentary state of relief.

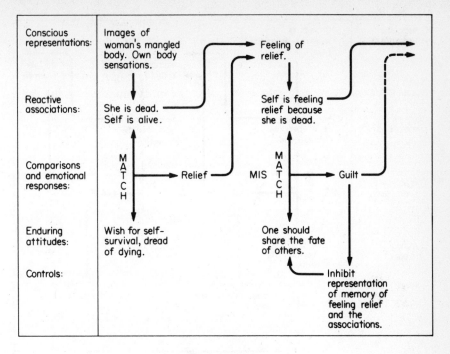

Figure 10.2

Inhibition of Representation of Specific Ideas as a Control Process

Even in such extreme stress, there may be momentary elation as one compares the fear of death with the awareness of being alive. This moment of elation gives way to other emotional reactions as other ideas occur. As conscious experience of relief, however, is remembered over time, it may come to seem very strange—as it did to Harry, whose memory of feeling relief was incongruent with his idea of how a moral person ought to behave upon finding another person has died. The appropriate moral feeling, according to Harry's value schema, was deep regret for the suffering of another, and even a readiness to absorb some of the bad fate so it would not be so harsh to the other.

INHIBITION OF IDEAS OF THE THEME

Once the feeling of relief has been consciously represented and perceived as discrepant with value schemas, it leads to guilty remorse (see figure 10.2). This guilt is so intense as to be unbearable if it continues to escalate. As preconscious processing assesses the ideas as possibly expanding feelings of guilt, anxiety about that threat is aroused. As a result, representations of the threatening ideas and emotions are inhibited.

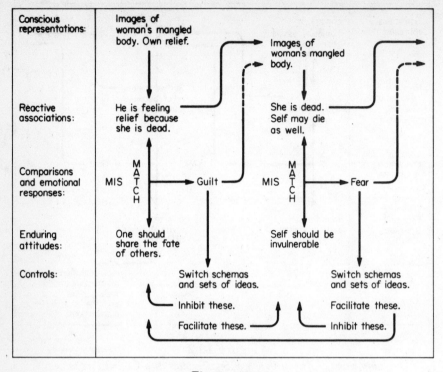

Figure 10.3
The Switching of Themes Represented as a Control Process

SWITCHING THEMES OR SUBTHEMES

In some instances, inhibition of representations is not sufficient to satisfy defensive purposes. Additional controls, such as switching between schemas and sets of ideas, may be added. Different associations to the images of the woman's dead body could lead Harry to feel guilty because he felt relief, or to fear that he might share her fate. He could switch back and forth between these themes, using the guilty set to reduce excessive fear, and the fearful set to reduce excessive guilt, as expressed diagrammatically in figure 10.3.

SLIDING OF MEANINGS

The third and last control process to be illustrated by Harry's case is *sliding,* one of a variety of ways to distort meanings in order to prevent a threatening state of mind (see figure 10.4). In the case of Harry, the idea

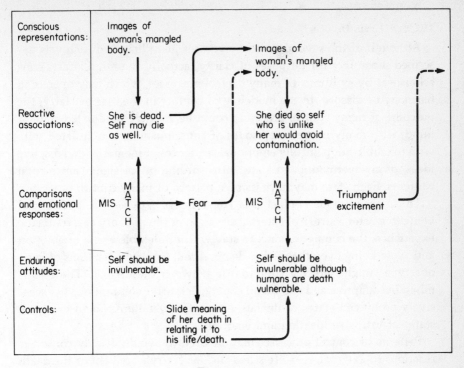

Figure 10.4
The Sliding of Meanings as a Control Process

that the young woman was dead led to the idea that he, too, might die, and so to fear. Motivated by the threat of a chaotically fearful state of mind, a Harry vulnerable to such a state might prevent it by sliding the meaning of personal vulnerability into an opposite direction, adopting an idea that her death confirmed his own immortality. In order to accomplish this defense, Harry might fantasize that the fates had selected her as a victim. She died so that he, who is unlike her, might avoid contamination with death as a victim. The irrational sequence of ideas becomes: she is dead; death is "in the air," but he is unlike her, so he will live. The escape from death is associated with triumphant excitement rather than fear. By sliding meanings, Harry uses the fact that she has died to prove that she is the kind who dies. That he has not died "proves" the irrational idea, "I am not the kind who dies. I am invulnerable!" This transition from ideas evoking fear to ideas evoking triumphant excitement is diagrammed in figure 10.4.

209

THE SYNTHESIS OF CONTROLS

Although of the several control processes just illustrated each was described separately for purposes of clarity, actually the mind affects consciousness by synthesis of many control processes, which may operate in harmony or discord. In the modeling of conflict in the case of Harry, the outcome of many control processes could be an undermodulated state of mind, with many intrusive episodes of consciousness; a modulated state with tolerable but painfully emotional sequences of memories and reactive ideas; or an overmodulated state with warding off of significant mental contents. Each state may have its own pattern of many control processes.

Thus, unconscious conflict is a competition between goals: one goal being to master a stressful external situation or the memory of a traumatic experience; the competing one, to stay within tolerable levels of emotion and avoid being overwhelmed or demoralized. Control operations of various types might effect a compromise between these goals. The results might be: adaptive and successful coping, defensive solutions (as in excessively prolonged states of denial), or regulatory failures (as in excessive states of intrusive ideation and emotion).

Patterns of control processes may be used to avoid not only conscious reactions to external, real-life stress such as Harry's accident or the death of Marilyn's mother but also such internal elements as arousal of conflicted motives that would lead to stressful conscious experiences or behavior. Some patterns of control are used habitually to avoid stressful ideas and emotions, as I shall discuss in the next chapter.

11

Unconscious
Neurotic Conflict

IN NEUROTIC DISTURBANCE of personality, one finds a tendency to repetition of the same unrewarding patterns in interpersonal behavior and to an enduring avoidance of conscious knowledge of unpleasant aspects of the self. This maladaptive combination can be changed during adult life, but the process of change is not easy. In this chapter, unconscious neurotic conflict is modeled, and the hard work of modifying personality considered. In such conflict, one uses certain of the defense mechanisms considered in the preceding chapter in habitual, if maladaptive, ways to prevent conscious recognition of conflicts within the self.

Personality consists in part, as I suggested in chapter 1, of a person's repertoire of states: those one desires, fears, or seeks to stabilize as a defensive compromise between wish and fear. One's personality has also a repertoire of schemas which organize wishes, fears, and defensive positions. In addition, personality is in part a repertoire of habitually used controls affecting the nature of consciousness.

In personality development, control styles that have worked well to master previous stressful situations tend to be repeated in response to new stress. Habitual control patterns become an aspect of character and are so automatic that one may be relatively unaware of one's own means of coping and defense. On the other hand, the person who becomes aware of unconscious avoidance and distortion can make new alternative choices.

New life experiences may also convince one that unconsciously expected dangers are not excessively threatening. The conscious intention to take risks can override the unconscious intention to "play it safe." The conscious intention to be cautious and realistic can override unconscious impulses toward immediate gratification. Characteristic defensive styles can be modified by repetition of such conscious efforts.

Of the many character styles, two prototypes—histrionic and compulsive—have become relatively well formulated and will serve to illustrate habitual defenses and issues of enduring conflict involving unconscious schemas. Psychodynamic psychotherapy can modify such habitual defensive styles and unconscious schematic conflicts, as I shall demonstrate for each prototype.

The Histrionic Style

In the hysterical or histrionic defensive style of avoiding knowledge, one has strongly emotional states of mind but experiences them as more under-modulated than do most people (Shapiro 1965; Horowitz 1977a,b). The habitual style of such persons seems to rest on a general aim of avoiding conscious recognition of why their experienced emotions occur. They seem especially to want to avoid an anxious or guilty knowledge of the self as having an active part in emotional situations with others. Such persons dread the responsibility of having bad thoughts, emotions, and actions. A defensive purpose is to avoid knowledge about such themes. The defensive outcome of control processes is conscious ignorance of what is going on. Because of the continuation of this ignorance over time, such persons often feel they are drifting aimlessly through life. The general avoidance of personal responsibility often leads one to have an existential sense that one's life experiences are not quite real and that one's current actions do not really count.

In this style, one inhibits at the level of processing information representation of conflicted themes and, at the level of schemas, role-relationship models in which the self is active. Because of the relative defensive inhibition of role-relationship models containing active, responsible self-schemas, such a person tends to excessive use of role-relationship models in which the self is passive and the other is active. In facilitating role-relationship models in which the self is passive, such persons tend to repeat interpersonal relationship patterns in which they take a childlike position and put others in parental surrogate roles.

Often this passivity includes repeated patterns of victim, aggressor, and rescuer scripts. The self gives in, suffers pain from the aggressor, and then expects either that the aggressor will feel guilty and be nice, or that—after one's suffering has been displayed—one will be rescued by someone who defeats the aggressor and cares for one.

The usual actions to obtain the care of an attentive, active, strong parental surrogate figure conspicuously and dramatically display some attribute of the self, or the body, to others. The fact that this is an active display for a deliberate purpose, and to satisfy personal wishes, is inhibited from conscious representation. The self-dramatizing aspect of this personality style has earned it the name *histrionic.*

One inhibits conscious awareness of the wish to get care and attention because the role-relationship models used for organizing this wish contain a fear: that is, that the care sought will be incestuous, destructive, or bad in some other way. Thus, one seeks the care through actions organized according to unconscious schemas. Any attribute that may attract interest from others may be used in setting up a desired but feared interpersonal situation. Sexuality is good for this purpose if the person has an attractive body. Sometimes this ploy leads to a kind of hyperfemininity or hyper-masculinity to excite others (Blacker and Tupin 1977). Underneath this flaunting of gender roles there may be less sexual desire than is apparent to the target person, with impairment of actual sexual performance or personal satisfaction.

A woman, for example, may be unable to have an orgasm; while a man may have difficulty getting or maintaining an erection. One reason for impairment in entering and continuing a sensuously erotic state of mind is fear of the activity of self during intercourse. In safer situations, such as masturbation, orgasm may occur, showing that the difficulty is not neurological or genital in origin.

Other attributes besides an attractive body may be a part of the attention seeking so apparent to others and so disavowed in one's own conscious reflections. Mental characteristics such as high creativity or brilliance may be displayed as "promise," seeking the nurturing mentorship of others. Handicaps—such as a tendency to disturbed states of mind, muscular paralysis, blindness, deafness, or susceptibility to seizures—may not only require realistic adaptation, but be used to get more than necessary attention from others.

Unfortunately, doctors sometimes see the person with a histrionic style only as manipulative when he or she has a real need for care and is expressing worries, fears, anger at helplessness, and frustrations over difficulties with communication.

The attention-seeking behavior of the histrionic style is motivated by wishes for care and organized by role-relationship models in which care is given by active others. Conscious recognition of such wishes and ways of action is ordinarily possible, especially as one takes note of maladaptive but recurrent consequences of the way in which one has sought attachment. But, as I have mentioned, conscious recognition leads to anxiety, shame, or guilt because of unconscious conflicts embedded in the role-relationship models in use. For example, the person may experience the wishes for care as morally taboo: a sexualized approach to a parental figure may be unconsciously felt as incestuous, as an overture to the actual parent. The wish for care itself is associated, however irrationally, with being bad.

Normal persons can tolerate feeling anxious, ashamed, or guilty without necessarily entering undermodulated states of mind. They can contemplate the ideas leading to such emotions, and separate reality from fantasy, rational belief from irrational belief. Persons with a hysterical or histrionic style of warding off self-knowledge have lower tolerance for negative feelings such as fear, shame, guilt, or sadness. While they feel such emotions, they associate them with being out of control. They experience the emotions not so much as being self-formed but as inflicted upon them from some alien source. They feel they cannot do anything about the formation of such emotions through thinking and acting, but instead seek to get out of the emotional state of mind by quickly entering some other state of mind. To avoid an out-of-control state, such persons withhold conscious representation from ideas that might otherwise occur.

Thus is created an enduring but maladaptive constellation. Conscious reflection, which could lead to the eventual revision of schemas, is inhibited in the exact areas of its greatest usefulness. The person is left with immature or primitive role-relationship models, which he or she repeats over and over again as working models of new situations. The conflict is repeated in actions because schemas are not changed by experience. The absence of learning can keep otherwise intelligent people in a state of ignorance about themselves and the interpersonal world.

Because of the irrational inability to tolerate self-knowledge and endure painful emotional experiences, one attempts to blot out conscious recognitions that might lead to problem solving and conflict resolution. Instead of clear consciousness, there is selective vagueness of perception. For example, a woman with this style may dress in a sexually exciting and inviting manner, but not notice that she was doing so and then feel bothered by overtures from others.

Attention may be selectively deployed more on other people than on the sensations derived from the self. The person with this style might be unconscious of fiddling with clothing, as in unbuttoning buttons, or rocking the pelvis or legs. Similarly, the ideas of wanting attention, planning to get it in certain ways, and worrying about excessive responses from others are inhibited from clear verbal representation, and from clear image representation as well. Only jumbles of partial fantasies may reach consciousness. Motives, intentions, and planned limits on how to respond to others seem to be relatively missing from conscious thought. This means that other people can indeed be actively bad: that is, they can manipulate and exploit the person who uses this style. The inner expectation becomes a self-fulfilling prophecy.

Such persons who do control mental set so as to contemplate a conflictual theme may still avoid subtopics of that theme leading to negative emotions such as anxiety or guilt. Only some possible associations to an idea are permitted, while other associational lines are inhibited. In this manner of control, one unconsciously short-circuits threatening emotions by consciously believing one has completed a period of contemplating the conflictual theme. One thinks in effect, "That's all there is to that," and—if asked in a therapeutic conversation what else is relevant—may say over and over, "I don't know."

I should like at this point to emphasize that this type of personality configuration contains a paradox that accounts for its repetition of maladaptive patterns rather than replacement of them with more adaptive ones. Although the schemas organizing such patterns are inappropriate to actual situations, one cannot consciously reflect clearly upon this fact because one's control processes are denying entry into unpleasantly emotional states of mind. When one does enter such a state of mind, one's control processes are inadequate, and one feels so out of control that one cannot think of any new alternative, especially if it involves an active self-schema. The defensive styles of global inhibition leave the pathological schemas uncorrected by either rational reflection or new experiences.

It is hard for the person to set aside habitual repressions, denials, and disavowals—defenses that are the result of unconscious choices. While possible to make conscious choices to counteract habitual unconscious controls, it is hard to do so because awareness of avoidance is limited and because of immature schemas which would result in self-criticism as being "bad" if the warded-off contents were to gain awareness.

Without new experiences and new working models one does not revise the enduring irrational attitudes that might lead to harsh and unwarranted self-criticism. One does not develop attitudes that might lead to more mature self-criticism. The immature schemas keep the repressions in place; the repressions keep the immature schemas in place. The person grows older in chronological but not in psychological age, and remains frozen in a maladaptive personality pattern which regards self and others as cardboard stereotypes rather than as flexible, resourceful adults.

A person whose emotional suffering has become intolerable may seek to change through psychotherapy guided by psychodynamic theory. Such psychotherapy addresses both the defenses and the schemas through work aimed at increasing conscious, reflective self-awareness (Schafer 1968a; Basch 1980; Malan 1979; Strupp and Binder 1984; Luborsky 1984). The work also aims at creating a role-relationship model in which the patient is active and responsible, and the therapist is non-exploitative and consistently concerned with the best long-range interests of the patient. This relationship may also lead to unconscious development of new role-relationship models through struggles to understand unrealistic projections onto the relationship, as in the interpretation of transference reactions.

The new schemas and the new modes of awareness operate hand in glove at both conscious and unconscious levels to revise controls and modes of behavior. In order to set aside such control processes as inhibition of representation of feared topics, the person has to learn new tolerance for emotional states of mind. Such tolerance rests on modification of enduring schemas and of habitual resistances to self-knowledge. The consequences of expressing an emotion such as anger have to be seen as less threatening than inscribed in primitive role-relationship models and their sequences that lead rapidly from anger expression to anxiety over harming another, or fear of retaliation from another. The case of Laura illustrates some aspects of such changes.

Laura was thirty years old when she came for psychotherapy for a histrionic personality disorder. She had symptoms of depression, agitation, and low self-esteem following the breakup of a relationship. Other breakups had occurred in somewhat the same way, and she felt defective and unlovable as a consequence. She also had been unable to experience sexual pleasure through orgasm except by masturbation. In addition, she seemed to be drifting in her career choices, and conflicts emerged repeatedly in her relationships with women as well as men. Laura manifested the habitual, defensive style I have described. When she approached a theme that bothered her, she prematurely closed her discussion of it by saying, "I don't know." She was usually unable to predict, when asked, how she might feel if a situation developed in a certain way—if, for example, she were not asked out a second time by a man she had just seen once. "I don't know," she might say, or just trail off in her communication.

Cause-and-effect sequences were poorly connected as she related stories about troublesome recent events. It was as if she did not associate her response with what another person did next. She did not think in terms that might deduce people's long-range intentions from their current behavior. She especially inhibited conscious representation of her own goals, although she might say what she had done in a relationship. If pressed for such details, she might enter a distracted state of mind in which communication was impoverished. Nonetheless, when not under emotional stress from conflicted themes, she thought and acted with superior intelligence.

In the course of treatment, clarifications and labels of feelings and actions provided by the therapist helped Laura in her own efforts to gain clearer conscious representation of usually warded-off themes. Her vagueness about labeling with words was at first countered by the therapist who provided specific words. Later, he clarified the nature and motives for her defensive ambiguities, and urged her to supply labels.

For example, in discussing her transition from states of erotic arousal to anxiety-filled tension states during sexual courtship, Laura referred to all sexual body parts as "it" or "things." The therapist repeated what she had said, using specific words such as *penis, nipple, labia,* and *vagina.* Then he indicated her fear of being specific, and its basis in deeper anxieties and a sense of guilt. At the same time, he was modeling with his calm tone of voice a different attitude toward sexual body parts than Laura had learned in her family, where the style was to be nervous but excited while speaking of "it."

Laura gradually became more aware of the times when she was speaking and thinking in a vague manner. At such times she made a conscious effort, in identification with the therapist, to be clear about what she meant: to stay on a topic rather than short-circuit it. She came to feel more and more comfortable speaking of the previously "unthinkable" matters of sexuality and interpersonal hostility that her family had treated as exciting, guilty, and fearful "unmentionables."

The therapist also repeated what Laura had just said, especially at times when she seemed about to change from an alert working state into a distracted and cloudy state as a defense against her mounting anxiety. Hearing in his voice the words she had just uttered, she seemed startled and surprised: when he spoke, it seemed real to her; when she spoke, it seemed not to count as a real idea. The therapist pointed out her attitude of experiencing herself as an inauthentic sham of a woman rather than as a meaningful person who deserved to speak of her own ideas and feelings.

When the therapist repeated her remarks, Laura learned to listen to herself in a new way, taking seriously her own motives, emotions, and ideas of what was of value to her. She enlarged her network of available associations. She began to understand the cause-and-effect sequences of who did what to whom in interpersonal situations. Such work helped Laura not only go farther down a train of thought about a troublesome topic, but also gradually to alter her habitual style of avoiding conscious knowledge of what was happening. She learned to think more clearly and to plan her actions more in accord with her desires.

At first, Laura was startled when the therapist made a clarification or interpretation. She sometimes misinterpreted his intentions according to her existing role-relationship models in which she was a passive person often assaulted by the desires or needs of another person. She feared she would enter a state of mind in which she was too excited and enthralled by the therapist, that she might then be used or hurt by him. She was frightened because the words of the therapist seemed to be inserting ideas into her mind, and because she was excited by these ideas. This pattern was a repetition of feelings she had about her father, whom she idealized, but who also had overstimulated her with rapid-fire ideas, accompanied by his insistence on being nude during discussions.

Laura feared listening too closely to the therapist as she had feared getting too enthralled with her strange father. The therapist was also strange, it seemed, and had farfetched psychoanalytic ideas about unconscious mental processes. Believing what he said, even tentatively, would make her dependent upon him. She had heard about transference love for therapists, and feared that was what he expected and what he was manipulating her to develop. She was also afraid to know that, due to her associative habits, she became sexually excited about the "intercourse of ideas."

Recognition of this set of ideas about the relationship allowed this view to be contrasted with another view: that of a relationship between a seeking patient and a helping expert who was neither manipulative, exploitative, and sexually aroused nor cold, detached, and abandoning. Gradually, the role-relationship model of seeking patient and helping expert became more prominent. It survived her anger at feeling abandoned and her excitement, fear, and guilt at feeling close. This allowed more work on lessening her defensive controls, which in turn allowed greater clarity about irrational expectations and neurotic interpersonal responses.

As Laura developed the role-relationship model of a safe therapeutic alliance, she could spend more time in the alert working state organized by this schema. This meant more time in consciously representing ideas and feelings that otherwise seemed to run away from her in under-modulated states in which she felt too emotional and so not in self-command. With more time, she could think of new solutions to interpersonal dilemmas as they occurred in her life. She could try out and practice these new solutions until they became more automatic.

Since Laura felt more in control during these working states, she could allow herself to associate more fully, thus increasing her level of felt emotion; but she had learned that she could tolerate emotion if she did not shift into a defective set of self-schemas when she experienced intense feeling. She could tolerate thinking about conflicting ideas, modeling in part this ability on the ability she watched in the therapist to accept and repeat what she had said without passing judgment, insisting on immediate decisions, or using her feelings to his advantage.

With this increase in tolerance for emotions, especially for sadness, fear, anger, and guilt, Laura could review her past life patterns and see a repetitive story to them. In recalling repressed memories about her father, mother, and other childhood figures, she got a clearer perspective on her own life history and personal development. Memories once organized from a child's frame of reference were now reorganized by the new meanings available from adult contexts. Thus, she was helped to understand some irrational fears she had about expressing wishes in her current relationships with men.

As Laura moved from a passive to an active self-concept, she changed her career to a more assertive and rewarding one. With continued work on her ideas based upon a defective body schema, she began to explore her own body and her bodily sensations. She developed self-schemas as an adult woman, rather than as an excited but endangered child. She was capable of sexuality without harm. She began to enjoy her sexuality and that in turn bolstered her self-confidence and self-esteem. Increased boldness led to increased and clearer confrontations with her fears, and rational readjustments to them. Active, strong, and sexually female self-schemas were now available for use as organizers of her states of mind.

Laura's treatment involved both conflict resolution through schematic change and modification of how she formed her thoughts and communicated with others. (For more details on this case, see Horowitz 1977a.)

The Obsessional Style

In contrast to the set of control processes typifying a histrionic style stands the set of character-based ways of coping with conflict called the *obsessional* or *compulsive style.* This set of defensive habits as a prototype is characterized by rigidity of thought and stifled feelings. Instead of the dramatic shifts in state of mind often seen in the histrionic style, one is stabilized in a narrower range of experience where one seems to overvalue thought at the expense of feeling.

The most dreaded states of mind are those of uncontrolled emotion. The person avoids undermodulated states of mind by maintaining over-modulated ones. Life is regimented into routines, sometimes pressured or strained ones. The strain occurs because of value schemas that emphasize perfection in terms of work productivity. Interpersonal transactions are dutiful rather than lively. Role-relationship models are often juggled in a way that accomplishes rapid reversals of role (Salzman 1968; Horowitz et al. 1984). The self moves back and forth from strong to weak positions, from weak to strong, to escape from the most threatening condition of the moment. This switching movement of self in working models is associated, with a rapid switching of ideas in consciousness and, often, in communications (see chapter 10).

Where the hysterical style may involve a global, cloudy focus on the big picture, the obsessional style has a sharp focus of attention upon details. Representations and communications are clear, but the detail presented is often at the periphery of a theme. It is as if one makes an unconscious appraisal of where conscious thought might go, and then gradually moves away from the emotional heart and central meaning of a given theme.

The rapid switching between different subthemes of a topic limits conceptual progress to reach solutions to dilemmas and conflicts about any one subtheme. Before the dilemma or conflict is clearly represented, one has felt its emotional consequences in small affective signals, and switches away the ideational routes to prevent more intense feeling. The derailment of thought from a central, emotional focus is disguised by logic that often amounts to generalization or rationalization rather than specification and reasoning through to the solution of a life problem.

Persons who have this pattern find it hard to reach clear choices unless they leap impulsively out of a paralysis of doubt. If they do take impulsive action, they then regret it, undo it, or ruminate endlessly about it. In conversations they change between pros and cons so often that they become confusing, irritating, or boring to listen to. Thus, in contrast to the histrionic style, there is an apparent superabundance of thought rather than an impoverishment of conscious reflection, and an underabundance of emotion since the full weight of a theme or a subtopic is not developed.

In unconscious neurotic conflict of long standing occur what R.D. Laing (1970) has aptly called *knots,* and John Dollard and Neal Miller (1950) have called *approach and avoidance conflicts.* In these situations, the solution to any one problem leads to another problem. The schemas contain dilemmas, and the personality is the result of one's being on the horns of these dilemmas. It is like being in a corridor faced with a charging bull: as one dodges to escape one horn, one is in danger of being gored with the other. The case of Brad, who approximated an obsessional prototype through his long-standing unconscious conflicts, exemplifies such dilemmas, which in this instance were schemas, and the symptoms formed the result of defensive compromises between wishes and fears.

Brad had the common conflict of wishing both to be dependent and to be independent. Instead of finding an adaptive way to satisfy both wishes, he used either position as a defense against the dangers embedded in schemas for the opposite wish. When threatened by the consequences of wanting a kind of dependency, he switched to schemas involving the self as independent. Then, when faced with the dreaded consequences of being independent, he switched to schemas of being dependent. It was not just that wishes to be dependent conflicted with Brad's wish to be independent; one may be both at different times even in a specific relationship. A problem in this case was that being dependent and being independent both had feared consequences, and that, as a result, Brad had no schema to be stabilized.

Brad was in his mid-thirties when he sought psychotherapy for personality-based symptoms—work inhibitions and sexual difficulties—that had started during adolescence and become clearer as recurrent maladaptive patterns in his twenties.

He wrote briefs for senior partners as a major part of his current work in a prominent law firm. His ambition to be promoted to partnership was thwarted by the fact that he could not make himself write the briefs. This problem was not new: at various times during law school and his college years, his ability was marred by periodic procrastination. This avoidance of completing work tasks was not joyful self-indulgence; it was painful rumination without progression.

Equally distressing was Brad's sexual life. Too frequently he experienced premature ejaculation or could not stay erect when his partner was most excited. He had anxious thoughts about his sexuality and, while with a woman, might turn his mind to work problems.

Brad had strong motives for the pleasures of being close and interdependent with another person and strong motives for being a person who had the satisfaction of being independent. He was conflicted both when seeking the pleasures of being dependent, and when seeking the satisfactions of being independent—goals he seemed to see as contradictory. In addition, conflicts were embedded in the role-relationship models he used to organize either pursuit.

DEPENDENCE CONFLICT

When thinking of dependent pleasures, Brad would often organize his ideas and feelings according to a role-relationship model in which he was affiliated with a powerful male figure, one who operated as mentor and leader. The sequence might begin with Brad as a loyal follower indicating his affiliation to the mentor. The expected response was one in which the mentor would be grateful for the affiliation and take care of Brad's next career plans by providing guidance and help. Brad's reaction was not satisfaction but rather fear that now he was positioned in a way that would render him always immature. This fear, linked with a wish in the sequence of a schema, presents a conflict. In actual transactions, Brad at first sought help from a mentor. Then, when help was offered, he would reject it—as a defense against the feared result of being diminished by and too enmeshed with the mentor. Some flaw in the leader would be used as a rationalization to cover over the compulsive withdrawal to avoid anxiety.

Earlier, in childhood and adolescence, Brad had feared not developing sufficiently to escape from his father's efforts to dominate him. Staying closely united to his father meant that Brad could not leave home and develop his own manhood. At an extreme, he also feared the insistent domination by his father which was sometimes revealed in the relationship of the father to Brad's mother. As Brad viewed it as a child, the father forced the mother to submit to his sexual desires. Brad interpreted sounds he had heard as a child from his parent's bedroom as his father's brutal sexual attacks on his mother. Deeply unconsciously, but emergent during dream images and symbols, Brad feared being forced into as submissive a role as his mother by his father.

INDEPENDENCE CONFLICT

The most prominent role-relationship model used to organize the theme of independent wishes was one in which Brad would remain related to others but with himself in the role of a powerful, strong leader. He would then obtain the admiration of other men and the love of women through extravagant displays of his skill at the law. Preparing a subtle but incisive legal argument was a way of showing off. Through such acts he planned to surpass his peers and gain partner status in the firm. Brad could not enjoy the fruits of such a sequence of events, even in daydreams of the increased salary and prestige he would gain. Embedded in this scenario was a fear.

When Brad reached the point where he was manifestly strong in the sequence, he then feared a response from others. They would feel he had harmed them by his triumph. He would have to feel either guilty over their sufferings from defeat in competition, or fearful of their subsequent efforts at retaliation. He had to interrupt his daydreams when his conscious images reached this point in the scenario. He would ruminate unpleasantly at that point about how badly others would feel about his success, and how to protect himself from them.

This role-relationship model, in which he was the strong victor and another male the defeated rival, also was developed in the past largely in the context of his internalized relationship with his father. Brad had in the past felt envious rage toward his father's position of dominance in the family, and wanted to surpass him.

The father had been at times excessive in putting Brad down in the pecking order, or in depreciating his boyhood attempts at emulating manly skills. In addition, as Brad became strong during adolescence, his success sometimes humiliated the father. After the father developed a chronic and mildly debilitating illness, both Brad and his father shared irrational beliefs that the son's development of strength and skills somehow diminished the father rather than providing him a source of pride. As this was coded in the role-relationship model, Brad had to feel guilt as a reaction to his father's envious and degraded responses to his own desired successes.

As a consequence of such unconscious schemas, Brad sometimes reacted at work in relationship to senior partners as if he were showing up his sensitive and vulnerable father. This attitude was inappropriate to the actual situation, since he was dealing with people who were tough and operating knowingly in an arena of both cooperation and competition.

Brad used the weak set of self-schemas to undo the threat of strong ones, and vice versa. When during psychotherapy he was describing a brief he was writing as a powerful, incisive tool, he became anxious and quickly began speaking of it as if in writing the brief he was only submissively following the dictates of his boss. When that idea seemed to make him anxious, he would switch back to speaking of the brief as his own powerful creation.

A similar pattern occurred when Brad attempted to explore his ideas and feelings about a current sexual relationship with a woman. When describing how strong and powerful he felt that he had performed well sexually, he seemed to get momentarily confused by rapid switches to other ideas. Sometimes the other ideas were on the same subtopic of his strength, with a switch from it being joyful to being potentially harmful to the woman. If so, he would speak of fear and guilt that he had degraded her by seducing her to sexual excitement.

Sometimes the other ideas were on the same theme but focused on a different subtopic. In such instances, he would organize his ideas by weak rather than strong self-concepts. By the sexual intimacy, he might say, he had fallen into the clutches of a woman. He would then speak of his fears of being trapped in the relationship. If that made him anxious, he might linger on weak self-concepts, but speak of the pleasures of being passively cared for; or he might switch to the various ideas containing strong self-concepts or organized by strong self-schemas.

These various switches might occur so rapidly, on a stressful topic, that Brad himself became confused; and it was usually difficult to follow the emotional thread of his meaning. Brad at times became so anxious and confused about the implications of his relationships with women that he avoided sexual encounters on one or another pretext. Abstinence led to states of loneliness, depression, and low self-esteem but reduced the likelihood of painfully anxious and obsessive rumination.

Brad consciously knew that he was in a damned-if-he-did and damned-if-he-didn't dilemma involving his work life and his love life. He did not consciously know the entangled schemas that he rigidly imposed on life situations, and was not clear about the sequential aspects of his recurrent behavioral patterns. Becoming aware of these sequences, and making inferences about the schemas that might lead to the repetitions, were the first goals for his treatment. Then the goals would be trials of new kinds of behavior. All these goals would require modification of his habitual modes of conscious experience and communication. Instead of switching back and forth, he might have to stay on a specific subtopic of a theme.

Brad habitually spoke in a constricted, emotionless, flat tone of voice. A quaver of anxiety occasionally crept in, however, allowing the therapist to know a stressful topic had been touched on. Brad behaved toward the therapist in an excessive, exaggerated manner of courteous consideration, but also had an opposite tendency—to interrupt or to insist on setting the topic no matter what the therapist might suggest or ask.

A prominent conceptual style was to edge away from the emotional heart of a current issue. Brad presented his ideas in a seemingly clear way, setting the stage for a story by describing the background, and then giving in great detail the sequence of events. Nothing cloudy or disjointed here. But he ignored the juice of the story and progressed to ever more peripheral details. This movement away from the core conflicts in describing his problems during therapy was just like his movement away from the central thrust of a brief he might be writing at work. He could not maintain concentration down a center path, but was deflected by mounting anxiety about the conflicts along the way. Only the emergency of a deadline would force him to complete the main line of an argument in a brief.

When the therapist confronted Brad with his pattern of avoiding the emotional and personal implications of a story he was telling, Brad responded by courteously agreeing in words but without changing his behavior. Gradually the therapist became more persistent in inquiring about the central, emotional implications. Brad responded with a conscious attempt to increase time on such topics—an attempt to deal with emotional implications which increased the frequency and intensity of Brad's switching behavior.

Only gradually was this unconsciously mediated defensive style altered. Then Brad was able to stay longer on an emotional subtopic of a given theme, to confront some of his irrational views about current situations, and to relate these to previous views from the developmental past. He began to lose his courteous veneer and allowed himself to feel and reveal that he felt the therapist was forcing him to conform to the therapist's own model of how the treatment ought to proceed. Brad allowed himself to feel and reveal that he felt at other times that he was beating the therapist down, harming him by ignoring the usefulness of his clarifications and interpretations. He had difficulty comparing these ideas with the actual situation: that the therapist was neither dominating him nor submitting to him, neither rejoicing in molding him excessively nor feeling degraded and ineffectual.

Little by little Brad came to see both himself and the therapist as having different roles, but on an equal footing in terms of dominance and submission; in time, this became a working model, a therapeutic alliance. Against this standard, Brad could have and confront the irrationality of other working models based on his pre-existing repertoire of problematic role-relationship models. As he developed a new role-relationship model with the therapist, his trust in the relationship deepened, and bolstered his self-esteem.

Brad was then still more capable of reducing the frequency of his intellectualizations, rationalizations, and generalizations. He was able to acknowledge when he felt a momentary sense of inner confusion, rather than having to gloss it over with his previous habitual mannerism of fast, bright talking. He could stop, and try to tune up his inner representation of emotion in enactive and image systems, and to translate feelings into emotional words.

Unconscious conflict embedded in enduring schemas may be modified by the development of new schemas. For Brad, as with many neurotic patients, this outcome meant change both in the role-relationship models and in the controls used to regulate schemas and the modes of representation. As he learned to give up overmodulated states of mind, he found he did not have to enter, as he had feared, states of uncontrolled emotion. He learned to feel in an understanding, well-modulated way, even when what he was feeling was unpleasant. His unconscious defenses of warding off emotion by rapid switching of themes and subtopics, and by moving toward an emotion-free periphery of details, were set aside through a series of conscious efforts to represent the heart of a theme, facilitated by the attention-focusing maneuvers of the therapist.

This effort of the therapist was successful because of the development of the relationship in the therapy through interpretation of transference distortions of that relationship. These modifications allowed Brad to change his other behavioral patterns. His unconscious fears of dominance and of submission were reduced as he was able to practice and become habitually used to relationships in which both parties were on an equal level. He could change topics deliberately, without putting down the therapist; he could stay on a topic initiated by the therapist without feeling subjugated. He could "fight" safely with the therapist about the meaning of an episode.

Meanwhile, at work Brad began to recognize that equals might compete or even fight without the loser being destroyed and the winner devastated by guilt. In his love life, this recognition meant that both parties might enjoy or be frustrated by the other without loss of either individual identity or mutual commitment. He also came to realize that he repeated a pattern of acting like what he called an "incompetent jerk." While he would date a mature woman, such as another lawyer, who had previous sexual relationships with men, he did not treat the woman as an experienced equal. Instead of developing a working model that incorporated realistic aspects of the situation, he used a role-relationship model from his repertoire which led him to view the woman as a virginal, shy maiden. He enacted the role of a supergallant man not too interested in sex, which she must regard as dirty. His behavior, organized at times by this gallant man/virginal maid model, could be silly because it was so discrepant with the situation. Reviewing it later in therapy, he would call himself a jerk.

The role-relationship model of being a supergallant man to a virginal maid was developed through a repeated adolescent fantasy. Brad used it as a defense against organizing a state of mind by either one of two conflicted schemas. In one dreaded schema, the woman would be seen not, as in actual situations, as a strong, self-controlled woman but as a sexually enthralled woman degraded into the sexual practices of a whore. He would want to have her in a ruthless way. She would be submissive to his dominant and sadistic sexual aggressions. Thinking of himself as brutally persistent and self-seeking in sexuality was at first too dreadful to contemplate. It was like bad memories about his father. Because he had avoided this association and other conscious derivatives, Brad's unconscious beliefs had persisted. His assertive sexuality was held in check by the more conscious gallant-man-to-virginal-maid role-relationship model, and he did not refine his adolescent, somewhat sadistic, and lustful imagery as a source of erotic arousal.

The relatively unconscious sadistic-man-and-subservient-whore role-relationship model also had a defensive function: it was better to be the strong party than to be in the weak, masochistic, submissive position. And there was a role-relationship model in which that was his dreaded self-schema. He was a kind of passive, depersonalized boy being used sexually by a kind of "big nurse" figure, a powerful, domineering woman who would stuff him inside herself and take control of his identity. This dream imagery of the submissive, dependent boy controlled by the "big nurse" had derivatives in his daytime ruminations. He worried that a current woman would trap him into a marriage in which she would always be dominant as a result of their growing closeness and as a feared consequence of his own emergent loving feelings.

Brad was so rigid that he could not just enjoy the idea of being sexually strong and virile: any fantasy that began that way seemed destined to lead him to the point of feeling guilty over being too dominant or sadistic. And he could not enjoy a loving tender feeling without the ensuing fear of being trapped. As role-relationship models of more equality developed, Brad was able to behave less like a jerk and more like a mature man. He could have the strongly active, and tenderly passive, closeness feelings with less anxiety and could see situations in terms of their actual qualities and potentials rather than of the rigid inner stereotypes.

Unconscious neurotic conflict is conflict that has solidified into rigid schemas which are then not changed by new working models of situations. These schemas are associated with a habitual defensive style. In order to learn new working models, the person with such neurotic features requires help in modifying defensive styles as well as in modifying irrational beliefs. In our examples Laura learned new modes of awareness and reduced her inhibition of conscious knowledge of ideas; Brad learned new modes of going to the emotional heart of a theme and reduced his automatic tendency to avoid feeling by switching themes.

Conclusion

Change in schemas requires reduced avoidance and increased acceptance of "the way things are." Sometimes making such changes requires a special effort at new syntheses of alternatives and new clear choices between contradictions. Consciousness is a useful tool in achieving such new syntheses. With conscious choice, one may override automatic avoidances of anxiety and deliberately try some new forms of relating with others and confronting the self. With practice, the altered modes of awareness and action become smooth functions, rather than tense or fearful trials of novel approaches. With such learning of automatic functions, consciousness can turn to planning new functions.

Some years ago, hallucinogenic drugs were seen as a route to heightened consciousness. We now see that as a false hope. The consciousness to heighten is ordinary, rational, empathic, and open to authentic feeling. It may require a slowing down of thought rather than a speeding up. Heightening consciousness for individual development is thus to be viewed as a result of persistent hard work, since it often means facing conflicts and tolerating tense uncertainties until new solutions are both found and practiced. As this work enhances knowledge of self and understanding of others, such knowledge and understanding will then contribute new ideas to psychodynamic theory, a field always open to revision and growth.

BIBLIOGRAPHY

Abelson, R. P. 1981. "Psychological Status of the Script Concept." *American Psychologist* 36:715–29.

Abraham, K. 1924. "A Short Study of the Development of the Libido, Viewed in Light of the Mental Disorders." In E. Jones, ed., *Selected Papers of Karl Abraham.* London: Hogarth Press.

Ainsworth, M. 1973. "The Development of Infant-Mother Attachment." In B. Caldwell and H. Ricciute, eds., *Review of Child Development Research,* no. 3. Chicago: University of Chicago Press.

Ainsworth, M.; Blehar, M.; Waters, E.; and Wall, S. 1978. *Patterns of Attachment: A Psychological Study of the Strange Situation.* New York: Basic Books.

Alba, J. W.; and Hasher, L. 1983. "Is Memory Schematic?" *Psychological Bulletin* 93:203–31.

Amsterdam, B. K. 1972. "Mirror Self-Image Reactions Before Age 2." *Developmental Psychology* 5:297–305.

Anderson, J. R. 1983. *The Architecture of Cognition.* Cambridge, Mass.: Harvard University Press.

Anthony, E. J. 1975. *The Child in His Family at Psychiatric Risk.* International Association for Child Psychiatry Yearbook 3.

Appelgarth, A. 1971. "Comments on Aspects of the Theory of Psychic Energy." *Journal of American Psychoanalytic Association* 19:379–416.

Arieti, S. 1967. *The Intrapsychic Self: Feeling, Cognition, and Creativity in Health and Mental Illness.* New York: Basic Books.

Arlow, J. 1969. "Unconscious Fantasy and Disturbances of Conscious Experiences." *Psychoanalytic Quarterly* 38:1–27.

Baars, B. J. 1986. *The Cognitive Revolution in Psychology.* New York: Guilford Press.

Baars, B. J. 1987. *A Cognitive Theory of Consciousness.* London: Cambridge University Press.

Baddeley, A. D. 1976. *The Psychology of Memory.* New York: Basic Books.

Basch, M. F. 1980. *Doing Psychotherapy.* New York: Basic Books.

Beck, A. T.; and Emery, G. 1979. *Cognitive Therapy of Anxiety and Phobic Disorders.* Philadelphia: Center for Cognitive Therapy.

Beck, A. T.; Rush, A. J.; Shaw, B. F.; and Emery, G. 1976. *Cognitive Therapy and Emotional Disorders.* New York: International Universities Press.

Beck, A. T.; Rush, A. J.; Shaw, B. F.; and Emery, G. 1979. *Cognitive Therapy of Depression.* New York: Guilford Press.

Becker, E. 1973. *The Denial of Death.* New York: Free Press.

Beland, H. 1987. "Ego Alteration by Defensive Processes and the Limitations of Psychoanalysis." Presented at the 35th International Psychoanalytical Congress, Montreal, 30 July 1987.

Benson, R.; and Pryor, D. B. 1973. " 'When Friends Fall Out': Developmental Interference with the Function of Some Imaginary Companions." *Journal of the American Psychoanalytic Association* 21(3):457–73.

Berne, E. 1961. *Transactional Analysis in Psychotherapy.* New York: Grove Press.

Berne, E. 1964. *Games People Play*. New York: Grove Press.

Berne, E. 1972. *What Do You Say After You Say Hello? The Psychology of Human Destiny*. New York: Grove Press.

Bion, W. R. 1967. *Second Thoughts: Selected Papers on Psychoanalysis*. London: Heinemann.

Bixler, E. O.; Kales, A.; and Soldatos, C. R. 1979. "Sleep Disorders Encountered in Medical Practice: A National Survey of Physicians." *Behavioral Medicine* 6:1–6.

Blacker, K.; and Tupin, J. 1977. "Hysteria and Hysterical Structures: Developmental and Social Theories." In M. Horowitz, ed., *Hysterical Personality*. New York: Jason Aronson.

Blanck, G.; and Blanck, R. 1979. *Ego Psychology II: Psychoanalytic Developmental Psychology*. New York: Columbia University Press.

Blatt, S. J. In press. "The Configurations of Personality Development and Psychopathology." In J. L. Singer, ed., *Repression: Defense Mechanism and Personality Style*. Chicago: University of Chicago Press.

Blatt, S. J.; Lerner, H. 1983. "The Psychological Assessment of Object Representations." *Journal of Personality Assessment* 47:7–28.

Block, J.; with the collaboration of Hahn, N. 1971. *Lives Through Time*. Berkeley, California: Bancroft Books.

Bloom, F. E.; Cooper, J. R.; and Roth, R. H. 1982. *Biochemical Basis of Neuropharmacology*. New York: Oxford University Press.

Bloom-Feshbach, J.; and Bloom-Feshbach, S. 1987. *The Psychology of Separation and Loss*. San Francisco: Jossey-Bass.

Blos, P. 1979. *The Adolescent Passage: Developmental Issues*. New York: International Universities Press.

Bower, G. H. 1981. "Mood and Memory." *American Psychologist* 36:129–48.

Bower, G. H.; and Gilligan, S. G. 1979. "Remembering Information Relating to One's Self." *Journal of Research in Personality* 13:420–32.

Bowers, K.; and Meichenbaum, D. 1984. *The Unconscious Reconsidered*. New York: John Wiley.

Bowlby, J. 1969. *Attachment and Loss*. Vol. I: *Attachment*. New York: Basic Books.

Bowlby, J. 1973. *Attachment and Loss*. Vol. II: *Separation: Anxiety and Anger*. New York: Basic Books.

Bowlby, J. 1979. *The Making and Breaking of Affectional Bonds*. London: Tavistock.

Bowlby, J. 1980. *Attachment and Loss*. Vol. III: *Loss: Sadness and Depression*. New York: Basic Books.

Brauer, R.; Harrow, M.; and Tucker, G. J. 1970. "Depersonalization Phenomena in Psychiatric Patients." *British Journal of Psychiatry* 117:509–15.

Breger, L.; Hunter, I.; and Lane, R. W. 1971. "The Effect of Stress on Dreams." *Psychological Issues* 7 (3). Monograph 27.

Brenner, C. 1982. *The Mind in Conflict*. New York: International Universities Press.

Bretherton, I.; and Waters, E., eds. 1985. *Growing Points in Attachment Theory and Research: Monographs of the Society for Research in Child Development*.

Breuer, J.; and Freud, S. 1895. "Studies on Hysteria." In *The Standard Edition of the Complete Psychological Works of Sigmund Freud*, vol. II. London: Hogarth Press, 1955.

Broadbent, D. E. 1971. *Decision and Stress*. London: Academic Press.

Bruner, J. S. 1964. "The Course of Cognitive Growth." *American Psychologist* 19:1.

Cannon, W. B. 1929. *Bodily Changes in Pain, Hunger, Fear and Rage*. New York: Appleton.

Carlson, R. 1981. "Studies in Script Theory: I. Adult Analogs of a Childhood Nuclear Scene." *Journal of Personality and Social Psychology* 40:501–10.

Carlson, R. 1982. "Studies in Script Theory: II. Altruistic Nuclear Scripts." *Perceptual and Motor Skills* 55:595–610.

Charcot, J. M. 1877. *Lectures on Diseases of the Nervous System*, G. Sigerson, trans. London: New Sydenham Society.

Colarusso, C. A., and Nemiroff, R. A. 1981. *Adult Development*. New York: Plenum Press.

Crook, J. 1980. *The Evolution of Human Consciousness*. Oxford: Oxford University Press.

Davenport, R. K.; et al. 1979. "The Relevance of Object Categorization to Cross Modal Performance by Chimpanzees." *Neuropsychologia* 16:539–43.

Davis, K. E. 1981. *Advances in Descriptive Psychology*. Greenwich, Connecticut: Jai.

Dennet, D. C. 1986. *Content and Consciousness*, 2nd ed. International Library of Philosophy. London: Methuen.

Deutsche, H. 1965. *Neuroses and Character Types*. New York: International Universities Press.

Dixon, N. F. 1981. *Pre-Conscious Processing*. New York: John Wiley.

Dollard, J.; and Miller, N. E. 1950. *Personality and Psychotherapy: An Analysis of Learning, Thinking and Culture*. New York: McGraw-Hill.

Eagle, M. N. 1984. *Recent Developments in Psychoanalysis: A Critical Evaluation*. New York: McGraw-Hill.

Edelson, M. 1984. *Hypothesis and Evidence in Psychoanalysis*. Chicago: University of Chicago Press.

Eisnitz, A. J. 1984–85. "Father/Daughter Incest." *International Journal of Psycho-Analysis and Psychotherapy* 10.

Eisnitz, A. J. 1986. "The Perspective of the Self Representation in Dreams." In A. Rothstein, ed., *The Significance of the Interpretation of Dreams in Clinical Practice*. New York: American Psychoanalytic Association Press.

Ekman, P. 1982. *Emotion in the Human Face*, 2nd ed. New York: Cambridge University Press.

Ekman, P. 1984. "Expression and the Nature of Emotion." In P. Ekman and K. Sherer, eds., *Approaches to Emotion*. New York: Lawrence Erlbaum.

Ekman, P.; and Friesen, W. 1975. *Unmasking the Face*. Englewood Cliffs, N.J.: Prentice Hall.

Ellman, S.; and Antrobus, J. 1984. *The Mind in Sleep*, 2nd ed. Hillsdale, N.J.: Lawrence Erlbaum.

Emde, R. N. 1981. "Changing Models of Infancy and the Nature of Early Development." *Journal of the American Psychoanalytic Association* 29:179–219.

Emde, R. N. 1983. "The Prerepresentational Self and Its Affective Core." *Psychoanalytic Study of the Child* 38:165–92.

Emde, R. N.; Gaensbauer, T. J.; and Harmon, R. J. 1976. *Emotional Expression in Infancy: A Bio-Behavioral Study*. New York: International Universities Press.

Emde, R. N.; and Harmon, R. J. 1982. *The Development of Attachment and Affiliative Systems*. New York: Plenum Press.

Emde, R.N.; and Sorce, J. F. 1983. "Rewards of Infancy: Emotional Availability and Maternal Referencing." In J. Coll, E. Galenson, and R. Tyson, eds., *Frontiers of Infant Psychiatry*. New York: Basic Books.

Engel, G. L. 1975. "The Death of a Twin: Mourning and Anniversary Reactions." *International Journal of Psycho-Analysis* 56:23–40.

Erdelyi, N. H. 1984. *Psychoanalysis: Freud's Cognitive Psychology*. San Francisco: W. H. Freeman.

Erikson, E. H. 1950. *Childhood and Society*. New York: W. W. Norton.

Erikson, E. H. 1956. "The Problem of Ego Identity." *Journal of the American Psychoanalytic Association* 4:56–121.

Erikson, E. H. 1959. "Identity and the Life Cycle." *Psychological Issues*. New York: International Universities Press.

Erikson, E. H. 1982. *The Life Cycle Completed*. New York: W. W. Norton.

Fairbairn, W. R. D. 1952. *Psychoanalytic Studies of the Personality*. New York: Basic Books.

Fairbairn, W. R. D. 1954. *An Object Relations Theory of the Personality*. New York: Basic Books.

Fenichel, O. 1945. *The Psychoanalytic Theory of the Neuroses*. New York: W. W. Norton.

Ferenczi, S. 1950. *Further Contributions to the Therapy and Techniques of Psychoanalysis*. London: Hogarth Press.

Fischer, R. 1971. "A Cartography of the Ecstatic and Meditative States: The Experimental and Experiential Features of a Perception Hallucination Continuum Are Considered." *Science* 174:897–905.

Flavel, J. H. 1963. *The Developmental Psychology of Jean Piaget*. Princeton, N.J.: Van Nostrand.

Fodor, J. A. 1983. *The Modularity of Mind*. Cambridge: MIT Press.

Franz, C. E.; and White, K. M. 1985. "Individuation and Attachment in Personality Development: Extending Erikson's Theory." *Journal of Personality* 53(2):224–56.

Freud, A. 1946 (1936). *The Ego and the Mechanisms of Defense*. New York: International Universities Press.

Freud, S. 1900. "The Interpretation of Dreams." In *The Standard Edition of the Complete Psychological Works of Sigmund Freud* (hereafter *The Standard Edition*), vol. III. London: Hogarth Press, 1953.

Freud, S. 1901. "The Psychopathology of Everyday Life." In *The Standard Edition*, vol. VI. London: Hogarth Press, 1960.

Freud, S. 1903. "On Psychoanalysis." In *The Standard Edition*, vol. XII. London: Hogarth Press, 1958.

Freud, S. 1905. "Three Essays on the Theory of Sexuality." In *The Standard Edition*, vol. VII. London: Hogarth Press, 1953.

Freud, S. 1911. "Formulations on the Two Principles of Mental Functioning." In *The Standard Edition,* vol. XII. London: Hogarth Press, 1958.

Freud, S. 1912. "Totem and Taboo." In *Standard Edition,* vol. XIII. London: Hogarth Press, 1955.

Freud, S. 1914. "On Narcissism: An Introduction." In *The Standard Edition,* vol. XIV. London: Hogarth Press, 1957.

Freud, S. 1914–17. "The Complete Introductory Lectures on Psychoanalysis." In *The Standard Edition,* vols. XV and XVI. London: Hogarth Press, 1963.

Freud, S. 1915. "The Unconscious." In *The Standard Edition,* vol. XIV. London: Hogarth Press, 1957.

Freud, S. 1917. "Mourning and Melancholia." In *The Standard Edition,* vol. XIV. London: Hogarth Press, 1957.

Freud, S. 1920. "Beyond the Pleasure Principle." In *The Standard Edition,* vol XVIII. London: Hogarth Press, 1950.

Freud, S. 1923. "The Ego and Id." In *Standard Edition,* vol. XIX. London: Hogarth Press, 1961.

Freud, S. 1926. "Inhibitions, Symptoms and Anxiety." In *The Standard Edition,* vol. XX. London: Hogarth Press, 1959.

Freud, S. 1927a: "Humour." In *The Standard Edition,* vol. XXI. London: Hogarth Press, 1961.

Freud, S. 1927b. "Fetishism." In *The Standard Edition,* vol. XXI. London: Hogarth Press, 1961.

Freud, S. 1940. "Splitting of the Ego in the Process of Defense." In *The Standard Edition,* vol. XXIII. London: Hogarth Press, 1964.

Gaarter, K. 1971. "Control of States of Consciousness: Attainment Through External Feedback Augmenting Control of Psychophysiological Variables." *Archives of General Psychiatry* 25:436–41.

Gaensbauer, T. J.; Harmon, R. J.; Cytryn, L.; and McKnew, D. H. 1984. "Social and Affective Development in Infants with Manic Depressive parents." *American Journal of Psychiatry* 141:223–29.

Gallup, G. 1979. "Self Recognition in Chimpanzees and Man." In M. Lewis and R. Rosenblum, eds., *The Child in Its Family* 2:107–26. New York: Plenum Press.

Gardner, H. 1982. *Art, Mind, and Brain: The Cognitive Approach to Creativity.* New York: Basic Books.

Gazzaniga, M. S.; and Le Doux, J. E. 1978. *The Integrated Mind.* New York: Plenum.

Gedo, J.; and Goldberg, A. 1973. *Models of the Mind.* Chicago: University of Chicago Press.

George, C.; and Main, M. 1979. "Social Interactions of Young and Abused Children: Approach, Avoidance, and Aggression." *Child Development* 50:306–318.

Gill, M. M. 1963. "Topography and Systems in Psychoanalytic Theory." *Psychological Issues,* Monograph 10. New York: International Universities Press.

Gill, M. M. 1967a. *The Collected Papers of David Rapaport.* New York: Basic Books.

Gill, M. M. 1967b. "The Primary Process." *Psychological Issues* 5: 60. Monograph 18/19.

Goldsmith, H. H.; and Campos, J. J. 1982. "Toward a Theory of Infant Temperament." In R. N. Emde and R. J. Harmon, eds., *The Development of Attachment and Affiliative Systems.* New York: Plenum Press.

Goleman, D. 1985. *Vitalize, Simple Truths: The Psychology of Self-Deception.* New York: Simon & Schuster.

Green, R. 1987. *The "Sissy Boy Syndrome" and the Development of Homosexuality.* New Haven: Yale University Press.

Greenberg, J. R.; and Mitchell, S. A. 1983. *Object Relations in Psychoanalytic Theory.* Cambridge: Harvard University Press.

Greenson, R. 1967. *The Technique and Practice of Psychoanalysis.* New York: Hallmark Press.

Greenspan, S.; and Lourie, R. S. 1981. "Developmental Structuralist Approach to the Classification of Adaptive and Pathological Personality Organizations: Infancy and Early Childhood." *American Journal of Psychiatry* 136:725–35.

Groddeck, G., Reprint 1950. *The Book of the It.* New York: Funk & Wagnalls.

Grotstein, J. S. 1981. *Splitting and Projective Identification.* New York: Jason Aronson.

Gunderson, J. G.; and Singer, M. T. 1975. "Defining Borderline Patients: An Overview." *American Journal of Psychiatry* 132:1–10.

Haan, N. 1977. *Copying and Defending.* New York: Academic Press.

Haggard, E.; and Isaacs, K. 1966. "Micromomentary Facial Expressions As Indicators of Ego Mechanisms." In L. A. Gottschalk and A. H. Auerbach, eds., *Methods of Research in Psychotherapy.* New York: Appleton-Century-Crofts.

232

Hartmann, E. 1984. *The Nightmare: The Psychology and Biology of Terrifying Dreams.* New York: Basic Books.

Hartmann, H. 1939. *Ego Psychology and the Problem of Adaptation.* New York: International Universities Press, 1958.

Hartmann, H. 1950. "Comments on the Psychoanalytic Theory of the Ego." *Psychoanalytic Study of the Child* 5:74–96.

Hartmann, H. 1964. *Essays on Ego Psychology: Selected Problems in Psychoanalytic Theory.* New York: International Universities Press.

Hartmann, H.; Kris, E.; and Loewenstein, R. M. 1964. *Papers on Psychoanalytic Psychology.* New York: International Universities Press.

Hilgard, E. R. 1977. *Divided Consciousness: Multiple Controls in Human Thought and Action.* New York: John Wiley.

Holt, R. R. 1967. "The Development of the Primary Process: A Structural View." *Psychological Issues* 5: 344. Monograph 18/19.

Holt, R. R. 1976. "Drive or Wish? A Reconsideration of the Psychoanalytic Theory of Motivation." In M. Gill and P. Holzman, eds., *Psychology Versus Metapsychology: Psychoanalytic Essays in Memory of George S. Klein. Psychological Issues,* Monograph 36. New York: International Universities Press.

Holt, R. R. 1985. "The Current Status of Psychoanalytic Theory." *Psychoanalytic Psychology* 2:289–316.

Horowitz, M. J. 1964. "Body Buffer Zone: Exploration of Personal Space." *Archives of General Psychiatry* 11:651–56.

Horowitz, M. J. 1970. *Image Formation and Cognition.* New York: Appleton-Century-Crofts.

Horowitz, M. J. 1974. "Stress Response Syndromes: Character Styles and Dynamic Psychotherapy." *Archives of General Psychiatry* 31:768–81.

Horowitz, M. J. 1976. *Stress Response Syndromes,* 2nd ed. 1986. New York: Jason Aronson.

Horowitz, M. J., ed. 1977a. *Hysterical Personality.* New York: Jason Aronson.

Horowitz, M. J. 1977b. "Hysterical Personality: Cognitive Structure and the Processes of Change." *International Review of Psychoanalysis* 4:23–49.

Horowitz, M. J. 1977c. "Cognitive and Interactive Aspects of Splitting." *American Journal of Psychiatry* 134:549–53.

Horowitz, M. J. 1979, 1987: *States of Mind.* New York: Plenum Press.

Horowitz, M. J. 1983. *Image Formation and Psychotherapy,* rev. ed. New York: Jason Aronson.

Horowitz, M. J. 1986. *Stress Response Syndromes.* Northvale, London: Aronson.

Horowitz, M. J.; et al. 1984. *Personality Styles and Brief Psychotherapy.* New York: Basic Books.

Horowitz, M. J.; and Zilberg, N. 1983. "Regressive Alterations in the Self Concept." *American Journal of Psychiatry* 140(3):284–89.

Inhelder, B.; and Piaget, J. 1958. *The Growth of Logical Thinking from Childhood to Adolescence.* New York: Basic Books.

Izard, C. 1977. *Human Emotions.* New York: Plenum Press.

Jackendoff, R. 1987. *Consciousness and the Computational Mind.* Cambridge: Bradford/M.I.T. Press.

Jackendoff, R. 1988. "Exploring the Form of Information in the Dynamic Unconscious." In M. Horowitz, ed., *Psychodynamics and Cognition.* Chicago: University of Chicago Press.

Jacobson, E. 1946. "The Effects of Disappointment on Ego and Superego Formation in Normal and Depressive Development." *Psychoanalytic Review* 33:129–47.

Jacobson, E. 1964. *The Self in the Object World.* New York: International Universities Press.

Jacobson, E. 1971. *Depression: Comparative Studies of Normal, Neurotic and Psychotic Conditions.* New York: International Universities Press.

Janis, I. 1969. Stress and Frustration. New York: Harcourt, Brace, Jovanovich.

Jones, E. 1929. "Fear, Guilt and Hate." *International Journal of Psycho-Analysis* 10:383–97.

Jung, C. G. 1923. *Psychological Types.* London: Routledge and Kegan Paul.

Jung, C. G. 1933. *Modern Man in Search of a Soul.* New York: Harcourt.

Jung, C. G. 1939. *The Integration of Personality.* New York: Farrar & Rinehart.

Jung, C. G. 1959. *The Archetypes and the Collective Unconscious.* New York: Pantheon.

Jung, C. G. 1964. *Man and His Symbols.* New York: Doubleday.

Kagan, J. 1981. *The Second Year.* Cambridge: Harvard University Press.

Kagan, J. 1982. *The Developing Self.* Cambridge: Harvard University Press.

Kagan, J.; and Moss, A. 1983. *Birth to Maturity.* New Haven: Yale University Press.

Kandel, E. 1983. "From Metapsychology to Molecular Biology: Explorations into the Nature of Anxiety." *American Journal of Psychiatry* 140:1277–93.

Karpman, B. 1968. "Fairy-Tales and Script Drama Analysis." *Transactional Analysis Bulletin* 7: 39–43.

Kernberg, O. 1967. "Borderline Personality Organization." *Journal of the American Psychoanalytic Association* 15:41–68.

Kernberg, O. 1975. *Borderline Conditions and Pathological Narcissism.* New York: Jason Aronson.

Kernberg, O. 1976. *Object Relations Theory and Clinical Psychoanalysis.* New York: Jason Aronson.

Kernberg, O. 1980. *Internal World and External Reality: Object Relations Theory Applied.* New York: Jason Aronson.

Kernberg, O. 1984. *Severe Personality Disorders.* New Haven: Yale University Press.

Kernberg, O. 1985. *Internal World and External Reality.* New York: Jason Aronson.

Kernberg, O. 1987. "Projection and Projective Identification: Developmental and Clinical Aspects." *Journal of the American Psychoanalytic Association* 35:795–820.

Kihlstrom, J. F. 1987. "The Cognitive Unconscious." *Science* 237:1445–52.

Kihlstrom, J. F.; and Cantor, N. 1984. "Mental Representations of the Self." In L. Berkowitz, ed., *Advances in Experimental Social Psychology.* Orlando, FL: Academic Press.

Kihlstrom, J. F.; and Cantor, N. 1985. "Social Intelligence: The Cognitive Basis of Personality." *Review of Personality and Social Psychology* 6.

Klein, G. S. 1976. *Psychoanalytical Theory.* New York: International Universities Press.

Klein, M. 1948. *Contributions to Psychoanalysis.* London: Hogarth Press.

Knapp, P. H. 1974. "Segmentation and Structure in Psychoanalysis." *Journal of the American Psychoanalytic Association* 22:14–36.

Kohut, H. 1971. *The Analysis of the Self.* New York: International Universities Press.

Kohut, H. 1972. "Thoughts on Narcissism and Narcissistic Rage." *Psychoanalytic Study of the Child* 27:360–400.

Kohut, H. 1977. *Restoration of the Self.* New York: International Universities Press.

Kohut, H. 1978. *The Search for the Self: Selected Writings of Heinz Kohut 1950–1978,* P. H. Ornstein, ed. New York: International Universities Press.

Kohut, H. 1984. "How Does Analysis Cure?" In A. Goldberg and P. Stepansky, eds., *Contributions to the Psychology of the Self.* Chicago: University of Chicago Press.

Kosslyn, S. 1981. "The Medium and the Message in Mental Imagery: A Theory." *Psychological Review* 88:46–66.

Kosslyn, S. 1983. *Ghosts in the Mind's Machine: Creating and Using Images in the Brain.* New York: W. W. Norton.

Kris, E. 1955. "Neutralization and Sublimation." *Psychoanalytic Study of the Child* 30–46.

Kroeber, T. 1963. "The Coping Functions of the Ego Mechanisms." In R. White, ed., *The Study of Lives.* New York: Atherton.

Kubie, L. S. 1943. "The Use of Induced Hypnotic Reveries in the Recovery of Repressed Amnesic Data." *Bulletin of the Menninger Clinic* 7:172.

Kuhl, J.; and Beckmann, J., eds. 1985. *Action Control.* Springer Series in Social Psychology. New York: Springer-Verlag.

Laing, R. D. 1970. *Knots.* New York: Pantheon.

Lakoff, G.; and Johnson, M. 1980. *Metaphors We Live By.* Chicago: University of Chicago Press.

Lazarus, R. S. 1966. *Psychological Stress and the Coping Process.* New York: McGraw-Hill.

Leigh, H.; and Reiser, M. F. 1982. "A General Systems Taxonomy for Psychological Defense Mechanisms." *Journal of Psychosomatic Research* 26:77–81.

Levinson, D. 1978. *The Seasons of a Man's Life.* New York: Ballantine Books.

Lewis, H. 1971. *Shame and Guilt in Neurosis.* New York: International Universities Press.

Lewis, H. B. 1981. *Freud and Modern Psychology,* vol. 1. New York: Plenum Press.

Lewis, H. B. 1983. *Freud and Modern Psychology,* vol. 2. New York: Plenum Press.

Lewis, H. B., ed. 1987. *The Role of Shame in Symptom Formation.* Hillsdale, N.J.: Lawrence Erlbaum.

Lewis, W. C. 1974. "Hysteria: The Consultants' Dilemma." *Archives of General Psychiatry* 30:145–51.

Lewis, W. C.; and Berman, M. 1965. "Studies of Conversion Hysteria." *Archives of General Psychiatry* 13:275–82.

Libet, B. 1987. "Consciousness: Conscious, Subjective Experience." In G. Adelman, ed., *Encyclopedia of Neuroscience* 1:271–5. Boston: Birkhauser.

Libet, B.; Gleason, C. A.; Wright, E.; Pearl, D. 1983. "Time of Conscious Intention to Act in

Relation to Onset of Cerebral Activities (Readiness-Potential): The Unconscious Initiation of a Freely Voluntary Act." *Brain* 106:623–42.

Lichtenberg, J. D. 1975. "The Development of the Sense of Self." *Journal of the American Psychoanalytical Association* 23:453–84.

Lichtenberg, J. D. 1983. *Psychoanalysis and Infant Research.* Hillsdale, N.J.: Analytic Press.

Lifton, R. 1976. *The Life of the Self.* New York: Basic Books.

Loevinger, J. 1976a. *Ego Development.* San Francisco: Jossey-Bass.

Loevinger, J. 1976b. "Origins of Conscience." In M. M. Gill and P. S. Holzman, eds., *Psychology Versus Metapsychology: Psychoanalytic Essays in Memory of George S. Klein.* New York: International Universities Press.

Luborsky, L. 1977. "Measuring Pervasive Psychic Structure in Psychotherapy: The Core Conflictual Relationship." In N. Freedman and S. Grand, eds., *Communicative Structures and Psychic Structures.* New York: Plenum Press.

Luborsky, L. 1984. *Principles of Psychoanalytic Psychotherapy.* New York: Basic Books.

McKellar, P. 1957. *Imagination and Thinking.* New York: Basic Books.

Mahler, M. 1968. *On Human Symbiosis and the Vicissitudes of Individuation.* New York: International Universities Press.

Mahler, M.; Pine, F.; and Bergman, A. 1975. *Psychological Birth of Human Infants.* New York: Basic Books.

Main, M. 1975. "Mother-Avoiding Babies." Paper presented at biennial meeting of Society for Research in Child Development, April.

Malan, D. H. 1979. *Individual Psychotherapy and the Science of Psychodynamics.* London: Butterworth.

Mandler, G. 1975. *Mind and Emotion.* New York: John Wiley.

Mandler, G. 1985. *Cognitive Psychology: An Essay of Cognitive Science.* Hillsdale, N. J.: Lawrence Erlbaum.

Mandler, J. M.; and Mandler, G., eds. 1964. *Thinking: From Association to Gestalt.* New York: John Wiley.

Marcel, A. 1988. "Electrophysiology and Meaning in Cognitive Science and Dynamic Psychology—Comments on 'Unconscious Conflict: A Convergent Psychodynamic and Electrophysiological Approach.' " In M. Horowitz, ed., *Psychodynamics and Cognition.* Chicago: University of Chicago Press.

Markus, H.; and Nurius, P. 1986. "Possible Selves." *American Psychologist* 41:954–69.

Markus, H.; and Wurf, E. 1987. "The Dynamic Self-Concept: A Social Psychological Perspective." *Annual Review of Psychology* 38:299–337.

Marmar, C.; and Horowitz, M. J. 1986. "Phenomenological Analysis of Splitting." *Psychotherapy* 23:21–29.

Masterson, J. F. 1975. "The Splitting Defense Mechanism of the Borderline Adolescent: Developmental and Clinical Aspects." In J. E. Mack, ed., *Borderline States in Psychiatry,* pp. 93–101. New York: Grune & Stratton.

Mayman, M. 1968. "Early Memories and Character Structure." *Journal of Projected Techniques and Personality Assessment* 32:303–16.

Meares, R.; and Grose, D. 1978. "On Depersonalization and Adolescence: A Consideration from the Viewpoint of Habituation and 'Identity.' " *British Journal of Medical Psychology* 51:4, 335–42.

Metcalf, A. 1977. "Childhood: From Process to Structure." In M. J. Horowitz, ed., *Hysterical Personality.* New York: Jason Aronson.

Miller, G. A. 1962. *Psychology: The Science of Mental Life.* Harmondsworth: Penguin Books.

Modell, A. H. 1968. *Object Love and Reality.* New York: International Universities Press.

Modell, A. H. 1976. "Holding Environment and Therapeutic Action of Psychoanalysis." *Journal of the American Psychoanalytic Association* 24: 285–307.

Money, J.; and Ehrhardt, A. A. 1972. *Man and Woman, Boy and Girl: The Differentiation and Dimorphism of Gender Identity from Inception to Maturity.* Baltimore: Johns Hopkins University Press.

Motley, M. T.; Camden, C. T.; and Baars, B. J. 1979. "Personality and Situational Influences upon Verbal Slips: A Laboratory Test of Freudian and Pre-Articulatory Editing Hypotheses." *Human Communication Research* 5 (3):195–202.

Murray, E. 1937. *Explorations in Personality.* Cambridge: Cambridge University Press.

Mussen, P. H.; Conger, J.; and Kagan, J., eds. 1980. *Readings in Child and Adolescent Psychology: Contemporary Perspectives.* New York: Harper & Row.

Nagera, H. 1976. *Obsessional Neuroses.* New York: Jason Aronson.

Nathan, P. E.; Parsons, O. A.; Butters, N., eds. 1987. *Neuropsychology of Alcoholism: Implications for Diagnosis and Treatment.* New York: Guilford Press.

Newell, K. M. 1978. "Some Issues on Action Plans." In G. Stelmach, ed., *Information Processing in Motor Control and Learning.* New York: Academic Press.

Noy, P. 1969. "A Revision of the Psychoanalytic Theory of the Primary Process." *International Journal of Psychoanalysis* 50: 155.

Offer, D.; and Offer, J. B. 1975. *From Teenage to Young Manhood.* New York: Basic Books.

Olson, D.; and Bialystok, E. 1983. *Spatial Cognition.* Hillsdale, New Jersey: Lawrence Erlbaum.

Ornstein, P. 1986. "On Self State Dreams." In A. Rothstein, ed., *The Significance of the Interpretation of Dreams in Clinical Work.* New York: American Psychoanalytic Association Press.

Osterweis, M.; Solomon, F.; and Green, M. 1984. *Bereavement: Reactions, Consequences, and Care.* Washington, D.C.: National Academy Press.

Parkes, C. S. 1972. *Bereavement: Studies of Grief in Adult Life.* New York: International Universities Press.

Parkes, C. S.; and Weiss, R. S. 1983. *Recovery from Bereavement.* New York: Basic Books.

Pavlov, I. D. 1972. *Lectures on Conditioned Reflexes.* New York: International Universities Press. (Originally published 1928–41.)

Penman, J. 1954. "Pain as an Old Friend." *Lancet* 1:633–36.

Peterfreund, E. 1971. "Information, Systems, and Psychoanalysis." *Psychological Issues* 7: (1/2). Monograph 25/26.

Piaget, J. 1930. *The Child's Conception of Physical Causality.* New York: Harcourt.

Piaget, J. 1951. *Play Dreams and Imitation in Childhood.* New York: W. W. Norton.

Piaget, J. 1954. *The Construction of Reality in the Child.* New York: Basic Books.

Piaget, J. 1970. *Structuralism.* New York: Basic Books.

Pine, F. 1985. *Developmental Theory and Clinical Process.* New Haven: Yale University Press.

Plomin, R. 1986. *Development, Genetics, and Psychology.* New Jersey: Lawrence Erlbaum.

Pollack, G. H. 1978. "Process and Affect: Mourning and Grief." *International Journal of Psycho-Analysis* 59:255–76.

Pollack, G. H. 1982. "The Mourning-Liberation Process and Creativity." *The Annual of Psychoanalysis* 10:33–354.

Pope, K. S.; and Singer, J. L. 1978. *The Stream of Consciousness.* New York: Plenum Press.

Rangel, L. 1969. "Choice, Conflict, and the Decision-Making Function of the Ego: A Psychoanalytic Contribution to Decision Theory." *International Journal of Psychoanalysis* 50:599–602.

Rapaport, D. 1960. "The Structure of Psychoanalytic Theory: A Systematizing Attempt." *Psychological Issues* 6. New York: International Universities Press.

Rapaport, D. 1967a. See Gill, M. M., ed., 1967, *The Collected Papers of David Rapaport.* New York: Basic Books.

Rapaport, D. 1967b. "Cognitive Structures." In M. Gill, ed., *Collected Papers of David Rapaport.* New York: Basic Books.

Raphael, B. 1977. "Preventive Intervention with Recently Bereaved." *Archives of General Psychiatry* 34:450–54.

Raphael, B. 1982. "The Young Child and the Death of a Parent." In C. M. Parkes and J. S. Hinde, eds., *Place of Attachment in Human Behavior.* New York: Basic Books.

Raphael, B. 1983. *The Anatomy of Bereavement.* New York: Basic Books.

Reich, W. 1949. *Character Analysis.* New York: Farrar, Straus & Giroux.

Reiser, D. E.; and Rosen, D. H. 1984. *Medicine as a Human Experience.* Baltimore: University Park Press.

Reiser, M. 1984. *Mind, Brain, Body: Toward a Convergence of Psychoanalysis and Neurobiology.* New York: Basic Books.

Roiphe, H.; and Galenson, E. 1981. *Infantile Origins of Sexual Identity.* New York: International Universities Press.

Rosenfeld, S. K.; and Sprince, M. P. 1963. "An Attempt to Formulate the Meaning of the Concept 'Borderline.'" *The Psychoanalytic Study of the Child* 18:603–35.

Rothbart, M. K.; and Derryberry. 1981. "Measurement of Temperament in Infancy." *Child Development* 52:569–78.

Rothenberg, A. 1979. *The Emerging Goddess: The Creative Process in Art, Science and Other Fields.* Chicago: University of Chicago Press.

Rothstein, A. 1987. *The Reconstruction of Trauma.* Madison, Conn.: International Universities Press.

Rumelhart, D. E.; McClelland, J. L.; and the PDP Research Group. 1986. *Parallel Distributed Processing: Explorations in the Microstructure of Cognition,* vol. I: *Foundations.* Cambridge, Mass.: MIT Press.

Sacks, O. 1983. *Awakenings.* New York: E. P. Dutton.

Salk, J. 1983. *Anatomy of Reality: Merging of Intuition and Reason.* New York: Columbia University Press.

Salzman, L. 1968. *Obsessive Personality: Origins, Dynamics, and Therapy.* New York: Science House.

Sandler, J.; and Freud, A. 1985. *The Analysis of Defense: The Ego and the Mechanism of Defense Revisited.* New York: International Universities Press.

Sandler, J.; and Rosenblatt, B. 1962. "The Concept of the Representational World." *Psychoanalytic Study of the Child* 17:128–45.

Saperstein, J.; and Gaines, J. 1978. "Commentary on the Divergent Views between Kernberg and Kohut on Theory and Treatment of Narcissistic Personality Disorders." *International Review of Psycho-Analysis* 5:413–23.

Sarnoff, C. 1976. *Latency.* New York: Jason Aronson.

Schafer, R. 1968a. *Aspects of Internalization.* New York: International Universities Press.

Schafer, R. 1968b. "The Mechanisms of Defense." *International Journal of Psycho-Analysis* 49:49–62.

Schank, R.; and Abelson, R. 1977. *Scripts, Plans, Goals, and Understanding.* Hillsdale, N.J.: Lawrence Erlbaum.

Schilder, P. 1950. *The Image and Appearance of the Human Body: Studies in the Constructive Energies of the Psyche.* New York: International Universities Press.

Schmale, A. H.; and Engel, G. L. 1975. "The Role of Conservations—Withdrawal in Depressive Reactions." In E. J. Anthony and K. Benedek, eds., *Depression and Human Existence.* Boston: Little, Brown.

Schur, M. 1966. *The Id and the Regulatory Principles of Mental Functioning.* New York: International Universities Press.

Selye, H. 1976. *Stress in Health and Disease.* Boston: Butterworth.

Shapiro, D. 1965. *Neurotic Styles.* New York: Basic Books.

Shapiro, D. 1981. *Autonomy and Rigid Character.* New York: Basic Books.

Shengold, L. 1979. "Child Abuse and Deprivation: Soul Murder." *Journal of the American Psychoanalytic Association* 27:533–59.

Shevrin, H. 1988. "Unconscious Conflict: A Convergent Psychodynamic and Electrophysiological Approach." In M. Horowitz, ed., *Psychodynamics and Cognition.* Chicago: University of Chicago Press.

Singer, J. L. 1966. *Daydreaming.* New York: Random House.

Singer, J. L. 1984. *The Human Personality.* New York and San Diego: Harcourt, Brace, Jovanovich.

Singer, J. L. 1987. "Psychoanalytic Theory in the Context of Contemporary Psychology": The Helen Block Lewis Memorial Address. Presented to the Division of Psychoanalysis of the American Psychological Association, Annual Meeting, New York City, August.

Skinner, B. F. 1953. *Science and Human Behavior.* New York: Macmillan.

Slap, J. W.; and Saykin, A. J. 1983. "The Schema: Basic Concept in a Nonmetapsychological Model of the Mind." *Psychoanalysis and Contemporary Thought* 6:305–25.

Solomon, S. 1987. *Introduction to General, Organic and Biochemistry.* New York: McGraw-Hill.

Spence, D. P. 1987. *The Freudian Metaphor: Toward Paradigm Change in Psychoanalysis.* New York: W. W. Norton.

Sperry, R. W. 1966. "Brain Bisection and Mechanisms of Consciousness." In J. C. Eccles, ed., *Brain and Conscious Experience.* New York: Springer-Verlag.

Sperry, R. W. 1969. "A Modified Concept of Consciousness." *Psychological Bulletin* 76:532.

Spitz, R. A. 1960. *The First Year of Life.* New York: International Universities Press.

Sroufe, L. A. 1979. "The Coherence of Individual Development: Early Care Attachment, and Subsequent Developmental Issues." *American Psychologist* 34:834–41.

Sroufe, L. A.; and Fleeson, J. 1986. "Attachment and the Construction of Relationships." In W. P. Hartup and Z. Rubin, eds., *Relationships and Development.* Hillsdale, N.J.: Lawrence Erlbaum.

Steele, B. F.; and Alexander, H. 1981. "Long Term Effects of Sexual Abuse in Childhood."

In P. Mrazek and C. Kempe, eds., *Sexually Abused Children and Their Families*. Oxford: Pergamon Press.

Stern, D. N. 1985. *The Interpersonal World of the Infant*. New York: Basic Books.

Stern, M. M. 1961. "Blank Hallucinations: Remarks about Trauma and Perceptual Disturbances," *International Journal of Psycho-Analysis*, 42:205–15.

Stevens, A. 1982. *Archetypes: A Natural History of the Self*. New York: William Morrow.

Stoller, R. 1968. "Sex and Gender," vol I.: *The Transsexual Experiment*. New York: Jason Aronson.

Stoller, R. J. 1979. *Sexual Excitement: Dynamics of Erotic Life*. New York: Pantheon.

Stoller, R. 1985a. *Presentations of Gender*. New Haven, Conn.: Yale University Press.

Stoller, R. 1985b. *Observing the Erotic Imagination*. New Haven, Conn.: Yale University Press.

Stolorow, R. D.; and Lachmann, F. M. 1980. *The Psychoanalysis of Developmental Arrests*. New York: International Universities Press.

Stone, L. 1961. *The Psychoanalytic Situation: An Examination of Its Development and Essential Nature*. New York: International Universities Press.

Strupp, H. H.; and Binder, J. L. 1984. *Psychotherapy in a New Key*. New York: Basic Books.

Sullivan, H. S. 1953. *The Interpersonal Theory of Psychiatry*. New York: W. W. Norton.

Suppes, P.; and Warren, H. 1975. "On the Generation and Classification of Defense Mechanisms." *International Journal of Psycho-Analysis* 56:405–14.

Symington, N. 1986: *The Analytic Experience*. New York: St. Martin's Press.

Thickstun, J. T.; and Rosenblatt, A. D. 1977. "Monograph on Information Processing and PSA Theory." *Psychological Issues* 11 (2/3). Monograph 42/43.

Thickstun, J. T.; and Rosenblatt, A. D. 1978. *Modern Psychoanalytic Concepts in General Psychology*. New York: International Universities Press.

Thoma, H.; and Kachele, H. 1987. *Psychoanalytic Practice*, vol. I: *Principles*. Berlin: Springer-Verlag.

Thomas, A.; and Chess, S. 1977. *Temperament and Development*. New York: Brunner/Mazel.

Tolpin, M. 1972. "On the Beginnings of a Cohesive Self." *Psychoanalytic Study of the Child* 26:316–52. New York: Quadrangle Books.

Tomkins, S. S. 1962. *Affect, Imagery, Consciousness*, vol. I. New York: Springer.

Tomkins, S. S. 1963. *Affect, Imagery, Consciousness*, vol. II. New York: Springer.

Tomkins, S. S. 1979. "Script Theory: Differential Magnification of Affects." In H. E. Howe, Jr. and R. A. Dienstbier, eds., *Nebraska Symposium on Motivation, 1978*, vol. 26. Lincoln, Nebraska: University of Nebraska Press.

Turner, T. S. 1978. "Transformation, Hierarchy and Transcendence: A Reformulation of Van Gennep's Model of the Structure of Rites of Passage." In S. Moore and B. Myerhoff, eds., *Secular Ritual*. Amsterdam: Van Gorcum.

Turner, V. 1969. *The Ritual Process: Structure and Anti-Structure*. Ithaca, N.Y.: Cornell University Press.

Uznadze, D. N. 1966. *The Psychology of Set*. The International Behavioral Science Series. New York: Consultants' Bureau.

Vaillant, G. E. 1971. "Theoretical Hierarchy of Adaptive Ego Mechanisms." *Archives of General Psychiatry* 24:107–18.

Vaillant, G. E. 1977. *Adaptation to Life*. Boston: Little, Brown.

Vaillant, G. E. 1987. "Empirical Studies of Ego Mechanisms of Defense." *American Journal of Psychiatry* 48:131–35.

Van der Velde, C. D. 1985. "Body Images of One's Self and of Others: Developmental and Clinical Significance." *American Journal of Psychiatry* 142:527–37.

Vela-Bueno, A.; Soldatos, C. R. and Julius, D. A. 1987. "Parasomnias: Sleepwalking, Night Terrors, and Nightmares." *Psychiatric Annals* 17:465–69.

Viney, T. 1969. "Self: The History of a Concept." *Journal of History and Behavioral Science* 5:349–59.

Volkan, V. D. 1976. *Primitive Internalized Object Relations*. New York: International Universities Press.

Wachtel, P. 1980. "Transference, Schema, and Assimilation: The Relevance of Piaget to the Psychoanalytic Theory of Transference." *Annual of Psychoanalysis* 8:59–76.

Watson, R. I. 1965. *Psychology of the Child*. New York: John Wiley.

Watson, R. I. 1978. *History of Psychological and Behavioral Science*. New York: Springer.

Weisman, A. D. 1958. "Reality Sense and Reality Testing." *Behavioral Science* 3:228–61.

Weiss, J.; and Sampson, H. 1986. *The Psychoanalytic Process: Theory, Clinical Observation and Empirical Research.* New York: Guilford Press.

Werner, H. 1957. *Comparative Psychology of Mental Development.* New York: International Universities Press.

White, M. T. 1985. "Self-Constancy: The Illusive Concept." In R. L. Lax, S. Bach, and J. A. Burland, eds., *Self and Object Constancy: Clinician and Theoretical Perspectives.* New York: Guilford Press.

Whitmont, E. C. 1969. *The Symbolic Quest: Basic Concept of Analytic Psychology.* New York: G. P. Putnam's Sons for C. G. Jung Foundation.

Winnicott, D. W. 1953. "Transitional Objects and Transitional Phenomena: A Study of the First Not-Me Possession." *International Journal of Psycho-Analysis* 43:89–97.

Winnicott, D. W. 1957. *Mother and Child.* New York: Basic Books.

Winnicott, D. 1962. "Ego Integration in Child Development." In *Maturational Processes and the Facilitating Environment.* New York: International Universities Press.

Winson, J. 1985. *Brain and Psyche: The Biology of the Unconscious.* New York: Doubleday.

Wurmser, L. 1981. *The Mask of Shame.* Baltimore: Johns Hopkins University Press.

Zahn-Waxler, C.; Cummings, E. M.; McKneur, D. H.; and Radke-Yarrow, M. 1984. "Altruism, Aggression and Social Interaction in Young Children with Manic Depressive Parents." *Child Development* 55:112–22.

Zajonc, R. B. 1980. "Feeling and Thinking." *American Psychologist* 35:151–75.

INDEX

Abandonment, fear of, 69
Abelson, R., 35
Aberrant working models, 76–95; in borderline and narcissistic personality styles, 82–84, 93–94; case illustrations of, 77–81, 85–91; motivation for use of, 86; in neurotic states of mind, 84–85, 94; in psychotic states of mind, 77–82, 93; rigid script sequences and, 86–89
Abraham, K., 65, 114
Abused children, 119; *see also* Sexual abuse of children
Acting out, 165–66, 189–91
Action plans, 183
Active memory storage, 172
Adaptive regulation, 196, 197
Adolescence, 141–43; acting out in, 165–66, 191; obsessional style in, 221–23, 227; self-schematization in, 101–2; sexuality in, 145; twinship figures in, 107
Aggression, 36; and early caregiver transactions, 119; in role-relationship models, 54; sexuality and, 145
Aggressor, identification with, 105, 191
Aggressor-victim role-relationship model, 134–36
Ainsworth, M., 101, 118
Alexander, H., 136
"All-bad" working model, 82–83
Alter egos, 83

Altruism, 190, 191
Ambivalence: inability to tolerate, 110; in mourning, 71–73; ruminations and, 128
Amsterdam, B. K., 99
Anal phase, 113, 114, 118
Anger: grief and, 71–72; modulation of states of, 14–17
Anima and animus, 139
Annihilation, fear of, 131
Anorexia nervosa, 31
Anosognosia, 162
Anthony, E. J., 27
Anticipation, 190
Anxiety dreams, 167
Anxiously worried state, 18
Aphasias, 163
Appelgarth, A., 114
Appetites, 36
Approach and avoidance conflicts, 221
Aprosodias, 163
Arlow, J., 47, 181
"As if" identification, 83
Associational width, constriction of, 21
Associations, 190; inhibition of, 203, 206, 207
Attachment, 69; stranger anxiety and, 100, 101; and supplies of love and care, 118–19; temperament and, 98
Auditory images, 158; in dreams, 166
Automatic imagery, 158
Avoidant state, 27

241